MARVELOUS POSSESSIONS

The Clarendon Lectures (Oxford University)
and
The Carpenter Lectures (University of Chicago)
1988

MARVELOUS POSSESSIONS

The Wonder of the New World

STEPHEN GREENBLATT

THE UNIVERSITY OF CHICAGO PRESS

1991

The University of Chicago Press, Chicago 60637
Oxford University Press, Oxford

Paperback edition 1992
Printed in the United States of America

14 13 12 11 10 09 08 7 8 9 10

Library of Congress Cataloging-in-Publication Data

Greenblatt, Stephen Jay.
Marvelous possessions : the wonder of the New World / Stephen Greenblatt.
p. cm.
Includes bibliographical references and index.
1. America—Discovery and exploration.
2. America—Description and travel. 3. Marvelous, The—Social aspects. 4. Wonder—Social aspects.
5. Travel in literature. I. Title.
E121.G74 1991 91-3447
970.01′5—dc20 CIP
ISBN 0-226-30652-6 (pbk.)

♾ The paper used in this publication meets the minimum requirements of the American National Standard for Information Sciences—Permanence of Paper for Printed Library Materials, ANSI Z39.48-1992.

To

Natalie Zemon Davis

and

Robert Pinsky

Acknowledgments

AS befits a study of travel writing, this book owes its existence to exotic realms beyond the borders of California: specifically, to Oxford University, where I delivered versions of these chapters as the Clarendon Lectures, and to the University of Chicago, where I gave them as the Carpenter Lectures. Both visits were for me wonderful occasions, memorable for the extraordinary kindness and generosity of my hosts. How could the visits have been anything but wonderful? Thanks to the Dean and Students of Christ Church, I spent two splendid weeks in rooms that looked out on the Meadow. Chicago in January is not quite as green and mild as Oxford in May, but it has more than ample compensations, including *La Grande Jatte* and one of the best blues clubs I have ever set foot in.

And the people in both places! Among the many to whom I owe substantial debts of gratitude, let me mention only a few: in Oxford, Julia Briggs, Christopher Butler, John Carey, Stephen Gill, Malcolm Godden, Dennis Kay, Don McKenzie, David Norbrook, Nigel Smith, John Walsh; in Chicago, Leonard Barkan, Camille Bennett, David Bevington, James Chandler, Arnold Davidson, Philippe Desan, Bernadette Fort, Christopher Herbert, W. J. T. Mitchell, Janel Mueller, Michael Murrin, Carol Rose, Richard Strier, Pauline Turner Strong, and Frank Thomas. I would like to give special thanks to Kim Scott Walwyn of the Oxford University Press and to Alan Thomas of the University of Chicago Press for their encouragement, attentiveness, and patience. Patricia Williams generously added her own wise editorial counsel.

There are many other places and other people with whom this book is linked: Inga Clendinnen and Greg Dening in Melbourne, Guido Fink in Bologna, Salvatore Camporeale and Louise Clubb in Florence, Wolfgang

Iser and Jürgen Schlaeger in Konstanz, Michel de Certeau, Luce Giard, François Hartog, Louis Marin, and Tzvetan Todorov in Paris. I started to make a list of the others, closer to home, but when I filled several pages with names and had still not come to an end, I decided to abandon the attempt. The friends and colleagues who have been so generous with their time and their learning already know, I hope, what they mean to me. I must, however, at least thank by name those who have read and offered criticisms of the whole manuscript: Paul Alpers, Oliver Arnold, Sacvan Bercovitch, Homi Bhabha, Catherine Gallagher, Steven Knapp, Thomas Laqueur, Robert Pinsky, and David Quint. Rolena Adorno, Svetlana Alpers, Alfred Arteaga, Howard Bloch, Beatriz Pastor Bodmer, Theodore Cachey, Natalie Zemon Davis, Joel Fineman, Philip Fisher, Frank Grady, Ellen Greenblatt, Roland Greene, T. Walter Herbert, Jr., Jeffrey Knapp, David Lloyd, Laurent Mayali, Louis Montrose, Michael Palencia-Roth, José Rabasa, Michael Rogin, David Harris Sacks, Elaine Scarry, Candace Slater, Randolph Starn, Wendy Steiner, and Janet Whatley all read substantial chunks and made valuable suggestions. My research assistants, Lianna Farber, Paula Findlen, Lisa Freinkel, Wendy Ruppel, Eve Sanders, and Elizabeth Young, helped me get some control over voluminous materials that were always threatening to spin off into irremediable confusion. I also benefited greatly from the expertise of librarians at the University of California, Oxford University, the University of Chicago, Harvard University, the Bibliothèque Mazarine, the Bibliothèque Nationale, the British Library, the Warburg Institute, and the Newberry Library. And, of course, the University of California, Berkeley, has as usual provided not only generous support but also an immensely exciting intellectual network.

There is another place and set of people with whom this book is linked both directly and indirectly. I first drafted the chapters on Mandeville and Columbus as lectures to be given on separate occasions in Israel, the first at a conference on 'Landscape, Artifact, Text' at Bar Ilan University in Tel Aviv, the second at the Hebrew University in Jerusalem. Once again I want to acknowledge the hospitality, friendship, and intellectual generosity of many people, including Sharon Baris, Daniel Boyarin, Harold Fisch, Elizabeth Freund, David Heyd, Milly Heyd, Zvi Jegendorf, Ruth Nevo, and Ellen Spolsky. But I also want to acknowledge something else: the original destination of these two lectures is not a neutral fact. It never is, I suppose, for the situation or occasion of one's discourse always manages to shape its meanings, however careful, objective, and truthful one tries to be. At the end of one of my lectures in Chicago, a student challenged me to account for my own position. How can I avoid the implication, she asked, that I have situated myself at a very safe distance from the Europeans about whom I write, a distance secured by means of a sardonic smile that protects me from implication in the discursive practices I am describing? The answer is that I do not claim such protection nor do I imagine myself situated at a safe distance. On the contrary, I have tried in these chapters, not without pain, to register within the very texture of my scholarship a critique of the Zionism in which I was raised and to which I continue to feel, in the midst of deep moral and political reservations, a complex bond. The critique centers on the dream of the national possession of the Dome of the Rock and on the use of the discourse of wonder to supplement legally flawed territorial claims. The bond centers on the spiritual, historical, and psychological legacy of uprooting and genocide. Neither the critique nor the bond constitute the meaning of this book—which is, after all, about other times and other places—but their pressure makes itself felt, along with the question I am still struggling to resolve: how is it possible, in a time of disorientation, hatred of the other, and possessiveness, to keep the capacity for wonder from being poisoned?

Contents

List of Illustrations

Plates (between pages 82 and 83)

Text Illustrations

CHAPTER ONE

Introduction

WHEN I was a child, my favorite books were *The Arabian Nights* and Richard Halliburton's *Book of Marvels*. The appeal of the former, even in what I assume was a grotesquely reduced version, lay in the primal power of storytelling. Some years ago, in the Djeema El Fnah in Marrakesh, I joined the charmed circle of listeners seated on the ground around thc professional story-teller and attended uncomprehendingly to his long tale. In the peculiar reverie that comes with listening to a language one does not understand, hearing it as an alien music, knowing only that a tale is being told, I allowed my mind to wander and discovered that I was telling myself one of the stories from the Arabian Nights, the tale of Sinbad and the roc. If it is true, as Walter Benjamin writes, that every real story 'contains, openly or covertly, something useful',[1] then that tale, of diamonds, deep caverns, snakes, raw meat, and birds with huge talons, must have impressed itself upon my prepubescent imagination as containing something extremely useful, something I should never forget. The utility, in this particular case, has remained hidden from me, but I am reasonably confident that it will be someday revealed. And I remain possessed by stories and obsessed with their complex uses.

The appeal of Halliburton's *Book of Marvels* is less easy to explain. Halliburton was a popular American traveler and journalist. He wrote in what now seems to me a dismayingly exclamatory and hyperventilating manner, as if he believed in some part of himself that his marvels were not all that marvelous and needed to be rhetorically enhanced for the marketplace. But, even in a debased form, *The Book of Marvels* was in touch with what Michel de Certeau calls 'the joyful and silent experience of childhood: . . . *to be other and to move toward the other.*'[2] And I suppose that my suburban soul, constricted by the conventionality of the Eisenhower 1950s, eagerly embraced the relief that Halliburton offered, the sense that the real world was full of wonder, the wide-eyed account of exotic travels—Iguassu Falls, Chichén Itzá, the Golden Gate Bridge. It was Halliburton's trademark to put himself into danger in order to witness or verify his marvels: he flew a light plane perilously close to the raging waters of Iguassu Falls, he jumped into the Pool of Sacrifices at Chichen and swam to safety, I suppose he drove at rush hour across the Golden Gate Bridge. I shouldn't make light of his daring; as if to prove that the risks he was taking were real, Halliburton disappeared on one of his voyages and was never heard from again.

At a certain point I passed from the naïve to what Schiller calls the sentimental—that is, I stopped reading books of marvels and began reading ethnographies and novels—but my childhood interests have survived in a passionate curiosity about other cultures and a fascination with tales. It will not escape anyone who reads this book that my chapters are constructed largely around anecdotes, what the French call *petites histoires*, as distinct from the *grand récit* of totalizing, integrated, progressive history, a history that knows where it is going.[3] As is appropriate for voyagers who thought that they knew where they were going and ended up in a place whose existence they had never imagined, the discourse of travel in the late Middle Ages and the Renaissance is rarely if ever interesting at the level of sustained narrative and teleological design, but gripping at the level of the anecdote. The sense of overarching scheme is certainly present in this discourse, most often in the conviction of the inexorable progress from East to West of Christianity or empire or both, but compared to the luminous universal histories of the early Middle Ages, the chronicles of exploration seem uncertain of their bearings, disorganized, fragmentary. Their strength lies not in a vision of the Holy Spirit's gradual expansion through the world but in the shock of the unfamiliar, the provocation of an intense curiosity, the local excitement of discontinuous wonders. Hence they present the world not in stately and harmonious order but in a succession of brief encounters, random experiences, isolated anecdotes of the unanticipated. For the anecdote, which is linked at least etymologically with the unpublished, is the principal register of the unexpected and hence of the encounter with difference that is at once initiated and epitomized by Columbus's marvelous landfall in an unimagined hemisphere that blocked his access to the eastern end of the known world.

If anecdotes are registers of the singularity of the contingent—associated (to introduce the Mandevillian terms I will discuss in the next chapter) with the rim rather than the immobile and immobilizing center—they are at the same time recorded as *representative* anecdotes, that is, as significant in terms of a larger progress or pattern that is the proper subject of a history perennially deferred in the traveler's relation of further anecdotes. A purely local knowledge, an absolutely singular, unrepeatable, unique experience or observation, is neither desirable nor possible, for the traveler's discourse is meant to be useful, even if the ultimate design in which this utility will be absorbed remains opaque. Anecdotes then are among the principal products of a culture's representational technology, mediators between the undifferentiated succession of local moments and a larger strategy toward which they can only gesture. They are seized in passing from the swirl of experiences and given some shape, a shape whose provisionality still marks them as contingent—otherwise, we would give them the larger, grander name of history—but also makes them available for telling and retelling.

My own traveler's anecdotes are bound up with those that I study, shaped by a similar longing for the effect of the locally real and by a larger historicizing intention that is at once evoked and deflected. An example: in August, 1986, on a tourist's typical first night in Bali, I walked by moonlight on narrow paths through silent rice paddies glittering with fireflies. I reached a tiny village which in the darkness I identified less by the low, half-hidden huts and temples than by the frenzied barking of the dogs at my approach. I saw a light from the *bale banjar*, the communal pavilion in which I knew—from having read Clifford Geertz and Miguel Covarrubias and Gregory Bateson and Margaret Mead—that the Balinese gathered in the evenings. I drew near and discovered that the light came from a television set that the villagers, squatting or sitting cross-legged, were intent on watching. Conquering my disappointment, I accepted the gestured invitation to climb onto the platform and see the show: on the communal VCR, they were watching a tape of an elaborate temple ceremony. Alerted by the excited comments and whoops of laughter, I recognized in the genial crowd of television watchers on the platform several of the ecstatic celebrants, dancing in trance states, whom I was seeing on the screen.

We may call what I witnessed that evening the assimilation of the other, a phrase it is well to leave deliberately ambiguous.[4] For if the television and the VCR and, for that matter, my presence on the platform suggested the astonishing pervasiveness of capitalist markets and technology, their extension into the furthest corners of the earth, the Balinese adaptation of the latest Western and Japanese modes of representation seemed so culturally idiosyncratic and resilient that it was unclear who was assimilating whom.[5] The villagers had purchased a sophisticated version of international capitalism's representational machinery, its leading device at the moment for the production, reproduction, and transmission of cultural texts. The immense transformative power of that device, its ability to diminish difference by initiating relatively isolated and autonomous cultures into the imagery and values of the world system, has been amply demonstrated around the globe. But the VCR allows a surprising amount of local autonomy, and what I witnessed was the pleasure of self-representation, as the villagers had their own bodies and voices and music enter the machine and be projected back at them. Whose ideological triumph is being registered here? Whose possession is disclosed? Representational practices are ideologically significant—it is the purpose of this book to explore some aspects of this significance—but I think it is important to resist what we may call *a priori* ideological determinism, that is, the notion that particular modes of representation are inherently and necessarily bound to a given culture or class or belief system, and that their effects are unidirectional.

The alternative is not to imagine that representational modes are neutral or even that they give themselves over, like Chekhov's 'Darling,' to whoever has embraced them, but to acknowledge that individuals and cultures tend to have fantastically powerful assimilative mechanisms, mechanisms that work like enzymes to change the ideological composition of foreign bodies. Those foreign bodies do not disappear altogether but they are drawn into what Homi Bhabha terms the inbetween, the zone of intersection in which all culturally determinate significations are called into question by an unresolved and unresolvable hybridity.[6] Even representational technologies that require highly specialized equipment along with an infrastructure that includes electric generators, the accumulation of so-called hard currency, and the middlemen and customs bureaucracy in Tokyo, Jakarta, and Denpasar are not unequivocally and irreversibly the bearers of the capitalist ideology that was the determining condition of their original creation and their expansion throughout the world. In the case of the Balinese television set, there is not only the remarkable adaptive power of the local community but a distinct sense conveyed by that community that the adaptation is not all that remarkable, that nothing very novel is occurring, that no great expenditure of collective energy is engaged in the assimilation of the other.

At first I accounted for my impression as a consequence of the gracefulness for which the Balinese are justly famous, but a few days later it received a sharper focus when I milled about in the town of Amlapura with an enormous crowd celebrating Indonesian Independence Day. I had hoped to see some traditional *legong* dances, which were to take place on the stage of the large movie theater on the town square, but by the time I arrived the dances were over and the current movie, Charles Bronson's *Death Wish II*, was about to begin, a free screening that evening on the occasion of the holiday. Across the square another movie was already showing on a large makeshift screen—evidently a comedy about rich yuppies in Jakarta. The film, depicting people whose language, religion, and sense of identity are far different from those of the Balinese, was also being shown in honor of the celebration, a gesture then toward that cultural assimilation of Bali that Javanese have been attempting to achieve, most often by considerably less genial means, for centuries. Finally, against the side wall of the movie theater, and jutting into the square, someone had constructed a rough trestle stage on which had been erected yet another screen, stretched across a wooden frame. Behind this screen, which was lit by a coconut oil lamp, was an aged *dalang*, a mystic story-teller. The *dalang* sat cross-legged beside a coffin-like box out of which he took, one by one, exquisite puppets cut from buffalo parchment and arrayed them before him. He then began to perform with amazing dexterity a *wayang kulit*, a shadow puppet play based upon episodes from the *Ramayana* and *Mahabharata*.

The Balinese were moving gaily and apparently at random from one of these shows to another, crowding in to witness a few illuminating minutes of American screen violence, moving outside to listen to the chanting of the *dalang* and watch the shadow puppets flickering across the screen, squeezing in behind that screen to watch the *dalang* manipulate the puppets, crossing the square to see the gilded youth in Jakarta race around in red sports cars. In the context of this festive perambulation, the villagers whom on my first night I had seen huddled together before the television set seemed part of a larger Balinese fascination with images on screens. Though the *wayang* scaffold was propped against the movie house, it seemed far more plausible symbolically at least to imagine the movie house propped against the ancient puppet theater, with its intimations of the unreality of the world.

But it is not the question of cultural origins or priority that most interests me here.[7] Rather I want to emphasize the multiple sites of representation and the crowd's movement among them, for they suggest that the problem of the assimilation of the other is linked to what we may call, adapting Marx, *the reproduction and circulation of mimetic capital*. There are three reasons why it is worth invoking 'capital' here. First, and most obvious, I want to insist on the crucial connection between mimesis and capitalism, for, though the Roman Empire and Christianity provided impressive precedents, in the modern world-order it is with capitalism that the proliferation and circulation of representations (and devices for the generation and transmission of representations) achieved a spectacular and virtually inescapable global magnitude. This magnitude—the will and the ability to cross immense distances and, in the search for profit, to encounter and to represent radically unfamiliar human and natural objects—is the enabling condition for the particular experiences with which this book will be concerned. Second, I want to convey the sense of a stockpile of representations, a set of images and image-making devices that are *accumulated*, 'banked,' as it were, in books, archives, collections, cultural storehouses, until such time as these representations are called upon to generate new representations. The images that matter, that merit the term capital, are those that achieve reproductive power, maintaining and multiplying themselves by transforming cultural contacts into novel and often unexpected forms. And third, I want to suggest that mimesis, as Marx said of capital, is a social relation of production. I take this to mean that any given representation is not only the reflection or product of social relations but that it is itself a social relation, linked to the group understandings, status hierarchies, resistances, and conflicts that exist in other spheres of the culture in which it circulates. This means that representations are not only products but producers, capable of decisively altering the very forces that brought them into being.

This emphasis on the productive power of representation should not lead to a collapse of the distinction between mimetic practice and any other kind of social practice. It is important to grasp that mimetic capital—the stock of images, along with the means of producing those images and circulating them according to prevailing market forces—is differentiated from other, non-mimetic forms of capital. Cultures are not altogether an assemblage of screens, or texts, or performances. In concentrating on mimetic capital, we can get at certain important qualities—the multiple, interconnected sites of representation, the mobility of spectacle and spectator alike, the unreality of images paradoxically linked to the dazzling power of display—but we also risk ignoring other important qualities: modes of non-mimetic production as well as reproduction, presentation as well as representation, reality as well as simulation. It is, I think, a theoretical mistake and a practical blunder to collapse the distinction between representation and reality, but at the same time we cannot keep them isolated from one another. They are locked together in an uneasy marriage in a world without ecstatic union or divorce.

The authors of the anecdotes with which this book concerns itself were liars—few of them *steady* liars, as it were, like Mandeville, but frequent and cunning liars none the less, whose position virtually required the strategic manipulation and distortion and outright suppression of the truth. But though they were liars, European voyagers to the New World were not systematic, so that we cannot have the hermeneutic satisfaction of stripping away their false representations to arrive at a secure sense of reality. Instead we find ourselves groping uneasily among the mass of textual traces, instances of brazen bad faith jostling homely (and often equally misleading) attempts to tell the truth.

In the chapters that follow I have tried less to distinguish between true and false representations than to look attentively at the nature of the representational practices that the Europeans carried with them to America and deployed when they tried to describe to their fellow countrymen what they saw and did. I have been very wary of taking anything Europeans wrote or drew as an accurate and reliable account of the nature of the New World lands and its peoples. It is almost impossible, I find, to make this skepticism an absolute and unwavering principle—I catch myself constantly straining to read into the European traces an account of what the American natives were 'really' like—but I have resisted as much as I can the temptation to speak for or about the native cultures as if the mediation of European representations were an incidental consideration, easily corrected for. At this time and place it is particularly tempting to take the most admiring European descriptions of the 'Indians' as if they were transparent truths and to reserve epistemological suspicion for the most hostile accounts, but this strategy produces altogether predictable, if sentimentally appealing, results. We can be certain only that European representations of the New World tell us something about the European practice of representation: this seems like a modest enough claim, but I hope this book will show that it rewards exploration. I should add that if I do not put terms like 'New World,' 'Indian,' and 'discovery' in quotations, it is only because I think that in the texts I am considering such terms can never be detached from European projections.

But can we legitimately speak of 'the European practice of representation'? There were profound differences among the national cultures and religious faiths of the various European voyagers, differences that decisively shaped both perceptions and representations. Hence, for example, when the English Protestant Thomas Harriot describes the religious rites of the Algonquians, he notes that their carved posts resemble 'the faces of Nonnes couered with theyr vayles,' and his collaborator John White represents the scene accordingly. Similarly, the Calvinist Jean de Léry polemically compares the cannibalism of the savage Brazilian people known as Ouetaca with the Catholicism of the French expedition's leader, Nicolas Durand de Villegagnon, who 'wanted to eat the flesh of Jesus Christ raw.'[8] It is not only a matter of polemics: Catholics and Protestants tended to ask different questions, notice different things, fashion different images.[9] The differences are sufficiently great to allow a scholar of the seventeenth century to speak of a specifically 'Protestant poetics,' and, if it would be more difficult to do so for the earlier period with which we are concerned, there are from the inception of the Reformation ample reasons to make distinctions.[10] On crucially important matters—the significance of ritual and festivity, the process of conversion, the nature of gifts, the way Christians should deal with the false beliefs of others, and the authority that secured and legitimized interpretation—there had emerged, by the time of the second generation of European voyagers to the New World, highly visible divisions, divisions that not only marked the distinction between Catholic and Protestant but cut each of the groups into smaller fragments. Hence it would be possible to differentiate fruitfully between Franciscan and Dominican representations of the New World, and between Calvinist and Lutheran. And then, of course, these distinctions would have to be further elaborated with reference to the very considerable differences among national cultures and social classes and professions.

These differences figure importantly in my account, but I have tried not to lose sight of all that was shared by the quite diverse European voyagers to the New World. For European mimetic capital, though diverse and internally competitive, easily crossed the boundaries of nation and creed, and it therefore seemed to me a mistake to accord those boundaries an absolute respect. Certainly the age's greatest technological device for the circulation of mimetic capital, the printing press, was no respecter of national or doctrinal borders. Richard Hakluyt's intensely patriotic and staunchly Protestant *Principal Navigations, Voyages, Traffiques, & Discoveries of the English Nation* somehow managed to include Giovanni de Pian Carpini, William of Rubruck, and Odoric of Pordenone. Catholic and Protestant polemicists of the period made much of their differences, each accusing the other of atrocities, but both decency and horror, like the capacity to represent, seem distributed fairly evenly. In any case, after the momentous events of 1989 and 1990, it is easier than at any time since the late fifteenth century to perceive all of the ways that Europe has a common culture and destiny.

The Europeans who ventured to the New World in the first decades after Columbus's discovery shared a complex, well-developed, and, above all, mobile technology of power: writing, navigational instruments, ships, warhorses, attack dogs, effective armor, and highly lethal weapons, including gunpowder. Their culture was characterized by immense confidence in its own centrality, by a political organization based on practices of command and submission, by a willingness to use coercive violence on both strangers and fellow countrymen, and by a religious ideology centered on the endlessly proliferated representation of a tortured and murdered god of love. The cult of this male god—a deity whose earthly form was born from the womb of a virgin and sacrificed by his heavenly father to atone for human disobedience—in turn centered on a ritual (highly contested, of course, by the second decade of the sixteenth century and variously interpreted) in which the god's flesh and blood were symbolically eaten. Such was the confidence of this culture that it expected perfect strangers—the Arawaks of the Caribbean, for example—to abandon their own beliefs, preferably immediately, and embrace those of Europe as luminously and self-evidently true. A failure to do so provoked impatience, contempt, and even murderous rage.

With a very few exceptions, Europeans felt powerfully superior to virtually all of the peoples they encountered, even those like the Aztecs who had technological and organizational skills that Europeans could recognize and greatly admire. The sources of this sense of superiority are sometimes difficult to specify, though the Christians' conviction that they possessed an absolute and exclusive religious truth must have played a major part in virtually all of their cultural encounters. On many occasions, this conviction was bound up with what Samuel Purchas in the early seventeenth century called the Europeans' 'literall advantage'—the advantage, that is, of writing. The narcissism that probably always attaches to one's own speech was intensified by the possession of a technology of preservation and reproduction. It is not clear if the illiterate sailors and soldiers basked in the reflected glory of this technology, but those who wrote the books—

those therefore with whose testimony we are left—saw writing as a decisive mark of superiority. God gave man reason and speech, Purchas writes, a double endowment beyond the natural capacity of any other 'sensitive Creatures.' The two special gifts function together: speech distinguishes man from the animals by uniting diverse individuals into a social community founded on reason. But there is another divine endowment and another distinction: 'God hath added herein a further grace, that as Men by the former exceed Beasts, so hereby one man may excell another; and amongst Men, some are accounted Civill, and more both Sociable and Religious, by the Use of letters and Writing, which others wanting are esteemed Brutish, Savage, Barbarous.'[11]

Purchas's use of the term 'barbarous' signals an important shift from the Greek distinction between self and other, a distinction based on the difference between those who spoke Greek and those who did not. In Purchas the linguistic community is assumed to have a legitimate multiplicity; the crucial difference is a technological one—the achievement of literacy—but this technology is understood to have implications well beyond a certain quantitative difference. For Purchas the key to 'the litterall advantage' is the fact that speech, as he conceives it, is limited to the present moment and the present auditors:

> by speech we utter our minds once, at the present, to the present, as present occasions move (and perhaps unadvisedly transport) us: but by writing Man seemes immortall, conferreth and consulteth with the Patriarks, Prophets, Apostles, Fathers, Philosophers, Historians, and learnes the wisdome of the Sages which have been in all times before him; yea by translations or learning the Languages, in all places and Regions of the World: and lastly, by his owne writings surviveth himself, remaines (litera scripta manet) thorow all ages a Teacher and Counsellor to the last of men: yea hereby God holds conference with men, and in his sacred Scriptures, as at first in the Tables of Stone, speakes to all. (p. 486)

For Purchas, then, as for many other Europeans, those who possess writing have a past, a history, that those without access to letters necessarily lack.[12] And since God 'speakes to all' through writing, unlettered cultures (as distinct from illiterate individuals) are virtually excluded by definition from the human community: 'Want of Letters hath made some so seely as to thinke the Letter it selfe could speak, so much did the Americans herein admire the Spaniards, seeming in comparison of the other as speaking Apes' (pp. 486–7).[13] Seeming so to whom—to the Americans themselves, to the Catholic Spaniards, or to the Protestant Purchas? Purchas doesn't bother to specify, because the difference between Spaniard and Englishman, Catholic and Protestant, fades before the massive cultural difference, as he conceives it, between European and American, lettered and unlettered, and therefore 'civilized' and 'barbarous.'

Purchas's overweening cultural confidence and religious dogmatism have somewhat receded, at least in academic circles,[14] but his notion of the 'literall advantage' continues to find powerful support. In a thoughtful and disturbing book that has helped to set the agenda of my own study, Tzvetan Todorov has argued that the crucial cultural difference between European and American peoples was the presence or absence of writing, and that this difference virtually determined the outcome of their encounter: 'the absence of writing is an important element of the situation, perhaps even *the* most important.' Todorov drastically minimizes Mayan and Aztec writing: the pictograms used by the latter 'are not a lesser degree of writing,' he writes; 'they note the experience, not the language.'[15] Even the most culturally sophisticated of the Mesoamerican peoples, in this account, did not merely lack certain important refinements in the art of writing; they lacked the thing itself, the essential concept, and hence they lacked the communicative, symbolic, and interpretive skills that at once fashion and are fashioned by writing.

In Todorov's view, the consequence for American cultures was not (as Purchas or Léry thought) a loss of the past—their production of formal discourse, he observes, was dominated by memory—but rather a fatal loss of manipulative power in the present. The absence of writing determined the predominance of ritual over improvisation and cyclical time over linear time, characteristics that in turn led to disastrous misperceptions and miscalculations in the face of the *conquistadores*. The unlettered peoples of the New World could not bring the strangers into focus; conceptual inadequacy severely impeded, indeed virtually precluded, an accurate perception of the other. The culture that possessed writing could accurately represent to itself (and hence strategically manipulate) the culture without writing, but the reverse was not true. For in possessing the ability to write, the Europeans possessed, Todorov argues, an unmistakably superior representational technology: 'There is a "technology" of symbolism, which is as capable of evolution as the technology of tools, and, in this perspective, the Spaniards are more "advanced" than the Aztecs (or to generalize: societies possessing writing are more advanced than societies without writing), even if we are here concerned only with a difference of degree' (p. 160).

The slight uneasiness registered in the quotations placed around the word 'advanced' is well-taken,[16] for there seems to me no convincing evidence that writing functioned in the early encounter of European and New World peoples as a superior tool for the accurate perception or effective manipulation of the other. Monuments to writing are built by writers: from the midst of the system within which our knowledge of the world is organized, we take legitimate pleasure in our own tools. But it is a leap from this pleasure to faith in what Todorov calls 'the evolution of the symbolic apparatus proper to man' (p. 160), a leap that should give us pause. And it is a further leap—across a chasm at least as great—from this general celebration of writing to the particular dealings between Cortés and Montezuma. In his encounter with Cortés, Montezuma made fatal strategic mistakes; the outcome suggests that Cortés evidently made fewer mistakes. But where is the link between his success and his culture's possession of writing or, for that matter, between the Aztec failure and their supposed lack of writing? There is a demonstrable linguistic element to the Spanish triumph which I will discuss in Chapters 4 and 5 at some length, but that element is the possession not of writing but of competent translators.[17] Montezuma had no one who was even remotely the equivalent of Cortés's loyal bilingual informants and go-betweens, Geronimo de Aguilar and the indispensable Doña Marina.[18]

Translation and communication were crucial, but the ability to communicate effectively is a quite different matter from the ability through writing or any other means to perceive and represent reality. It may be that the Europeans' possession of writing (and their impression that the New World natives did not) increased the *conquistadores*' self-confidence, but neither confidence nor success is a reliable indicator of superior access to reality. On the contrary, it has been persuasively argued that the Spanish misperceived some of the fundamental principles of Aztec culture.[19] It is equally likely that the Aztecs misperceived the other—for example, by assuming initially that Cortés was somehow linked to the culture-hero Quetzalcoatl—but there is no evidence that this misperception was caused by their supposed lack of writing. In other words, there is nothing in the available symbolic technology of either of the peoples that would determine a greater or lesser access to the truth of things.

My book is about early European responses to the New World and hence about the uses of symbolic technology, but I am skeptical of any attempt to translate the historical record of these uses into conclusions about the relative epistemological merits of the tools with which the Europeans were endowed in comparison with those of the Americans. The responses with which I am concerned—indeed the only responses I have been able to identify—are not detached scientific assessments but what I would call engaged representations, representations that are relational, local, and historically contingent. Their overriding interest is not knowledge of the other but practice upon the other; and, as I shall try to show, the principal faculty involved in generating these representations is not reason but imagination.

Great as the difference was between themselves and the natives, almost all European voyagers believed that they could communicate across it through the giving of gifts and the display of representations. An entry in Columbus's log-book for December 18, 1492, will serve to introduce these attempts at communication, which I will examine at some length in the chapters that follow. On his ship, anchored off the island of Tortuga, Columbus is visited by a young and impressively dignified native 'king' and several of his 'counsellors':

> I saw that he was pleased with a coverlet that I had on my bed. I gave it to him and some very good amber beads that I wore on my neck, and some red shoes, and a flask of orange-flower water, with which he was so pleased that it was a marvel. And he and his tutor and counsellors were very troubled because they did not understand me nor I them. Nevertheless I gathered that he told me that if something from this place pleased me that the whole island was at my command. I sent for some beads of mine on which, as a token, I have a gold *excelente* on which Your Highnesses are sculptured, and I showed it to him; and again, as yesterday, I told him how Your Highnesses commanded and ruled over all the best part of the world, and that there were no other princes as great. And I showed him the royal banners and the others bearing the cross, which he esteemed greatly. What great lords Your Highnesses must be, he said (speaking toward his counsellors), since from so far away and from the heavens they had sent me here without fear; and many other things passed between them that I did not understand, except that I saw well that they took everything as a great wonder.[20]

I am fascinated by the move, here and elsewhere, from knowing nothing ('they did not understand me nor I them') to imagining an absolute possession ('the whole island was at my command'). Columbus could have simply appealed to his sense of overwhelming power: in his log-book he had just noted complacently (and, as it turned out, incorrectly) that a few armed Spaniards could easily command the entire population. But instead he represents the move toward sovereign possession as the result of an act of interpretation, a deciphering of the native's words and gestures: 'I gathered that he told me. . . .' Columbus imagines—and invites his readers, above all the king and queen, to imagine—a scene of legitimate appropriation, an appropriation enabled, through a mechanism at once institutional and psychic, by the giving of gifts and the display of what must have been to the natives utterly incomprehensible representations: the portrait of the king stamped on a gold coin, the royal banners, the cross. The weirdness of these displays is at once repressed in a palpable lie—

though he has just acknowledged that he did not understand the native 'king's' language nor the 'king' his, Columbus reports a speech flattering at once to himself and to the Spanish sovereigns—and at the same time registered at least indirectly in the natives' 'wonder.' Wonder is, I shall argue, the central figure in the initial European response to the New World, the decisive emotional and intellectual experience in the presence of radical difference: it is quite possible that the people whom Columbus was encountering also experienced, as he reports, a sense of wonder, but here as elsewhere in the account of the other we principally learn something about the writer of the account.

Nil admirari, the ancient maxim taught. But, in the presence of the New World, the classical model of mature, balanced detachment seemed at once inappropriate and impossible. Columbus's voyage initiated a century of intense wonder. European culture experienced something like the 'startle reflex' one can observe in infants: eyes widened, arms outstretched, breathing stilled, the whole body momentarily convulsed. But what does it mean to experience wonder? What are its origins, its uses, and its limits? Is it closer to pleasure or pain, longing or horror? Is it a sign and an agent of renunciation or possession? The ambiguities of wonder in the New World may be suggested by a passage from Jean de Léry's great *History of a Voyage to the Land of Brazil*. A Huguenot pastor, Léry lived for several months in 1557 among the Tupinamba in the Bay of Rio. During this stay he and two other Frenchmen (one of them a Norman interpreter) had occasion, he writes, to witness a solemn religious assembly of the natives. What he saw and heard amazed and frightened him:

> While we were having our breakfast, with no idea as yet of what they intended to do, we began to hear in the men's house (not thirty feet from where we stood) a very low murmur, like the muttering of someone reciting his hours. Upon hearing this, the women (about two hundred of them) all stood up and clustered together, listening intently. The men little by little raised their voices and were distinctly heard singing all together and repeating this syllable of exhortation, *He, he, he, he*; the women, to our amazement, answered them from their side, and with a trembling voice; reiterating that same interjection *He, he, he, he*, let out such cries, for more than a quarter of an hour, that as we watched them we were utterly disconcerted. Not only did they howl, but also, leaping violently into the air, they made their breasts shake and they foamed at the mouth—in fact, some, like those who have the falling-sickness over here, fell in a dead faint; I can only believe that the devil entered their body and that they fell into a fit of madness.[21]

For Léry the spectacle is the very embodiment of what his culture views not only as otherness but as evil: the intimations of bestiality and madness merge with an overarching, explanatory image of demonic possession. The reference to the devil is not a metaphor; it is the deep truth of the natives' condition: 'the Americans are visibly and actually tormented by evil spirits' (p. 138). This torment is deeply significant, for in Léry's view the natives' religious fear and suffering is both a divine punishment—proof that 'even in this world there are devils to torment those who deny God and his power'—and justification for their future damnation: 'one can see that this fear they have of Him whom they refuse to acknowledge will render them utterly without excuse' (p. 139). In the Kafka-like logic of this argument, the Tupinamba will be justly condemned through all eternity precisely because they fear the one true God whom they do not and cannot know and whom for this reason they refuse to acknowledge. Léry reports, as the most vivid example of this refusal, that he and his fellows chose the natives' intense fear of thunder as an opportunity to evangelize: 'Adapting ourselves to their crudeness,' he writes, 'we would seize the occasion to say to them that this was the very God of whom we were speaking, who to show his grandeur and power made heavens and earth tremble; their resolution and response was that since he frightened them in that way, he was good for nothing' (p. 135).

Such a response, in Léry's view, condemns the Tupinamba to fear, credulity, and superstition. It is not an accident that the Protestant Léry thought that the low chanting from the men's house sounded at first 'like the muttering of someone reciting his hours' (p. 141); we have already glimpsed his condemnation of the Catholic Mass as cannibalism.[22] For Léry, whose *History of a Voyage* was published in Calvinist Geneva, Catholic rituals are occasions in which the devil is doing his work, and he invites his readers to interpret the Tupinamba ceremony in the light of that Mass: in both the experience of wonder is linked to a violation of all that is most holy.

In the 1585 edition of the *History of a Voyage*, Léry added to his account a description taken from Jean Bodin's *De la démonomanie des sorciers* (1578) of a witches' sabbath. Bodin was one of the most learned, influential, and uncompromisingly punitive of the Renaissance witchmongers, the most articulate of those who insisted that the devil was literally present in what appeared to be fantastic and imaginary claims. Léry evidently felt he had found in Bodin's account the European ritual that most closely resembled the astonishing scene he had witnessed more than twenty years earlier, a resemblance that transcended the immense cultural and geographical distance he himself continually remarks: 'I have concluded,' Léry writes, 'that they have the same master: that is, the Brazilian women and the witches over here were guided by the same spirit of Satan; neither the distance between the places nor the long passage over the sea keeps the father of lies from working both here and there on those who are handed over to him by the just judgment of God.'[23]

What Léry has seen in Brazil then is nothing less than the active and literal manifestation of Satan, and like Bodin he insists that those who would take this manifestation as a delusion, imagination, or metaphor are 'atheist dogs,' 'worse than the devils themselves' (p. 139). And yet it is precisely here, at the moment in which the wonder aroused by the religious assembly is fully disclosed as a justifiable shudder of revulsion, a prelude to flight, that the mood shifts radically:

Although I had been among the savages for more than half a year and was already fairly well used to their ways, nonetheless (to be frank) being somewhat frightened and not knowing how the game might turn out, I wished I were back at our fort. However, after these chaotic noises and howls had ended and the men had taken a short pause (the women and children were now silent), we heard them once again singing and making their voices resound in a harmony so marvelous that you would hardly have needed to ask whether, since I was now somewhat easier in my mind at hearing such sweet and gracious sounds, I wished to watch them from nearby. (p. 141)

Avoidance is transformed into approach, as Léry and his fellows draw nearer to the dancing, singing men:

At the beginning of this witches' sabbath, when I was in the women's house, I had been somewhat afraid; now I received in recompense such joy, hearing the measured harmonies of such a multitude, and especially in the cadence and refrain of the song, when at every verse all of them would let their voices trail, saying *Heu, heuaure, heura, heuraure, heura, heura, oueh*—I stood there transported with delight [*tout ravi*]. Whenever I remember it, my heart trembles, and it seems their voices are still in my ears. (pp. 142–4)

Wonder is now not the sign of revulsion but of ravishment, an ecstatic joy that can be experienced anew even twenty years later through an act of remembrance. The authenticity of the recovery is confirmed in Léry's body itself, in the trembling of his heart, for this trembling is the authentic sign of wonder, proof that the marvelous Tupinamba voices are still in his ears: wonder, as Albertus Magnus wrote, is like 'a systole of the heart'.[24] As Albertus' brilliant figure and Léry's experience make clear, the marvelous gestures toward the world by registering an overpowering intensity of response. Someone witnesses something amazing, but what most matters takes place not 'out there' or along the receptive surfaces of the body where the self encounters the world, but deep within, at the vital, emotional center of the witness. This inward response cannot be marginalized or denied, any more than a constriction of the heart in terror can be denied; wonder is absolutely exigent, a primary or radical passion.

But what is the meaning of this passion for Léry? What is the relation between the experience of exquisite beauty and the horror of satanic evil? It would be possible to reconcile the two by reminding the reader, as Renaissance clerics frequently did, that the angel of darkness disguised himself as an angel of light. The beauty of the music would be revealed then to be a lure. But, though he can be an alert and even relentless moralist, Léry does not interpret his experience as a temptation; he seems eager to provide not a warning but a reflection of his own intense pleasure. Thus in later editions of his *History of a Voyage* he even includes musical notation for the Tupinamba chant, as if he longed for his reader actually to hear the music and share his ravishment. Nor does he quite turn this ravishment, as he elsewhere does, into a lesson for atheists, a sign that even the benighted savages have some higher vision, some practice of religious adoration. He does, to be sure, learn from the Norman interpreter that the songs he has just heard mingle laments for the dead and threats against enemies with something else: a tale of a flood in ancient times that had covered the world and drowned everyone except their ancestors who climbed to safety in the highest trees. Not surprisingly, Léry believes that this tale is a corrupt oral version of the biblical Flood—'being altogether deprived of writing, it is hard for them to retain things in their purity' (p. 144)—but the scriptural echo is not what gives the chant its power, for it had ravished his senses before he knew its meaning.

Léry presents his appreciation of the beauty of the savage music as a triumph over his own panic fear in the presence of the demonic. Perhaps we should interpret his response then as a version of the aesthetic recoding by means of which medieval Christians neutralized the images of the ancient pagan deities. In Michael Camille's account of this recoding, 'the aesthetic anesthetizes': medieval admiration for the wonders of pagan art, he writes, 'was really a phenomenon of distancing, a taking out of context.'[25] It is certainly true that Léry's ravishment takes the ceremony—which he has identified as a witches' sabbath—out of context, but his response does not seem to be the same as distancing: on the contrary, he takes it out of context—any context, including his own beliefs—in order to approach more closely, to draw it into himself, to remember it in the very beating of his heart. The experience of wonder seems to resist recuperation, containment, ideological incorporation; it sits strangely apart from everything that gives coherence to Léry's universe, apart and yet utterly compelling. This passage in the *History of a Voyage*, Michel de Certeau

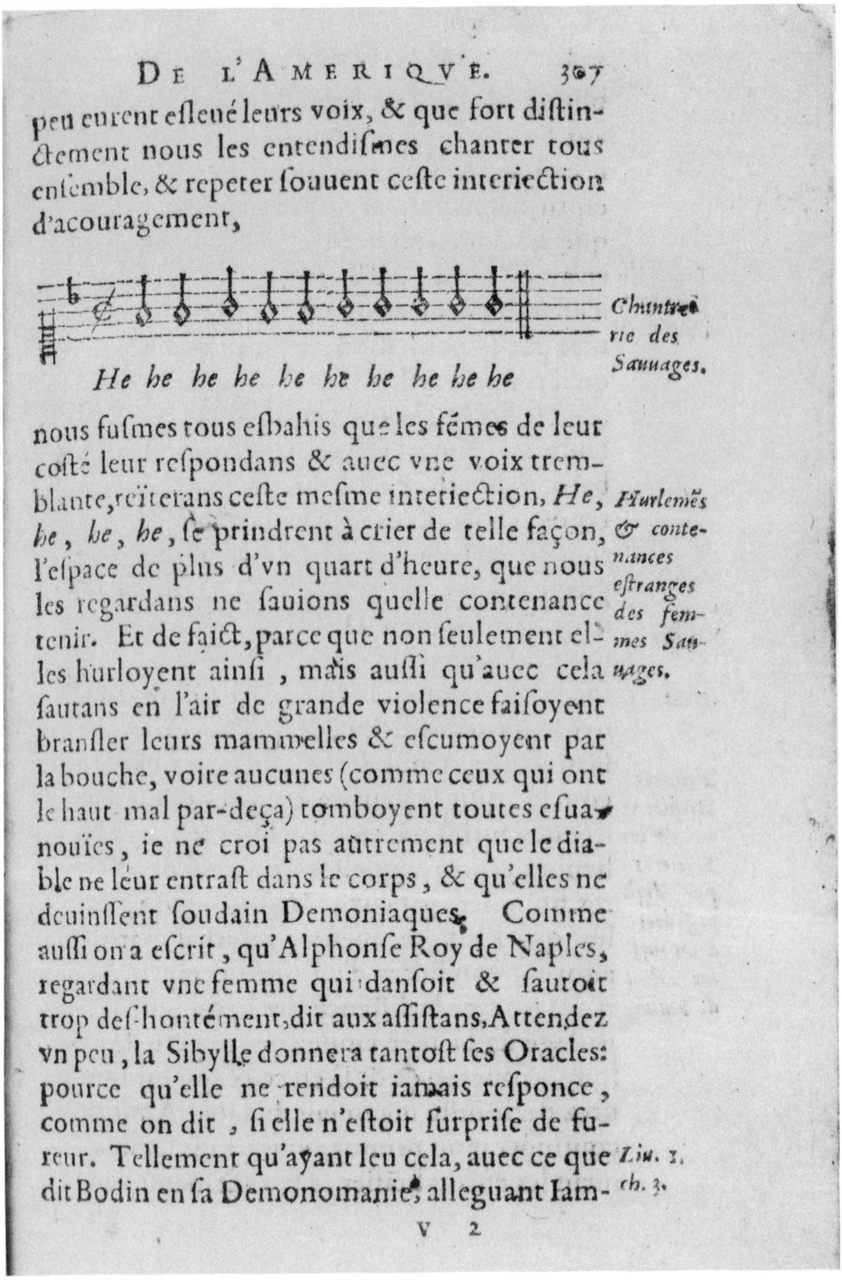
DE L'AMERIQVE. 307

peu eurent eſleué leurs voix, & que fort diſtinctement nous les entendiſmes chanter tous enſemble, & repeter ſouuent ceſte interiection d'acouragement,

He he he he he he he he he he

Chantrerie des Sauuages.

nous fuſmes tous eſbahis que les fémes de leur coſté leur reſpondans & auec vne voix tremblante, reïterans ceſte meſme interiection, *He, he, he, he*, ſe prindrent à crier de telle façon, l'eſpace de plus d'vn quart d'heure, que nous les regardans ne ſauions quelle contenance tenir. Et de faict, parce que non ſeulement elles hurloyent ainſi, mais auſſi qu'auec cela ſautans en l'air de grande violence faiſoyent branſler leurs mammelles & eſcumoyent par la bouche, voire aucunes (comme ceux qui ont le haut mal par-deça) tomboyent toutes eſuanouïes, ie ne croi pas autrement que le diable ne leur entraſt dans le corps, & qu'elles ne deuinſſent ſoudain Demoniaques. Comme auſſi on a eſcrit, qu'Alphonſe Roy de Naples, regardant vne femme qui danſoit & ſautoit trop deſ-hontément, dit aux aſſiſtans, Attendez vn peu, la Sibylle donnera tantoſt ſes Oracles: pource qu'elle ne rendoit iamais reſponce, comme on dit, ſi elle n'eſtoit ſurpriſe de fureur. Tellement qu'ayant leu cela, auec ce que dit Bodin en ſa Demonomanie, alleguant Iam-

Hurlemẽs & contenances eſtranges des femmes Sauuages.

Liu. 2. ch. 3.

V 2

Musical notation of a Tupinamba song. From Jean de Léry, *Histoire d'un voyage fait en la terre du Brésil, dite Amerique* (Geneva: Vignon, 1600). Bancroft Library, University of California, Berkeley.

writes, is 'a stolen instant, a purloined memory beyond the text.' The fact that Léry does not securely attach a meaning to his experience—and that we cannot do so for him—is the source of its mysterious power: 'An absence of meaning,' de Certeau remarks, 'opens a rift in time.'[26]

This rift, this cracking apart of contextual understanding in an elusive and ambiguous experience of wonder, is a central recurring feature in the early discourse of the New World. It is the feature that most decisively links this discourse, stylistically unambitious and conceptually muddled though much of it is, to both philosophical and aesthetic discourse. For wonder plays a decisive role in the period's philosophy and art, theorized by the former as a principal cause and by the latter as a principal effect. That is, philosophy (as Socrates had already formulated it) begins in wonder, while the purpose of poetry (as innumerable poets said) was to produce the marvelous. This theoretical conceptualization of the marvelous was already under way before the discourse of the New World, but it was by no means fully articulated. It is not, in other words, only or even primarily as an intellectual background to Columbus and other early voyagers that I find discussions of the marvelous important. Something like the reverse is also the case: the frequency and intensity of the appeal to wonder in the wake of the great geographical discoveries of the late fifteenth and early sixteenth centuries helped (along with many other factors) to provoke its conceptualization.[27]

This conceptualization can be read back into the discourse of travel in order to explicate some of its most persistent and puzzling features. According to Descartes—to choose the philosopher who marks the end-point of the mental world of the early modern voyagers and the inception of a different and more familiar world—wonder is not, as Albertus had thought, registered in the heart and blood; unlike the other passions that have good or evil as their objects and hence involve the heart, wonder has only knowledge as its object and thus occurs strictly in the brain. This relocation would seem to detach wonder from the source of its somatic authority—the experience of something very much like a heart attack—but Descartes too insists on its immense strength, a strength that derives from the element of surprise, 'the sudden and unexpected arrival of this impression.'[28] This surprise does not cause the heart to contract, in Descartes's view, but at its most extreme it causes a drastic alteration in the spirits of the brain which rush, as it were, to bear witness to the object of wonder:

> And this surprise has so much power in causing the spirits which are in the cavities of the brain to take their way from thence to the place where is the

impression of the object which we wonder at, that it sometimes thrusts them all there, . . . and this causes the whole body to remain as immobile as a statue, and prevents our perceiving more of the object than the first face which is presented, or consequently of acquiring a more particular knowledge of it. This is what we commonly call being astonished, and astonishment is an excess of wonder which can never be otherwise than bad. (pp. 363–4)

A moderate measure of wonder is useful in that it calls attention to that which is 'new or very different from what we formerly knew, or from what we supposed that it ought to be' and fixes it in the memory, but an excess of wonder is harmful, Decartes thought, for it freezes the individual in the face of objects whose moral character, whose capacity to do good or evil, has not yet been determined. That is, wonder precedes, even escapes, moral categories. When we wonder, we do not yet know if we love or hate the object at which we are marveling; we do not know if we should embrace it or flee from it. For this reason wonder, Descartes argues, 'has no opposite and is the first of all the passions.' Similarly for Spinoza—in whose account wonder was not, strictly speaking, a passion at all, but rather a mode of conception (*imaginatio*)—wonder depends upon a suspension or failure of categories and is a kind of paralysis, a stilling of the normal associative restlessness of the mind. In wonder, 'the mind comes to a stand, because the particular concept in question has no connection with other concepts.'[29] The object that arouses wonder is so new that for a moment at least it is alone, unsystematized, an utterly detached object of rapt attention.

Wonder—thrilling, potentially dangerous, momentarily immobilizing, charged at once with desire, ignorance, and fear—is the quintessential human response to what Decartes calls a 'first encounter' (p. 358). Such terms, which recur in philosophy from Aristotle through the seventeenth century, made wonder an almost inevitable component of the discourse of discovery, for by definition wonder is an instinctive recognition of difference, the sign of a heightened attention, 'a sudden surprise of the soul,' as Descartes puts it (p. 362), in the face of the new. The expression of wonder stands for all that cannot be understood, that can scarcely be believed. It calls attention to the problem of credibility and at the same time insists upon the undeniability, the exigency of the experience.

It is in this spirit that Milton invokes wonder when he describes the rebel angels shrinking themselves in scale in order to enter the council chamber of Pandemonium:

> Behold a wonder! they but now who seemed
> In bigness to surpass Earth's giant sons
> Now less than smallest dwarfs, in narrow room

Throng numberless, like that pygmean race
Beyond the Indian mount, or faerie elves,
Whose midnight revels, by a forest-side
Or fountain some belated peasant sees,
Or dreams he sees, while overhead the moon
Sits arbitress, and nearer to the earth
Wheels her pale course, they on their mirth and dance
Intent, with jocund music charm his ear;
At once with joy and fear his heart rebounds.
(*Paradise Lost* 1.777–88)[30]

The transformation of the rebel angels is at once unbelievable and true—hence a wonder, akin to the marvelous beings, giants and pygmies, long associated with voyages to the Indies. The experience of beholding such a wonder is, in Milton's account, profoundly ambiguous: the exalted spectacle of radical evil is likened to a belated peasant's hallucinatory encounter with fairies, likened then to moon-struck Bottom who tells his mates, 'I am to discourse wonders; but ask me not what' (*Midsummer Night's Dream* v. ii. 29–30). For a moment epic is confounded with comedy, as are giant with dwarf, torment with mirth, demonic with harmless, what lies outside the mind with what lies within. Magical charms, compelling and dangerous, are fleetingly lodged within the pleasures of art, as the fairies 'charm his ear' with their music. The whole experience produces the somatic effect that is, as we have seen, the hallmark of wonder: 'At once with joy and fear his heart rebounds.'

With this rebounding of the heart we are back to Jean de Léry and the wonder of Tupinamba music and dance. Experiences such as those he wishes to describe pose a serious rhetorical problem, a problem akin to that Milton faced in describing events in Heaven and Hell. At the beginning of his account, Léry asks how his French readers can be made to 'believe what can only be seen two thousand leagues from where they live: things never known (much less written about) by the Ancients; things so marvelous that experience itself can scarcely engrave them upon the understanding even of those who have in fact seen them?' (p. lx). The skepticism that educated Europeans have developed must somehow be suspended; they must be made to revise their sense of what is possible and what is only fabulous.

In Guiana in the 1590s Sir Walter Ralegh hears of a people who 'are reported to have their eyes in their shoulders, and their mouths in the middle of their breasts.' Ralegh knows that this 'may be thought a meere fable,' precisely the kind of report that had given Mandeville—who writes of 'foul men of figure without heads, and they have eyes in either shoulder one, and their mouths are round shaped like a horseshoe, y-midst their breasts' (p. 142)—a reputation for lying. But for Ralegh it is skepticism rather than credulity that is likely to be misleading: 'Such a nation was written of by Mandevile, whose reports were holden for fables many yeeres, and yet since the East Indies were discovered, we find his relations true of such things as heretofore were held incredible.'[31] Similarly, Léry writes, with a sarcastic glance at his great enemy Friar Thevet, 'I do not endorse the fabulous tales found in the books of certain people who, trusting to hearsay, have written things that are completely false,' but, he goes on to declare, 'I am not ashamed to confess that since I have been in this land of America, where everything to be seen—the way of life of its inhabitants, the form of the animals, what the earth produces—is so unlike what we have in Europe, Asia, and Africa that it may very well be called a "New World" with respect to us, I have revised the opinion that I formerly had of Pliny and others when they describe foreign lands, because I have seen things as fantastic and prodigious as any of those—once thought incredible—that they mention' (pp. lx–lxi).

The discovery of the New World at once discredits the Ancients who did not know of these lands and, by raising the possibility that what had seemed gross exaggerations and lies were in fact sober accounts of radical otherness, gives classical accounts of prodigies a new life. Léry's text depends for its authority precisely on its claim to sober accuracy ('simply to declare what I have myself experienced, seen, heard, and observed'), on its refusal of the lies, hearsay, and exaggerations of Thevet; but at the same time, he is writing not in testimony to the ordinariness and familiarity of Brazil but to its utter strangeness, the strangeness of 'lands completely unknown to the Ancients' (p. 3). His work can only be believed if he arouses in his readers something of the wonder that he himself has felt, for that wonder will link whatever is out there with inward conviction. For the early voyagers, wonder not only marked the new but mediated between outside and inside (Milton's 'sees|Or dreams he sees'). Hence the ease with which the very words *marvel* and *wonder* shift between the designation of a material object and the designation of a response to the object, between intense, almost phantasmagorical inward states and thoroughly externalized objects that can, after the initial moments of astonishment have passed, be touched, cataloged, inventoried, possessed.

The marvelous is a central feature then in the whole complex system of representation, verbal and visual, philosophical and aesthetic, intellectual and emotional, through which people in the late Middle Ages and the Renaissance apprehended, and thence possessed or discarded, the unfamiliar, the alien, the terrible, the desirable, and the hateful. By a 'system of representation,' I do not mean to suggest that there was a single, perfectly integrated mimetic practice. In this period, as in many others, philosophy and art are distinct and often opposed—the former seeking to pass through the wonder that the latter seeks to enhance—and each is in turn distinct from discourses like history, theology, natural history, and law. Each of the discursive regimes has its own characteristic concerns, intellectual and procedural boundaries, specialized languages. But each of these also touches and interacts with the others in a loose but powerful association, an association driven by certain mimetic assumptions, shared metaphors, operational practices, root perceptions.

Interpreters of literature are trained to analyze the imagination at play; in most early European accounts of the New World we are dealing instead with the imagination at work. It would be foolish to conflate the two modes and to proceed as if interpretive practice could be the same with both; I am painfully aware of all of the ways in which a literary critic is ill-equipped to deal with a text such as Columbus's letter to Santangel. But the European encounter with the New World, with its radical displacement of routines, brought close to the surface of non-literary texts imaginative operations that are normally buried deep below their surface (unlike works of literature where these operations are prominently displayed). Consequently, it may be possible to use some of the concerns of literary criticism to illuminate texts written with anything but literary ambitions and actions performed with anything but theatrical intentions—texts and actions that register not the pleasures of the fictive but the compelling powers of the real.

Let me try to be clear: I am not identifying an overarching Renaissance ideology, a single way of making and remaking the world. Any of the individual national cultures of early modern Europe, let alone the fantastically complex whole, had so many different and conflicting ways of seeing and describing the world that any attempt to posit a unified perceptual field will prove a gross distortion. But the variety is not infinite, and in the face of the New World—the epitome of Descartes's 'sudden and unexpected arrival'—the differing responses disclose shared assumptions and techniques. Struggling to grasp hold of the immense realms newly encountered, Europeans deployed a lumbering, jerry-built, but immensely powerful mimetic machinery, the inescapable mediating agent not only of possession but of simple contact with the other. For this reason, the early modern discourse of discovery, as I shall try to show, is a superbly powerful register of the characteristic claims and limits of European representational practice.

The qualities that gave wonder its centrality to this practice also gave it its ideological malleability. For the perception in Descartes or Spinoza that wonder precedes recognitions of good and evil, like the perception in Aristotle or Albertus Magnus that it precedes knowledge, conferred upon the marvelous a striking indeterminacy and made it—like the imagination to which it is closely linked—the object of a range of sharply differing uses. The chapters that follow explore two of these uses. With Mandeville, I argue in Chapter 2, the language of the marvelous is part of a renunciation of possession, the critical pathway in a circulation of plagiarized, unstable signifiers through which a crusading drive toward the sacred rocks at the center of the world is transformed into a tolerant perambulation along its rim. With Columbus, by contrast, the language of the marvelous is subtly revised, enabling it, as I show in Chapter 3, to function strategically as a redemptive, aestheticizing supplement to a deeply flawed legal ritual of appropriation. I do not think that this possessive use of the marvelous is decisive or final: as I try to show in the latter part of the book, the experience of wonder continually reminds us that our grasp of the world is incomplete.

The most palpable sign of this incompleteness for the early voyagers was an inability to understand or be understood. Such language difference perhaps always has some element of the marvelous. (A Tuscan farmer once told me he could not quite get past his astonishment that *pane* was not called *pane* in English; all other words might possibly differ, but *pane*?) Europeans were particularly struck by encountering peoples who spoke languages, as one observer put it, 'neither knowen nor understood of any.' This linguistic encounter, I show, was caught up in the larger possessive project on which Europeans had embarked. Chapter 4 turns from the legal rites of possession discussed in the preceding chapter to the ruthless appropriation of language. Kidnapping, of course, was not the only possible response to linguistic difference. Trade, based on a more mutual exchange of words and gestures along with objects, offers some limited relief from the relentless, one-way pressure of linguistic appropriation, but I note that trade in the early discourse of the New World always seems to slide toward the oppressiveness and inequality of colonial relations. Hence I end the chapter with the emblematic fate of an Eskimo kidnapped in the act of trading and caught up as a wonder in the European representational machinery.

The trajectory these chapters follow then is from medieval wonder as a sign of dispossession to Renaissance wonder as an agent of appropriation: the early discourse of the New World is, among other things, a record of the colonizing of the marvelous. But my book emphatically does not end here, for an historical trajectory is not a theoretical necessity. In my final chapter, I return to the marvelous as a sign of the eyewitness's surprising recognition of the other in himself, himself in the other. I start with Herodotus, for whom such wonderful recognition is the very condition of history. I then look for a comparable acknowledgment of the other in Bernal Díaz's eyewitness account of Cortés's conquest of Mexico and try to understand why it does not break through. In Bernal Díaz wonder is, in effect, at war with itself: on the one hand, it provokes an uneasy perception of the similitudes hidden in otherness, on the other hand it becomes a blocking agent that continually prevents the perception of the other as brother. Finally, I find in Montaigne a sophisticated version of the mobile, unsettling, tolerant wonder that characterized *Mandeville's Travels*. This recovery of the critical and humanizing power of the marvelous does not magically make up for its use in the discourse of those who came to the New World to possess and enslave—as if art could redeem the nightmares of history—but it does suggest that wonder remains available for decency as well as domination.

I want to return to what I witnessed, or dreamed that I witnessed, in Bali: a sense at once of plenitude and ease, as if everything were possible, as if the festive crowd were freely choosing its pleasures and remaining unconstrained by the choice, as if one's culture were more securely one's own by virtue of a refusal of possession, as if wonder could be prolonged into the ebb and flow of delight. If this eyewitness testimony is suspect, my readers can perhaps agree that what I claim to have seen is a displaced and exotic and idealized image of the cultural mobility of late twentieth-century Europe and America. The displacement enables us to recover the wonder that is latent in our own practices, a wonder that has become flattened by familiarity and yoked depressingly to the ordinary, half-visible regulation of class and status in which museums, movies, paperback books, and schools all play a part. This is the utopian moment of travel: when you realize that what seems most unattainably marvelous, most desirable, is what you almost already have, what you could have—if you could only strip away the banality and corruption of the everyday—at home.

CHAPTER TWO

From the Dome of the Rock to the Rim of the World

INITIALLY I was interested in *Mandeville's Travels* simply as background to an attempt to understand Columbus. If Columbus thought that he had arrived in the East, it would be important to know what the concept of the 'East' meant. In the late fifteenth century that concept depended principally on Marco Polo and Sir John Mandeville, whose books Columbus read and quite possibly carried with him on his first voyage.[1] But as I often find, the background refused to be subordinated to the foreground. *Mandeville's Travels* had its own claims, or rather in this case its own non-claims, for in contrast to Marco Polo, who is constantly weighing the possibilities for trade, and to Columbus, who imagines that he is acquiring for his sovereigns an outlying corner of the Great Khan's empire, Mandeville takes possession of nothing. This abstinence is not only a matter of insufficient power but also of self-definition, a way of aligning himself not with merchants and adventurers but with the great Franciscan voyagers like William of Rubruck and Odoric of Pordenone. William, for example, recounts the awkwardness of appearing empty-handed before a Mongol lord: 'We stood before Sartach and he sat in all his glory, having the lute played and the people dance before him. . . . [I] offered my excuses explaining that as I was a monk, neither possessing nor receiving nor handling gold or silver or any precious thing, with the sole exception of the books and sacred objects with which we served God, we were therefore bringing no gift to him or his lord, for I who had renounced my own possessions could not be the bearer of those belonging to others.'[2]

Mandeville is not a monk—he is a knight and a man of the world—but he has his own version of renunciation in the service of the Christian faith: the Sultan of Egypt, whom Mandeville purports to have served for several years, 'would have married me richly with a great prince's daughter and given me many great lordships, so that I would have forsaken my belief and turned to theirs; but I would not.'[3]

The dream of riches and ennoblement, which burns in Columbus, Cortés, and others, is present here as something that must be renounced in order to keep the faith. And even this faith is not trumpeted as a possession; the refusal of the Sultan's offer is represented not as a heroic holding fast to the truth but as a simple, quiet negation: 'I would not.' Near the book's close, Mandeville recounts another moment of renunciation. Having first confessed, heard Mass, and taken Communion, he and his companions entered the Vale Perilous where they seemed to see gold, silver, and precious jewels all around them. 'But whether it were as it seemed, or it was but fantasy, I wot not.' He gives up the possibility of knowledge—the ability to distinguish between truth and illusion—because he will not reach out to possess any of the alluring things he sees around him: 'But for the dread that we had and also for it should not let [i.e. hinder] our devotion, we would lay hand on nothing that we saw' (i. 198).[4] Curiosity and acquisitiveness both are stilled by the linked emotions of fear and devotion. And once again the devotion is carefully understated, so as not to suggest a stable possession: 'for we were more devout then than ever we were before or after' (i. 198).[5]

This is a chapter about what it means not to take possession, about circulation or wandering as an alternative to ownership, about a refusal to occupy. For possession in Roman law was based largely upon the principle of bodily occupation: 'possession is so styled,' the Digest of Justinian explains, 'from "seat," as it were "position" [*a sedibus quasi positio*], because there is a natural holding, which the Greeks call *katoche* by the person who stands on a thing.' By means of a striking inversion, this principle of positioning—that is, occupation by virtue of placing one's body upon a piece of property—is then made to apply to the placing of a piece of property upon one's body: 'the ownership of things originated in natural possession,' the Digest continues, and 'a relic thereof survives in the attitude to those things which are taken on land, sea, or in the air; for such things forthwith become the property of those who first take possession of them. In like manner, things captured in war, islands arising in the sea, and gems, stones, and pearls found on the seashore become the property of him who first takes possession of them.'[6] As we have just seen, Mandeville abstains from picking up and hence taking possession of the unclaimed treasures that litter the Vale Perilous, and he similarly abstains from establishing a seat or position, a 'natural holding,' on any territory. Sir John Mandeville is the knight of non-possession.

Or rather he becomes the knight of non-possession in the course of his travels. For in fact the opening of his book is not about renunciation but about the dream of recovery, return, reoccupation, and hence repossession. If Mandeville appears to want nothing for himself alone, he wants something very precious for all of Christendom: he wants the land in which Jesus Christ was born and lived and traveled and died, and in particular he wants Jerusalem.[7] Of course, all places belong to God, but the Holy Land is special, for Jesus chose 'to environ that land with his blessed feet' (i. 1). We might note that in the *Glossa ordinaria* the Bolognese jurist Accursius recorded Justinian's definition of possession as 'a pedibus quasi positio,' rather than 'a sedibus'—quite possibly a simple error of transcription, but one that laid a particular emphasis upon possession by the placing of the feet, that is, by standing or perambulation.[8] Hence Mandeville imagines in a very literal sense that Jesus is the owner of the Holy Land; it is the land

> that is hight [i.e. promised] til us in heritage; and in that land he would die seised therein [i.e. possessing it as a freehold] to leave it to his childer. For the which land ilk a good Christian man that may and has whereof, should enforce him for to conquer our right heritage and chase out thereof them that are mistrowing. For we are called Christian men of Christ our father; and if we be right childer of Christ, we owe for to challenge the heritage that our father left to us, and for to do it out of strange men's hands. (i. 2)

But Mandeville issues this call for a Crusade in the first moments of the text, only to swerve from it immediately toward an attack on Christendom's ruling elite.[9] For the common people, Mandeville writes, 'would put their bodies and their chattels in jeopardy for to conquer our heritage,' but the 'lords of the world' are so inflamed by 'pride, envy and covetise . . . that they are more busy for to disherit their neighbours than for to challenge or conquer their right heritage' (i. 2). With aggression thus turned back from the misbelievers who occupy an inheritance that is not rightfully theirs to his fellow Christians who are greedily trying to possess an inheritance that is even less rightfully their own, Mandeville altogether stops talking about a Crusade.[10] He travels to Jerusalem not as a conqueror reclaiming his heritage but as a pilgrim dependent upon the special protection of the

Sultan whom he depicts as the wise and temperate ruler of an obedient, devout, and for the most part honest people.

At the close of his description of the Holy Land, Mandeville presents an extended account of Muslim beliefs which he regards at once as false and as tantalizingly close to Christian truths: 'And for als mickle as they go thus near our faith in these points and many other, methink that mickle the titter [more quickly] and the lightlier they should be converted til our law through preaching and teaching of Christian men' (i. 95).[11] Once again the prospect opens of a repossession, here of the Saracens' souls, and once again it is immediately closed. In place of the Christian preaching and instruction which he has just invoked, Mandeville offers to tell his readers 'what the Sultan did tell me upon a day in his chamber.' In a scene that anticipates Gulliver by some four hundred years, the Sultan asks Mandeville how Christians govern themselves in their own countries, to which Mandeville replies, '"Lord well, thanked be God."' '"Sickerly, nay. It is not so,"' rejoins the Sultan, who then launches into a devastating attack on the hypocrisy, greed, and ignorance of Christian princes and priests. When he finishes, Mandeville can only ask him 'with great reverence, how he came to thus mickle knowing of the state of Christianity' (i. 98). The dream of repossession is not abandoned—Mandeville claims that the Sultan spoke of prophecies 'that Christian men shall recover this land again in time coming, when ye serve your God well and devoutly'—but, in the face of Christian sinfulness, the political and military project proclaimed at the start has been evacuated, transformed into an appeal for moral renewal and a vague, chiliastic hope for redemption. And it is here, at almost the exact mid-point in his text, that Mandeville makes his decisive, peculiar, and unexplained move, turning abruptly from the Holy Land to the rest of the world:

> Here have I told you and declared of the Holy Land and of countries thereabout, and of many ways thither and to the Mount Sinai, to Babylon and other places, of which I have spoken of before. And now will I pass furthermore and speak of divers lands and isles that are beyond the Holy Land. For there are many divers kingdoms and countries and isles toward the east part of the world, wherein are many divers folk and divers kinds of beasts, and many other marvellous things. (i. 102)[12]

This move may seem modest enough, but it implies a renunciation more momentous than those at which we have glanced, an abandonment of the dream of a sacred center upon which all routes converge and a turning instead toward diversity, difference, the bewildering variety of 'marvellous things.' Among the first of these marvels is a castle between Trebizond and

Armenia about which Mandeville relates a particularly fantastic story involving a magical sparrowhawk and 'a fair lady of fairy'; this castle, he writes, is not on 'the right way'—the direct route—to the countries he has just named; 'but he that will see such marvels, him behoves some time thus wend out of the way' (i. 105). From the mid-point of *Mandeville's Travels* onward, the journey is a virtual succession of detours; indeed the very concept of the 'right way' begins to seem a mirage, for there is no longer a clear destination. In the East, to be sure, lies Paradise, but in that direction the roads give out, and there are only 'wastes and wildernesses and great rocks and mountains and a murk land, where no man may see, night ne day . . . . And that murk land and those deserts last right to Paradise terrestrial' (i. 214).

But if Mandeville cannot reach Eden—'Of Paradise can I not speak properly,' he ruefully concedes, 'for I have not been there' (i. 214–15).—his endless detours offer narrative compensations in the celebrated richness of the marvels of the East.[13] From antiquity, these marvels served as one of the principal signs of otherness and hence functioned not only as a source of fascination but of authentication.[14] The treatment of the marvelous in *Mandeville's Travels*—a by no means crude blend of spectacular credulity and genial skepticism—evidently contributed to the author's early reputation as a distinguished authority. Indeed for several centuries Sir John Mandeville, knight of St Albans and physician, was regarded throughout Europe as one of the greatest travelers in history and the most influential witness to the customs of the alien peoples beyond the Holy Land. He was celebrated as a heroic Englishman, cited as an authority on geography and ethnography, represented in manuscript illuminations, held up as a model of human knowledge and daring. Mandeville's account of his travels, written in the mid-fourteenth century, was immensely popular. Manuscripts circulated in English, German, Dutch, French, Spanish, Italian, Latin, Danish, Czech, and Old Irish: some three hundred manuscripts survive. As late as the sixteenth century he could be praised by the patriotic Leland as a greater traveler than Marco Polo, Columbus, or Cortés, and in the early seventeenth century Samuel Purchas could still write that Mandeville was 'the greatest Asian traveller that ever the world had.'[15]

But well before Purchas the number of errors and impossibilities in Mandeville's text had begun to awaken doubts. Hakluyt includes a Latin text of Mandeville in the first edition of *The Principal Navigations*, but marvels were becoming more embarrassing than authenticating. 'When we see something we have not seen before,' declares an interpolated passage in Hakluyt's Mandeville, 'our spirit is amazed not because it is wonderful of itself, but because it is new to us.'[16] This remark, which strikingly anticipates Prospero's words to Miranda, is evidently meant to still not wonder but skepticism. Those who have never left their birthplace will mock travelers' tales, but 'if a man will only go to the next state, he will find differences of speech, customs, fruits, animals; the further he goes the greater the difference. Therefore, despite the fools and unbelievers, the author will continue to describe what he saw' (pp. 8–9).

Not, however, in Hakluyt, for by the second edition Mandeville has been dropped. In general, the doubts about *Mandeville's Travels* hardened either into polite suggestions of textual corruption or into direct charges of lying. These charges in turn gradually expanded from particular 'whoppers'—the gravelly sea, the dog-headed men, the Indians whose testicles hang down to the ground, and so forth—to the content of the work as a whole. Intermingled with the extravagant fantasies were reasonably persuasive geographical or ethnographic descriptions, but the passages that were convincing seemed to derive from other travelers: William of Boldensele, Odoric of Pordenone, Giovanni de Pian Carpini, Albert of Aix, and others. Mandeville not only failed to acknowledge his sources; he concealed them—'coolly and deliberately,' as his great Victorian editor Sir George Warner puts it—in order to claim that he himself had personally undertaken the dangerous voyages to the Middle East and Asia. He was an unredeemable fraud: not only were his rare moments of accuracy stolen, but even his lies were plagiarized from others. Or worse still, they were made into lies in the act of appropriation, for what earlier travelers often presented only as hearsay or local myth, Mandeville made bold to have personally experienced. Thus there had been many reports of a Well of Youth, but Mandeville claimed to have located it and drunk from it himself.[17] Such claims are dangerous, of course, since they strain even eager credulity, but Mandeville is by no means a crude liar. By suggesting that only *continual* drinking from the well will make one seem forever young, he rationalizes the fantasy—brings it down, let us say, to the level of the label on a bottle of Italian mineral water—and then can deliver his testimonial with a pious glance not toward eternal springtime but toward his own mortality: 'I, John Mandeville, saw this well and drank thereof thrice, and all my fellows, and evermore since that time I feel me the better and the wholer and suppose for to do till the time that God of his grace will make me pass out of this deadly life' (i. 121–2).

The cunning with which this little lie is told may help to explain why it took hundreds of years for Mandeville to be transformed definitively from a hero to a calculating rogue. And even by the time of the Enlightenment when he was utterly discredited, his career was not over. In popular culture, he had already passed into the sphere of ballads and jest books.[18] In elite culture he was about to enter the sphere of scholarly editions. Due to a resonant conjunction of imperialism and medieval scholarship, *Mandeville's Travels* was of considerable interest to the nineteenth century, but the author could scarcely be regarded as a distinguished forbear of those indefatigable travelers who were then busily charting Africa and Asia for their grateful countrymen. Rather the work came to be treated as a 'case,' a fascinating old crime to be solved by the inspired scholarly detective work of Warner, Bovenschen, Hamelius, and others.

But the pursuit of obscure clues and the disclosure of forgotten thefts led in a disquieting direction, not toward the discovery of the motive but toward the disappearance of the criminal. By the early nineteenth century most of Mandeville's 'facts' about the world had been disclosed as fantasies, leaving only the author himself as a reality; by the late nineteenth century that author too had been disclosed as a fiction.

Mandeville's appropriations are signalled, we have remarked, by an intensification of the personal; the principle of the eyewitness received in this text an unusual elaboration, perhaps in imitation of the wonderful note of intimacy struck by the great Franciscan travelers of the thirteenth century. 'The married women [among the Tartars] make for themselves really beautiful carts which I would not know how to describe for you except by a picture,' writes William of Rubruck; 'in fact I would have done you paintings of everything if I only knew how to paint.'[19] Or again, 'That evening the fellow who was our guide gave us cosmos [koumiss] to drink, and as I drank it I sweated all over from fright and the novelty of it, for I had never before drunk of it. However it struck me as being very tasty, as in truth it is' (pp. 107–8).

Evidently, the author of *Mandeville's Travels* thought that it was not enough simply to declare 'I saw' or even, like William, 'I felt'; he took it upon himself to explain who the 'I' was. We are told where the author was born and raised, the precise date he left England to begin his travels, for how many years he served the Sultan of Egypt, when he returned to write his account, his state of health, and so forth. But each of these details on inspection turns out to be a fabrication, most often a theft: 'The date of departure is taken from William of Boldensele's letter of dedication to his patron, Cardinal Talleyrand-Périgord; the name "Mandeville" is probably borrowed from the satiric French romance *le Roman de Mandevie*, written about 1340; the service in the court of the Great Khan is copied from

Odoric.'[20] The abundant identifying marks vanish on approach like mirages, and the extraordinarily ingenious efforts to name the author have failed.

The actual identity, the training, the motives, even the nationality of the person who wrote *Mandeville's Travels* have become, under scholarly scrutiny, quite unclear. To be sure, the work begins and ends with clearly articulated public and private motives: the opening exhortation to Christians to retake the Holy Land is matched by a closing appeal for the readers' prayers on behalf of the author's immortal soul. But like everything else in the book, these motives too begin to waver under scrutiny: as I have already noted, *Mandeville's Travels* gives a more sympathetic account of the Saracens than the Christians, and prayers on behalf of an author who turns out to be fictitious have a peculiar status. The pious close takes the form of an offer to exchange prayers with the reader—to 'all those that say for me devoutly a *Pater Noster* and an *Ave*, that God forgive me my sins, [may] he grant them part of all my pilgrimage and all other good deeds that I have done or may do in time coming unto my life's end' (i. 222–3). This holy bargain may be straightforward: 'there is no reason,' writes Mandeville's most distinguished modern editor, M. C. Seymour, 'to doubt the sincerity of the author's final prayer.'[21] But Seymour also writes that the work 'contains a sufficient number of inaccuracies and inconsistencies to make it extremely improbable that its author ever left his native Europe' (p. xiv). Wouldn't this make 'a share' in the author's pilgrimage rather less valuable than it might at first appear? If a reader were to pray for the soul of Sir John Mandeville, knight of St Albans and pilgrim to the Holy Land, what kind of spiritual exchange would actually be taking place? An exchange not with a being created by God but with a human fabrication, a textual artifact.

Most recently it has been argued that the figure of Mandeville was a persona created by an impressive literary artist.[22] This predictable move to a traditional conception of the literary has its advantages: it can categorically redeem the author's errors and lies and unacknowledged debts, and it produces its share of critical 'insights.' We are called upon to notice moments when the hidden 'artist' contrives a particularly ironic effect or turns a traditional bit of lore in an 'original' direction. But, though I follow in its wake, there is something at once misleading and sentimental about this saving invocation of art. Misleading because it detaches the work from its truth claims and from the history of its reception, a history based not upon a willing suspension of disbelief but upon trust; sentimental because it reinforces familiar modern conceptions of intentionality and originality exactly where they are most powerfully challenged. Nineteenth-century fulminations against Mandeville's lies—he was no gentleman!—now seem rather quaint, but they are in touch with the fact that for the modern reader at least there is something disturbing in this work, a toying with trust, an undermining of propriety, a primary and extreme dispossession, a violation of the presumption of a unitary material body that has produced the text, breathed life into its signs, set it in the world. With a travel narrative or an eyewitness history, this presumption is particularly irresistible. Herodotus, the 'father of history,' may have been, as some said, the 'father of lies,' but the notion of fatherhood implies a principle of generative embodiment that recuperates what the lying appears to give away. But Mandeville is radically empty; his name is a textual effect, signalling only the absence of an authentic traveler, an absence that now serves to call forth a compensatory faith in an anonymous artist.

No such aesthetic faith was evoked in the fourteenth century, but would an early reader of *Mandeville's Travels* have shared what I have called the presumption of a unitary material body? Would a contemporary reader expect that a travel text was written by an authentic traveler? What is the nature and source of the text's claim on the reader? The answer is unclear because the ontological categories and institutional structures that are implicit in such questions were themselves only in the process of being formed, the object more of exploration than dogmatic assertion. We can sense the equivocality in a passage at the end of several of the early manuscripts. Mandeville professes to be concerned that some readers might not believe him, for 'many men trow not but that at they see with their eyes, or that they may conceive with their own kindly wits' (p. 222). The problem with eyewitness accounts is that they implicitly call attention to the reader's lack of that very assurance—direct sight—that is their own source of authority. The undermining of credibility is intensified in an account such as Mandeville's, with its tales of exotic wonders beyond what men can normally 'conceive with their own kindly wits.' Therefore, writes Mandeville,

> I made my way in my coming homeward unto Rome to show my book til our holy father the Pope. And I told him the marvels which I had seen in divers countries, so that he with his wise counsel would examine it with divers folk that are in Rome, for there are evermore dwelling men of all nations of the world. And a little after, when he and his wise counsel had examined it all through, he said to me for certain that all was sooth that was therein. For he said that he had a book of Latin that contained all that and mickle more, after which book the *Mappa Mundi* is made; and that book he showed to me. And therefore our holy father the Pope has ratified and confirmed my book in all points. (i. 222)

This, remarks one critic, 'was exactly the circular system of authentication by which the Middle Ages accepted *Mandeville's Travels*: because he seconded the wildest rumors of Pliny or Vincent of Beauvais, because there was nothing new in him, he must be telling the truth.'[23] The operation of the medieval system of authentication is more complex than this comment implies; Mandeville's strategy here is not to dismiss the question of personal presence but to suspend it playfully. The text receives papal ratification—'all was sooth that was therein'—because all that is in it is already written down in another book; but the existence of *that* book is verified once again by Mandeville's eyewitness testimony: 'and that book he showed to me.' At the very moment that the search for Mandeville—the living, bodily source of authenticity, the 'author' of 'his' book—is called off, it is aroused again.

What difference would it make if someone today definitively identified the 'real' author of *Mandeville's Travels*—say, Hamelius's candidate, Jean d'Outremeuse? The effect would be to devalue the innumerable additions and variations, to locate the 'authentic' text in the 'original' language, to concentrate critical attention on the changes that the author introduced into the textual 'raw materials' from which he fashioned his work, to appreciate 'Mandeville' not as a traveler but as an artfully achieved fictive persona. In short, the effect would be to make *Mandeville's Travels* a literary property, the creation and hence the possession of its author. This way of construing a text is comfortably familiar—and, after all, *someone* (or was it some group?) must have assembled and framed the travel fragments that initiated *Mandeville's Travels*—but I think the failure to discover the originator has had its advantages. Not only does it force us to think about this text as an unstable, open-ended, collective production, but it calls attention in a particularly focused way to the discrepancy between written words and the missing body that these words attempt to conjure up.

I could, I suppose, in the manner of Barthes speak not of Mandeville but of the 'Mandeville-effect,' but this locution would only displace critical faith onto the anonymous creator of this effect and hence lose something of the text's paradigmatic power of imposition. For *Mandeville's Travels* is only an extreme version of the transformation of empty words into subjects and bodies. Even knowing that there was no Mandeville, I will continue to use the name to gesture toward the missing body, the fictive body made up of fragments of other bodies, the body that tastes and walks and sees toward which the language of this fourteenth-century text insistently if fraudulently refers.[24]

So strong is the reality claim based upon the eyewitnessing body that over the years it was reinforced and elaborated in the various transcriptions and translations. Hence, for example, to the account of the fish produced by the sea of sand and the lambs that grow on trees, an early English translator added, 'I John Mandeville ate of them, and therefore trow it, for sickerly it is sooth' (i. 190).[25] Why the insistence? To heighten the authority and pleasure of the text. But why should that authority and pleasure be enhanced for medieval readers by such insistence? The answer, I suggest, is to be found in a travesty of Anselm's proof: the most perfect wonder is the wonder that is also a material reality, and the reality-claim is stronger than reality itself.

We continue, as a consequence, to speak of Mandeville as if he existed, and as if the text referred back to his bodily existence. To do so is not simply to submit to an imposition; it is to participate in one of the founding desires of language, the desire to refer us to the world. And if language in this case, as in so many others, works deviously, it is not altogether empty even here. For it betokens not material existence as such but a circulation of signs that makes material existence meaningful, comprehensible, resonant. *Mandeville's Travels*, and the textual phenomenon we call Mandeville himself, is stitched together out of bits and pieces of human experience, most of them pieces that had passed like well-thumbed coins or rather like old banknotes through many hands.

Otto von Diemeringen, who translated the work into German in 1484, reports, according to a modern editor, that 'merchants from two dozen kingdoms, who gathered in Bruges, liked to listen to readings from Mandeville.'[26] It is tempting to say that the merchants sensed in Mandeville a capacity for fraud to which they felt themselves drawn, but his appeal is more likely to lie elsewhere. We might think that medieval merchants would have been more likely to celebrate a famous traveler who was one of their own—I refer to Marco Polo whose family first voyaged east 'in the hope of a profitable venture.'[27] Marco Polo's account of his travels, written in a Genoese prison in collaboration with a fellow prisoner, the professional romance writer, Rustichello of Pisa, is the product of a mercantile sensibility, a keen capacity not only for observing but for reckoning: 'So I, Marco Polo, who have often heard the reckoning made, can assure you personally that the sum total of the [Great Khan's] revenue from all these sources [in the city of Kinsai alone], excluding salt, amounts in normal years to 210 *tomauns* of gold, equivalent to 14,700,000 gold pieces. This is surely one of the most inordinate computations that anyone has ever heard made'

(p. 229).[28] But Marco Polo's obsession with computations seems to have awakened suspicions far more readily than Mandeville's vague visions of fabulous wealth and quiet gestures of pious renunciation. Marco Polo became known as 'Il Milione,' and his merchant friends gathered around his deathbed to urge him to retract his lies.

To judge from the surviving manuscripts, *Mandeville's Travels* was far more widely circulated and credited. *Mandeville's Travels*, we are told, 'was accepted in Paris, Bruges, and London as a fair medium of exchange' (Krasa, p. 13). This claim suggests that the work could be *imagined* not only as current but as currency, like the Chinese paper money that Mandeville, like Marco Polo, describes with wonder and admiration: 'This emperor may dispend als mickle as him list spend, for he makes no money but out of leather, or of paper, or of barks of trees. And when this money is waxed old, and the print thereof defaced because of using, it is brought to the king's treasury, and his treasurer gives new for old. This money is printed on both the sides, as money is of other countries, and it goes through all the Great Caan's lands. For they make no money there of gold ne silver . . .' (i. 165–6). 'Therefore,' adds the Cotton manuscript, the Great Khan 'may despende ynow and outrageously' (p. 172).[29]

Mandeville appears to believe that the use of paper money frees the emperor from the material limitations of coinage, that is, from the scarcity of gold and silver. Representation in the realm of the Great Khan is liberated from constraining material reality but does not, as a consequence of that liberation, lose its value. On the contrary, the paper (and the leather and bark that in Mandeville's times would have been even cheaper than paper) function exactly like the coins stamped on both sides in the West. But when the images on coins are worn away, the defacing signifies a loss of value, since some of the precious metal has been lost; by contrast, when the images on paper money are defaced, the king's treasury simply replaces and hence renews the value. Replacement and renewal are possible precisely because the representation does not depend upon the claim of an intrinsic, material value (or, for Mandeville, upon productivity or revenue) but solely upon the authority of the Great Khan. Conversely, the magnitude of that authority is constantly reaffirmed in the subjects' willingness to treat worthless objects as signs of wealth and tokens of exchange.

In the dream that is figured here we glimpse, I think, a fantasy at the heart of *Mandeville's Travels*: a representation of the external world that does not so much depend upon as call into being an external reality, a self-authorizing, self-authenticating representation that cannot be falsified or diminished in value through circulation; at the same time, a representation whose self-authorizing power does not empty it of material content, a representation that intensifies imaginative possession of the world. Perhaps it was this latent utopian fantasy that made *Mandeville's Travels* singularly appropriate as medium of exchange; a self-authorizing representation would be as good as gold. The agents of mobility had found their secular saint. For *Mandeville's Travels* is above all a hymn to mobility, a reverie of free movement in a world that is paradoxically at once materialized and disembodied.[30]

The image that renders this reverie concrete is that of the passport, and Mandeville characteristically exaggerates his source, in this case William of Boldensele, in order to give himself a perfect *laissez-passer*. The Saracens will not ordinarily allow Christians or Jews to enter the Temple of the Lord in Jerusalem, 'for they say that so foul men should not come into so holy place,' but Mandeville gains admission, 'for I had letters of the sultan with his great seal, in the which he commanded straitly til all his subjects, that they should let me see all the places where I came, and that they should show me the relics and the places at my will' (i. 58).[31] Usually, he writes, the sultan gives pilgrims only his signet—in itself a powerful token of authority, for men do such reverence to his signet, Mandeville writes, 'that, when they see it pass before them, they kneel down thereto, as we do when the priest passes by us with the pyx' (i. 58).[32] The comparison invokes what for Christians is the supreme self-authorizing material sign, but the Saracens treat the sultan's letters with an even greater reverence: 'when they come til any lord or til any other man, alsone as he sees them, he inclines thereto reverently and receives them and lays them upon his head, and syne he kisses them and reads them kneeling, and then proffers him to do all things that the bringer will' (i. 58–9). Such is the authority of the sign under which Mandeville travels.

What the sultan's letters permit the Christian traveler to see is his own lost heritage, a series of holy places that possess a staggering density of associations. These associations culminate in Jerusalem, where their density hardens, as it were, into two extraordinary rocks, one in the Church of the Holy Sepulcher and the other in the Temple of the Lord or the Dome of the Rock.[33] These objects are natural features in the landscape, but they are features that have been transformed by the momentous events that have occurred on them and still more by the simple physical presence, the literal weight, of certain remarkable persons. At times Mandeville imagines that this presence has actually left its mark; in Bethlehem, for example, when the nursing Virgin's breasts were engorged, she expressed some milk on certain red slabs of marble: 'and yet the spots of the white milk are seen upon the stones' (i. 51); or, similarly, Jesus stood on the Mount of Olives when he mounted into heaven: 'and yet may men see the step of his left foot in a stone that he stood on' (i. 68). But even without such 'traces,' as the Çotton manuscript calls them, the weight of sacred events and persons has a profound effect, an effect related to but distinct from the principle of possession by virtue of physical occupation. Where Roman law had seen objects transformed into possessions through bodily presence, here objects—the mute rocks—are transformed through such presence into sacred artifacts, that is, into objects infused with the manifest will and residual power of their maker. This transformation (which is never absolute, since the rocks remain rocks) is intensified—as it were, marked out—by virtue of the carefully wrought structures that frame the rocks, and the rocks are then further transformed into texts by virtue of their embeddedness in sacred stories. The core of the inheritance from which Mandeville is dispossessed consists of the rocks in which landscape, artifact, and text are fused, and he lovingly catalogs their significance.

The Temple of the Lord, for example, contains the rock 'that men called sometime Moriac, but syne was it called Behel.' This is the place where 'the ark of God stood, and other relics of the Jews.' In the ark were the tablets with the Ten Commandments, and Aaron's wand, and the 'yard of Moses, with the which he departed the Red Sea' (i. 60–1), and a gold vessel filled with manna, along with sacred objects and priestly ornaments and vestments. It was on this rock that Jacob slept and had the dream of the angelic stairway and wrestled with the angel and was renamed Israel;[34] that David saw the angel smiting the people with a sword. 'And on this rock our Lord set him when the Jews would have stoned him to death, and the rock clave in two, and in that rift he hid him, and a star came down and gave him light' (i. 61). It was also on this rock that Our Lady sat 'and learned her Psalter'; that Jesus forgave the woman taken in adultery; that Jesus was circumcised; that the angel showed the nativity of John the Baptist; that Melchisedech offered the bread and wine 'in token of the sacrament that was to come' (i. 62); that David prayed to God.[35] It should be noted that these associations are not listed in chronological order; there is no sense of digging down through the sequential layers of the past, no historical framing. Instead there is a sense of semiological thickness, of opacity, of holiness solidified.

The rocks function then as tangible materializations of sacred stories. Mandeville and his contemporaries are saturated with such stories, circulating not as chronologies or sources but as radiances that attach to material existence. In Jerusalem, those radiances become concrete, solid, objectified. The sacred places are clearly linked to the cult of relics; indeed the rocks constitute a species of immovable super-relic. So powerful is their appeal that even this immovability is called into question; in the case of Christ's sepulcher, the sultan, we are told, had to put up a wall to keep pilgrims from breaking off pieces to take away with them.

Mandeville assumes a lively interest in such relics: he reports extensively on some of the most important and warns his readers against misrepresentations:

> Some men trow that half the cross of Christ be in Cyprus, in an abbey of monks that men call the Hill of the Holy Cross; but it is not so. For that cross that is in Cyprus is the cross on which Dismas, the good thief, was hanged. But all men wot not that; and that is ill done. For by cause of getting of offerings they say that it is the cross of our Lord Jesu Christ. (i. 6–7)

This and similar warnings are far from constituting an Erasmian critique of relics; on the contrary, they reinforce their power by making distinctions within an overarching system of meaning that Mandeville complacently accepts. Indeed his one significant claim to possession in the book is of a thorn from the Crown of Thorns; it did not come to him through purchase or conquest, but was given to him, he says, 'for great friendship' (i. 9). In the case of the false cross, the monks lie in order to make money, but the relic in question is not even a fake: it is rather a marginal relic that has been wrongly moved to the center.

On occasion Mandeville is willing to acknowledge the possibility of fraudulence: 'The shaft of the spear with which Christ was stanged [pierced] to the heart has the emperor of Almayne; but the head thereof is at Paris. The emperor of Constantinople says that he has the spear head; and that spear head have I oft seen, but it is greater than that of Paris' (i. 10).[36] Even here, however, there is no direct grappling with fraud: the implication is that the relic at Constantinople is bogus, but Mandeville does not quite say so. Similarly, when he reports that half of Saint John's head is at Constantinople and the other half is in Rome, he adds that 'Some men say that Saint John's head is at Amiens in Picardy; and some say that it is the head of Saint John the bishop' (i. 76). The phrase 'Some men say' enables the author to raise doubts without directly implicating himself in those doubts. He concludes safely, 'I wot not; God wots.' And the Cotton manuscript adds, 'But in what wyse that men worschipen it the blessed Saynt John holt him apayd' (p. 78).

The tactic here is not principally one of caution; elsewhere Mandeville is willing to go quite far in his criticisms of the Catholic Church. Rather, I suggest, it is very difficult for Mandeville to believe that a sign, any sign, does not have some legitimate claim, however marginal, to reality. If a relic is not quite what it is said to be, it is likely that it is a relic of someone or something else. For virtually everything in Mandeville leans up against something else, and by doing so participates, if only glancingly, in the real. The rock, and the other holy sites Mandeville describes in Jerusalem, are extreme instances of this principle, as if the imbrication grows denser the closer one approaches the religious core. The Holy Land for Mandeville is the place of sacred metonymy: one Biblical story or holy legend is propped tightly against another, and it seems as if the major events of Jesus' life, along with careers of the patriarchs and prophets, transpired in a confused rush within a space of some ten square meters.[37]

This sacred metonymy is set against the very different secular metonymy figured in the traveler's movements from one place to another. The contrast is not explicitly thematized: Mandeville does not wish to oppose sacred and secular; on the contrary, he wants them to lean against each other in an uncomplicated, uncritical way. 'Here have I told you . . . of the Holy Land,' he writes half-way through his book; 'And now will I . . . speak of divers lands and isles that are beyond the Holy Land' (i. 102). Nothing could be simpler, more simple-minded even; yet there is an unacknowledged but powerful tension between the mobility that leads the pilgrim toward Jerusalem and the mobility that leads the traveler beyond the Holy Land. The pilgrim describes several different routes, but they all lead toward the same place: 'Many ways,' he writes, 'come all to one end' (i. 4). And that end is the geographical center of the world.

For Mandeville Jerusalem is not the geographical center because it is the spiritual center; it was made the spiritual center precisely because it lay at the geographical mid-point: 'For he that will do anything that he will be known openly til all men, he will ger [cause] cry it openly in the middle of a town or of a city, so that it may be known til all the parts of the city. On the same wise he that was king of all the world would suffer death at Jerusalem, that is in the midst of the world' (i. 1).[38] The space that is invoked in this passage is shaped in a moral and ideological form that pulls against the global vision that will later be articulated in *Mandeville's Travels*. Cartographically, the world is imaged here in the ancient 'T in O' plan, that is a circular disk or wheel ringed at the periphery by the ocean and divided by T-shaped interior rivers and seas into the three continents, with Jerusalem at the perfect center of the 'T'. Metaphorically, it is imaged as a global city with a rounded central space from which the king can announce his decrees. Everything in this view will be oriented toward this central space, everything will be measured in relation to it.

This is the universe in which Mandeville sets out, his mobility an attempt to locate the traces of the Savior who chose 'to environ that land with his blessed feet' (i. 1).[39] This choice confers upon the Holy Land the highest honor, so that 'among all other lands' it is 'the most worthy land and sovereign of all other.' The world then is organized not simply around a central space, but that space is the space of the greatest honor—as if the whole world were like a royal court with a distribution of rank and title. The superiority in honor of the Holy Land existed before Jesus' choice and is inherent in its centrality, so that the theological signification is nested in a geographical and cosmological signification. The philosophical principle that Mandeville cites is from Aristotle: 'the virtue of things is in the midst.' And the underlying scriptural principle is from Isaiah: 'It is He that sitteth upon the circle of the earth.'

This belief is not necessarily incompatible with a belief in the earth's sphericality: Mandeville may have imagined that the world was spherical but that its habitable land masses had the T–O shape—hence Jerusalem could well be the center of a symmetrically distributed set of continents, a center at whose perfect mid-point are the sacred rocks.[40] An uneasy compromise of this kind, projecting the Hebraic symbology of the earth on the sphere of Greek geography, seems to have obtained for Christians through much of late antiquity and the Middle Ages and was not definitively discarded until the wake of the discoveries of the late fifteenth century.[41] But something decisive happens when the vertical, sacramental metonymy that hardens into those rocks gives way to the horizontal, secularizing metonymy that is figured in the traveler's footsteps as he turns away from Jerusalem. One place continues to be linked to another, but instead of the solidifying pull toward the center of the circle, there is a pacing or measuring of the outer rim. And that pacing becomes the mark not of legitimate possession but of the absence of the proper: 'to walk,' Michel de Certeau writes in a visionary essay, 'is to lack a place.'[42] The tension between the two conceptions is registered in the revealing wavering about directions when Mandeville approaches the Earthly Paradise, east of the empire of Prester John. 'And that place is toward the east at the beginning of the earth. But that is not our east, where the sun rises til us; for, when the sun rises in those countries, then is it midnight in our country, because of the roundness of the earth. For . . . God made the earth all round in the midst of the firmament' (i. 214).

In place of a world in which all paths lead to the perfect center,

Mandeville comes to imagine a world in which every point has an equal and opposite point:

> And therefore I say sickerly that a man might go all the world about, both above and beneath, and come again to his own country, so that he had his health, good shipping and good company. . . . And alway he should find men, lands, isles, and cities and towns, as are in their countries. For ye wot well that those men that dwell even under the Pole Antarctic are foot against foot to those that dwell even under the Pole Arctic, as well as we and those men that dwell against us are foot against foot; and right so it is of other parts of the world. For ilk a part of the earth and of the sea has his contrary of things which are even against him. (i. 129)

What is happening here goes beyond a shift from the centralizing and vertical to the expansive and horizontal. Metonymic movement, pace by pace, place by place, one signifier giving way to the signifier contiguous to it, curves round on itself and becomes something different. Each point in the world is balanced by an antipodean point to which it is at once structurally linked and structurally disjoined.[43] 'And right as that star may not be seen here,' Mandeville writes of the Pole Antarctic, 'on the same wise this star [the Arctic Pole] may not be seen there' (i. 128). The absent or occulted signifier cannot be seen, but through an imaginative extension of the metonymic chain it is continually evoked, making the strange familiar and the familiar strange. There is no longer a mystical center, a unique place of honor: in the spherical world, when you have one landscape, you always have the shadowy presence of another, when you glimpse one artifact, you conjure up its strange simulacrum somewhere else, and when you invoke one text, you hear the echo of another. In the passage from the center of the earth to its curved rim, from the Dome of the Rock to the sphere, from the dream of recovery to an endless circulation, the metonymic has been transformed into the metaphoric.

The consequence, in Mandeville's writing, is a transformation in the representation of the human as well as the physical world. In the first half of the book, Mandeville describes peoples—Greek Orthodox Christians, Samaritans, and Muslims—whose beliefs are deviations from his own, true belief.[44] In the second half, the peoples he encounters are at once radically, often horrifyingly different from himself and uncannily connected. At certain moments the connections are reversals, on the antipodean principle of foot to foot. Thus, for example, the Numidians, Mandeville writes, consider black skin beautiful, and 'the blacker they are the fairer them think them. And they say that and [i.e. if] they should paint an angel and a fiend, they would paint the angel black and the fiend white' (i. 33). Or again, in India, 'the women drink wine and not the men. And women shave their beards, and not men' (i. 123); or again there is an isle in the Great Sea Ocean 'where women make mickle sorrow when their childer are born, and mickle joy when that they are dead' (i. 200). But many of these reversals are themselves subject to revisionary explication, so that we are told that 'the cause why they weep and make sorrow at the birth of their childer and make joy when they die is for, when they are born into this world, they come to sorrow and to travail, and when they die, they go to the joy of Paradise' (i. 201). Hence a practice that at first seems a simple inversion of Mandeville's ideology can come to seem instead its appropriate and clarifying enactment.

More resonant still are those metaphoric linkages that hover between inversion and enactment: throughout the second half of his travels Mandeville finds such linkages in a series of anathematized practices including idolatry, devotional self-maiming, ritualized suicide, and cannibalism. The accounts of these practices that come to characterize the strange world beyond the Holy Land insist on mimetic likeness even as they register profound cultural difference and on difference even as they acknowledge profound cultural similitude. They give voice to a peculiar blend of estrangement and familiarity, a collapse of the other into the same and an ironic transformation of the same into the other. Hence, for example, in a passage indebted to Odoric of Pordenone, Mandeville initially describes Tibet as if it were Burgundy: 'a good land and a plentifous of corn, of wine, and of many other things.' The inhabitants of this land do not live in houses, however, but rather in tents made of black felt. But this nomadic imagery immediately gives way to the urban, a description of a city 'walled about with black stones and white' and with paved streets. Within these walls, Mandeville writes, 'is no man so hardy to shed blood, neither of man ne of beast, for love of a mawmet [i.e. idol] that is worshipped there. In this city dwells the pope of their law, whom they call Lobassi. And he gives all the dignities and benefices that fall to their mawmets; and all the priests and ministers of idols are obedient to him as our priests are til our pope' (i. 218). Mandeville is establishing here a kind of metaphoric circulation, so that the idolatrous city seems at once the double and the ironic antithesis of the Christian city, the two contrary views constantly oscillating.[45]

The oscillation intensifies in the remarkable description, based on Odoric, of burial customs. When a man's father dies, Mandeville writes, his son invites his kin and friends to a ceremony. Together with priests and minstrels, they carry the corpse to a hill; there the chief priest cuts off the head and then hews the body into small pieces which are fed to ravenous birds. 'And then,' writes Mandeville, right as priests in our country sing for souls, *Subvenite, sancti Dei*, so those priests there sing with a high voice on their language . . . 'Take tent [attend] now and see how good a man this was, whom the angels of God come to fetch and bear into Paradise.' And then think the son and all his friends that his father is greatly worshipped, when fowls have thus eaten him. And aye the more fowls there come, the more joy have all his friends, and the more think them the dead man is worshipped. And then wends the son home and takes with him all his friends and makes them a great feast. . . . The son gers seethe his father's head, and the flesh thereof he parts among his special friends, ilk man a little, for a dainty. And of the scalp of the head he gers make him a cup, and thereof he drinks all his lifetime in remembrance of his father. (i. 219)[46]

Here the signs of extreme horror and dishonor in Mandeville's Europe—dismemberment, the eating of the corpse by birds, cannibalism—are regarded, in a radical transvaluation of values, as signs of grace. And yet this difference is collapsed in the explicit acknowledgment of liturgical parallels and the tacit acknowledgment of structural parallels with the Christian practice of transforming parts of saintly bodies into artifacts, with pious rituals of remembrance, and with a eucharistic piety that ardently celebrated the eating of the sacred flesh and the drinking of the sacred blood.[47] Sensitivity to the parabolic quality of otherness, to its inverted, metaphoric representation of the central rituals of Christian culture, leads Mandeville beyond the interest in metonymic swervings from orthodoxy that he detected in Islam. Or rather, in a process that closely resembles the movement from the center of the world to its rim, from the dream of possession to a dispossessed wandering, Mandeville passes from a possessive insistence on the core orthodox Christian belief to an open acceptance of many coexisting beliefs. 'And if all there be many divers laws and divers sects in the world,' he writes, 'never the latter [i.e. nevertheless] I trow that God evermore loves well all those that love him in soothfastness and serve him meekly and truly. . . . Men [should] despise no men for the diversity of their laws. For we wot not whom God loves ne whom he hates' (i. 207).[48]

It is tempting to close with this early and eloquent expression of tolerance, for it seems a remarkable human achievement. But should we call Mandeville's attitude tolerance?[49] Tolerance, we could argue, is only genuinely possible with those with whom one has to live; the customs of those at a vast distance in space or time or of imaginary beings may be admired or despised, but such responses are independent of tolerance. They are, in effect, the attitudinal equivalent of the act of categorizing: one may decide that other peoples scarcely merit the name of human beings or that they are models of virtue. In neither case do significant life choices, entailing political decisions with historical consequences, have to be made. A metaphoric embrace of the other is no doubt wonderful, but what is its exigency in the real world? What is to keep it from vanishing into thin air? From this perspective, Mandeville's open and lively interest in the customs of exotic peoples, his refusal to invoke demonic causality for unfamiliar or even repellent practices, and his willingness to impute internal coherence to superficially irrational behavior is not tolerance but rather an early instance of what Hans Blumenberg calls 'theoretical curiosity'.[50]

Yet in the fourteenth century such curiosity, as Blumenberg's magisterial *Legitimacy of the Modern Age* amply demonstrates, is itself heterodox.[51] A refusal to grant the universal authority and ontological priority of Christian orthodoxy, a set of interests that spin away from the centrifugal force of Christian beliefs, a narrative that does not secure the rock-like centrality of Christian order threatens to undermine the values upon which the intellectual and moral life of the faithful was to be constructed. Playfully to entertain the logic of idolatry or cannibalism in faraway lands may seem to have nothing to do with actual practice, but Mandeville, as I have argued, reaches those lands by pacing the rim of the world: there is no decisive break, no epistemological barrier that has to be crossed. Hence the traveler can move, almost imperceptibly, closer and closer to home: if the semi-fabulous inhabitants of Gynoscriphe can be admired, so too can the less imaginary Muslims; if the Muslims can be admired, so too can the Jacobite Christians who 'affirm that confession should be made all only to God and not to man' (i. 84).[52] When in the sixteenth century the inquisition demanded that the heretic Menocchio—who rejected the sacraments as human inventions and called for tolerance of all forms of religious belief—reveal his accomplices, Menocchio replied, 'Sir, I am not aware that I ever taught anyone, nor has anyone shared my opinions; and what I have said came from the book of Mandeville that I read.'[53] Menocchio was burned at the stake in 1599.

Mandeville's Travels then takes a position that could have lived consequences. It is not known if these consequences were actually realized in the late fourteenth century. Menocchio after all read Mandeville, among other books, in the wake of the Reformation, and we might note that several of the books he reported having read would seem in their own original setting to have had little or no subversive power. Hamelius's claim that *Mandeville's Travels* was in its own time a dangerously heterodox work, a kind of anti-papal satire, seems unsupported by the evidence he presents. But if we think of *Mandeville's Travels* as an encyclopaedia of interpretive possibilities, an open-ended articulation of theoretical curiosity based on the principle that we know not whom God loves nor whom he hates, we can usefully complicate the rather crude attempt to determine whether it was or was not a subversive text. Mandeville seems to have reached that principle by giving up one version of his travels—the version committed to the repossession of the sacred place in which all landscape, artifact, and text are conjoined in the solid rock at the center of the world—and embracing another: the version committed to girdling a sphere in which there are multiple landscapes, endlessly diverse artifacts and proliferating texts, each of which echoes another on the opposite side of the globe. But, though I honor the generosity of *Mandeville's Travels*, I want to look briefly at two odd shadows that are unexpectedly cast over it or perhaps by it during the latter half of the book.

The first is a sense of estrangement. In the pages on the Holy Land, Mandeville is highly critical of actual Christian practices, but the ideal origins that hover behind these practices have a clarity and solidity that is figured in the sacred rocks. By contrast, in the account of the marvels and odd beliefs of the East, this solidity appears to weaken, so that it becomes increasingly difficult to find a stable signified to which the whole thesaurus of exotic signifiers may be referred. Christianity remains a continuous half-occulted reference, but the metaphoric substitutions have a way of unsettling the point of origin. Hence, for example, the Eucharist is not so much confirmed as rendered strange by the Tibetan mortuary ritual that it resembles. Or again consider the effect of this description of Indian idol worshipers:

> To that image men come from far in pilgrimage with great devotion, als commonly als Christian men come to Saint James. And some of them, for the great devotion they have to that mawmet, aye as they go, are looking downward to the earth and will not look about them, for they should see nothing that should let their devotion. There come some also thither in pilgrimage that bear sharp knives in their hands, with which, aye as they go by the way, they wound themselves in the legs and the arms and in other places of their body, that the blood runs down from their wounds in great fuysoun. And this they do for the love of that idol, and say that he is full blessed that will die for the love of his mawmet. And some of them bring with them their childer and slay them and make sacrifice of them to their mawmet; and they take the blood of their childer and sprinkle it upon the image. . . . And they bring with them incense and other things sweet smelling for to thurify that image, as we do here to God's body. . . . And sickerly they suffer so mickle pain and martyrdom upon their bodies for the love of that ilk mawmet that unnethe will any Christian man suffer half so mickle, ne the tenth part, for the love of our Lord Jesu Christ. (i. 124–6).

Mandeville could have represented the Indian practices as demonic, but instead they appear to him as an extreme version of Christian practices, as if the language of religious adoration were now literalized, as if the homiletic force of saints' lives were acted out in the pilgrimages of the devout, as if the Indians took seriously, in their bodies as well as their souls, the Christian cult of suffering love. The effect is less to commend Christian moderation or to confirm the universal truth of Christian rituals than to translate those rituals, in the face of such martyrdom, into half-hearted metaphors.

The self-estrangement here, linked with the hollowness at the heart of the fictive traveler himself, is given its perfect emblem in the story told by Mandeville to prove that a man can 'environ' the round earth. The story is of a young man 'who went on a time to see the world.' He passed India and the many isles beyond India until he found an isle where his own language was being spoken to oxen. At this he marveled greatly and then turned back and retraced his immense journey. Only when he returned home did he realize that he had circumnavigated the globe and actually been at the boundaries of his own land; he had simply heard one of his countrymen encouraging his cattle. The story shows, Mandeville writes, that men can travel on what appears to be the underside of the globe without falling off into the firmament—'for as us think that those men are under us, so think them that we are under them' (i. 131)—but it also suggests that this relativizing understanding is purchased at the price of never again feeling quite at home, the price of what Heidegger called an 'uprooting in one's origins.'[54]

For readers of *Mandeville's Travels* from the late Renaissance onwards, this uprooting is linked to the very existence of the text as an unstable collage of pieces fraudulently appropriated and translated or rather mistranslated.[55] 'The translation,' Paul de Man wrote in a well-known essay on Walter Benjamin, 'is the fragment of a fragment, is breaking the fragment—so the vessel keeps breaking, constantly—and never reconstitutes it; there was no vessel in the first place, or we have no knowledge of this vessel, or no awareness, no access to it, so for all intents and purposes there has never been one.'[56] *Mandeville's Travels* is the articulation of a perpetual displacement, the expression, again to quote de Man, of 'a wandering, an *errance*, a kind of permanent exile if you wish, but it is not really an exile, for there is no homeland, nothing from which one has been exiled' (p. 92).

The body of John Mandeville is a set of pieces that are set in motion, carried from one place to another, endlessly exchanged. And a combination of philology and close reading discloses that there was no body to begin with, only the naïve or fraudulent illusion of a body. There is no original, no authorizing self, no authentic text; all texts are translations of fragments that are themselves translations. Still less is there an original experience, an extralinguistic meaning, a primal act of eyewitnessing that is subsequently copied, paraphrased, or imitated in Mandeville's collage of translations. Translation here and everywhere else is not a relation of a text to human experience but what de Man calls 'a relation from language to language' (p. 82), a metonymic chain of signifiers permanently excluded from a return home. Again, close reading of this intralinguistic exchange disarticulates any claim to wholeness, challenges any pretense to canonical authority.

The merchants of language travel with neither gold nor goods; they travel with paper currency, and no ruler will authorize—that is to say, *underwrite*—the medium of exchange. There are, to be sure, legends of such a ruler, but he has at best a shadowy existence, like the distant emperor in Kafka's parable, 'The Great Wall of China.' That emperor, you will recall, on his death bed sent you a message, a message only for you. The message is set in motion, but there are too many courtyards in the imperial palace and too many streets in the city beyond its gates and too many villages and houses in the world beyond its walls, and the emperor's dying words will never reach you: at nightfall, seated at your window, you ceaselessly dream this message.

'Now it is this motion,' writes Paul de Man, 'this errancy of language which never reaches its mark, which is always displaced in relation to what it meant to reach, it is this errancy of language, this illusion of a life that is only an afterlife, that Benjamin calls history' (p. 92). Read from this perspective, *Mandeville's Travels*, with its spurious allusions to defunct dynasties, its invocations of illusory authorities, its false claims to eyewitness authenticity, and above all its errancy, is an allegory of the text of history; and the absence of Mandeville from the work that bears his name is a figure for the absence of the human from history. For history, writes de Man, 'is not human, because it pertains strictly to the order of language; it is not natural, for the same reason; it is not phenomenal, in the sense that no cognition, no knowledge about man, can be derived from a history which as such is purely a linguistic complication; and it is not really temporal either, because the structure that animates it is not a temporal structure.' How, we might ask, could there be a history without temporality? 'Those disjunctions in language do get expressed by temporal metaphors,' de Man acknowledges, 'but they are only metaphors' (p. 92).

With the surprising appearance of the metaphorical in the space of metonymy, we are returned to the peculiar tolerance that is Mandeville's distinctive achievement: a capacious, theoretical, alienated tolerance that abjures possession. And we are brought as well to what is in de Man the rhetorical equivalent of this tolerance: a capacious, theoretical, alienated irony. In Mandeville's work as in de Man's, a half-smile, embracing everything, laying claim to nothing, seems linked to the inescapable errancy of language, an errancy that inscribes difference everywhere, not only at the margins but at the center, not only in the other but in the self.

But this acceptance and mutual celebration of difference is complicated in de Man's work by the history of which he never spoke, the history that was not 'purely a linguistic complication,' the history that led to the suicide of Benjamin. And now I turn to the second shadow that falls across *Mandeville's Travels* and darkens the generous accounts of Brahmin mystics, Tibetan cannibals, and Chinese idolaters. Such peoples were, of course, completely fantastic for a fourteenth-century European audience, but there was a strange people, an other, actually living in their midst. I am referring to the Jews, and toward them Mandeville is surprisingly ungenerous. The Jews of his own time scarcely figure in his account of the Holy Land—it is as if they had vanished, leaving only the ancient textual traces attached to the landscape.[57] But when Mandeville turns away from the Dome of the Rock to the sphere beyond, the Jews make several peculiar and highly charged appearances. He claims that a Jew had personally confessed to him that with a deadly poison that grows in Borneo his people had plotted to kill all of Christendom. This charge, in the context of fourteenth-century Europe with its waves of anti-Semitic persecutions centered (particularly after 1321 and 1348) on the charge of poisoning wells, is especially horrible and dangerous. Moreover, Mandeville writes that in a land beyond Cathay the Ten Lost Tribes are shut up within steep hills. The narrow exit from the hills is guarded by the Queen of the Amazons, and 'if it happen that any of them pass out, they can speak no language but Hebrew, ne they not speak with other men when they come among them' (i. 185). But it is prophesied, Mandeville writes, that in the time of the Antichrist these Jews—known as Gog and Magog—will sally forth from the hills and, aided by Hebrew-speaking Jews dispersed elsewhere in the world, will bring Christendom under their sway, just 'as they have been under Christian men' (i. 185–6).

Why are the Jews made the most significant exception to the tolerance that is so impressively articulated elsewhere in Mandeville's travels? Why can they not be included in the larger sphere of metaphoric understanding? Why must they be made into the other of the other? Because they are located, in a way Mandeville evidently finds intolerable, between the realms of the secular and the sacred, metonymy and metaphor, because they embody the estrangement that continually threatens to surface in relation to his own beliefs, because they are at once rivals in the dream of repossession and rivals in the dream of wandering. As unredeemable enemies, they secure the identity that always threatens to slip away from Mandeville's text, and their presence enables us to glimpse the seeds of the militancy that would, in a different time and place, inspire the Expulsion and the *Reconquista* and push outward on the round rim of the earth toward the New World.

In the year that Moorish Granada fell and that the Jews were driven from Spain, Columbus set sail for the East. On December 26, 1492, moored off Hispaniola, Columbus made an entry in his log-book that Las Casas transcribed with particular care. The Admiral will leave some of his men behind in the hope that when he once again returns to the newly discovered lands these men would have obtained by barter a cask of gold, 'and that they would have found the gold mine and the spicery, and those things in such quantity that the sovereigns, before three years [are over], will undertake and prepare to go conquer the Holy Sepulcher [*la casa Sancta*]; for thus I urged your Highnesses to spend all the profits of this my enterprise on the conquest of Jerusalem, and Your Highnesses laughed and said that it would please them and that even without this profit they had that desire. These are the Admiral's words.'[58]

Columbus's voyage on the round rim of the world would lead, he thought, back to the rocks at its sacred center.

CHAPTER THREE

Marvelous Possessions

LET us begin at the most famous of beginnings:

> As I know that you will be pleased at the great victory with which Our Lord has crowned my voyage, I write this to you, from which you will learn how in thirty-three days, I passed from the Canary Islands to the Indies with the fleet which the most illustrious king and queen, our sovereigns, gave to me. And there I found very many islands filled with people innumerable, and of them all I have taken possession for their highnesses, by proclamation made and with the royal standard unfurled, and no opposition was offered to me. To the first island which I found, I gave the name *San Salvador*, in remembrance of the Divine Majesty, Who has marvelously bestowed all this; the Indians call it 'Guanahani'. To the second, I gave the name *Isla de Santa María de Concepción*; to the third, *Fernandina*; to the fourth, *Isabella*; to the fifth, *Isla Juana*, and so to each one I gave a new name.[1]

Thus begins Columbus's celebrated account, in a letter to Luis de Santangel, of his first voyage.[2] The moment, of course, has become fixed in the popular imagination: the great adventurer on the beach, unfurling the royal standard and taking possession of the New World. Columbus's words are filled out by what we know to have followed: other voyages, widening discoveries, the dawning realization that classical geography was wrong and that a whole new hemisphere had been discovered, the violent encounter of civilizations, the missionary enterprise, mass enslavement and death, the immense project of colonization.

Apart from the determination to return, Columbus could not have known or anticipated any of this subsequent history; what from this distance is striking is how little he could grasp in 1492 where he was or what he was initiating. His words then, like the words of the Articles of Agreement with which he set sail, were in some important sense written as empty place-holders for uncharted lands and unimaginable future events—*todo esto*, 'all this,' as he puts it, with an expansive gesture that prudently avoids any specification of what 'all this' amounts to. And yet Columbus's letter does seem to anticipate and to promote the mythic sense with which time has invested his account. We can sense his myth-making already in the flourish with which he proclaims 'la gran vitoria', a phrase more appropriate in 1492 to the conquest of Granada than to landfall in the Caribbean,[3] and in the term used to describe God's bestowal of the discovered islands: 'marvelously' (*maravillosamente*). I shall argue that Columbus had a highly self-conscious interest in the marvelous.

Why did Columbus, who was carrying a passport and royal letters, think to take possession of anything, if he actually believed that he had reached the outlying regions of the Indies? It did not, after all, occur to Marco Polo in the late thirteenth century to claim for the Venetians any territorial rights in the East or to rename any of the countries; nor in the fourteenth century did Sir John Mandeville unfurl a banner on behalf of a European monarch. Indeed, as we have seen, in the climactic moment of Mandeville's account the knight and his companions piously refuse to pick up the gold and precious stones that litter the valley through which they pass. Columbus, who almost certainly had carefully read the travel accounts of both Marco Polo and Mandeville, behaved startlingly differently.

The difference may be traced of course to the fact that, unlike Marco Polo or Mandeville, Columbus was neither a merchant nor a pilgrim: he was on a state-sponsored mission from a nation caught up in the enterprise of the *Reconquista*. But the objective of this mission has been notoriously difficult to determine. Columbus's passport appears to suggest that he is to proceed to a known place—the Indies—on business concerning the orthodox faith.[4] The original of his *Diario* or log-book has disappeared, but the transcription by his contemporary Las Casas indicates that Columbus was charged to go to the city of Quinsay—that is, Hangzhou—'to give Your Highnesses' letters to the Grand Khan, and to ask for, and to come with, a reply.'[5] At the same time, the grant that Columbus received from Ferdinand and Isabella speaks of Columbus as 'going by our command, with certain vessels of ours and with our subjects, to discover and to gain certain islands and mainland in the Ocean Sea' (p. lxxii). This language—

'descobrir é ganar'—suggests something more than a diplomatic or commercial voyage, but neither the sailors nor the ships of the first expedition were appropriate for a serious military campaign, so that it is difficult to envisage what kind of 'gaining' the monarchs had in mind.[6] I have no solution to these famous enigmas, but I propose that we look carefully at the action Columbus reports and that we consider the extraordinary extent to which that action is *discursive*.

The claim of a 'great victory' and the unfurling of the royal standard suggest that we are about to hear an account of a battle, but what we get instead is an account of a series of speech acts: a proclamation (*pregón*) by which Columbus takes possession of the islands followed by the giving of new names. These speech acts—*he tomado posesión*, *puse nombre*—are so familiar to us that it is difficult to find anything in them worth remarking, but we would do well to look at them more closely.[7] Here, and throughout the early discourse of the New World, the reassuring signs of administrative order—bureaucratic formulas already well established in a very large number of earlier military, diplomatic, and juridical encounters in Europe and Africa—are deceptive; consciously or unconsciously, they draw us away from a sense of all that is unsettling, unique, and terrible in the first European contacts with the peoples of America.

It is important, I think, to resist the drift toward normalizing what was *not* normal. We can demonstrate that, in the face of the unknown, Europeans used their conventional intellectual and organizational structures, fashioned over centuries of mediated contact with other cultures, and that these structures greatly impeded a clear grasp of the radical otherness of the American lands and peoples. What else would we expect? But such demonstrations do not—or should not—efface the incommensurability, the astonishing singularity, of the contact initiated on October 12, 1492. Virtually all prior recorded encounters between Europeans and other cultures took place across boundaries that were to some degree, however small, porous; this means that all prior encounters had been to some degree, however small, anticipated. To be sure, there were many earlier occasions on which European voyagers experienced the shock of extreme cultural difference: 'And so on the third day after leaving Soldaia,' writes William of Rubruck in the thirteenth century, 'we came across the Tartars; when I came among them it seemed indeed to me as if I were stepping into some other world.'[8] But however strange the Tartars seemed to William, there had been a sporadic history of contact; William expected them to be there and knew roughly where to find them. Moreover, they were reached by a series of small stages that took William gradually away from his familiar world and toward the strange. Prior to Columbus there had been nothing comparable to the absolute break brought about by the exceptionally long ocean crossing, a break that effaced the process of acclimatization on the margins, the incremental signs of growing distance and difference that characterized earlier travel.[9] Alexander the Great managed to lead his army into India, but, as Arrian's biography makes clear, the advance consisted of innumerable smaller acts of reconnaissance, negotiation, and conflict. And this was the pattern for almost all episodes of expansion and warfare.

The European landfall in the Caribbean in 1492 was drastically different—the extreme length of the voyage, the invaders' total unfamiliarity with the land, and their absolute ignorance of its inhabitants' cultures, languages, socio-political organizations, and beliefs made it so. In consequence, all of the familiar procedures had, from the beginning, a quality of displacement. Detached from the world in which they had long functioned coherently (or at least routinely) and dropped into an entirely alien world, they have the odd air of quotations. Our initial interpretive move, I think, must be not to sweep away these quotations—the formularies and stereotypical gestures—but to realize how extremely strange they are or rather how strange they become in this unprecedented situation. Even if every detail is based on some precedent or other, each is destabilized, defamiliarized, uprooted. There are real bodies and real consequences, but the very conventions used to demarcate the real (in denoting sovereignty and legitimate possession) seem in the peculiar light of 1492 to be signs as much of the imaginary as of the real.

The display of the royal standard in the first moments after Columbus's landfall marks the formality of the occasion and officially designates the sovereign on whose behalf his speech acts are performed; what we are witnessing is a legal ritual observed by men whose culture takes both ceremony and juridical formalities extremely seriously. Columbus's journal entry for October 12 provides some of the details of the ritual: 'The Admiral called to the two captains and to the others who had jumped ashore and to Rodrigo Descobedo, the *escrivano* of the whole fleet, and to Rodrigo Sánchez de Segovia; and he said that they should be witnesses that, in the presence of all, he would take, as in fact he did take, possession of the said island for the king and for the queen his lords, making the declarations that were required, and which at more length are contained in the testimonials made there in writing.'[10] About twenty years later, in a royal instruction to Juan Díaz de Solís (a Portuguese navigator in the employ of the Crown of Castille), we get a more detailed account of the formal acts by which the crown's representatives took possession of 'new' lands:

The manner that you must have in the taking of possession of the lands and parts which you shall have discovered is to be that, being in the land or part that you shall have discovered, you shall make before a notary public and the greatest possible number of witnesses, and the best known ones, an act of possession in our name, cutting trees and boughs, and digging or making, if there be an opportunity, some small building [*edificio*], which should be in a part where there is some marked hill or a large tree, and you shall say how many leagues it is from the sea, a little more or less, and in which part, and what signs it has, and you shall make a gallows there, and have somebody bring a complaint before you, and as our captain and judge you shall pronounce upon and determine it, so that, in all, you shall take the said possession; which is to be for that part where you shall take it, and for all its district [*partido*] and province or island, and you shall bring testimony thereof signed by the said notary in a manner to make faith.[11]

As the phrase 'if there be an opportunity' suggests, this is less a description of actual Spanish practice than an ideal type, a compact anthology of legitimating gestures: actual presence in the land (mere sighting from shipboard does not suffice), the mechanism of legal recording (requiring a notary and witnesses), the physical alteration or marking of the land, the construction of an edifice on a distinctive site that is mapped (and hence can be verified and reoccupied), the formal exercise of justice. From other documents in the period one can expand the list of common symbolic acts: placing stones, cutting grass, raising mounds or pillars, erecting crosses, even drinking water. Captains would in effect select from the repertory and, within its generic limits, improvise a formal ceremony. Cortés, we are told, 'moved walking on the said land from one part to another, and throwing sand from one part to another, and with his sword he struck certain trees that were there, and he commanded to the people who were there that they should have him for governor of His Majesty of those said lands, and did other acts of possession.'[12] Pedro de Guzmán 'delegated his authority to a seaman who swam ashore and there erected a cross, cut down boughs of trees, and took possession of the island, his acts being witnessed by two other seamen who had swum ashore with him and whose testimony formed the basis of the formal notarial act that was subsequently drawn up on board the ship.'[13] Columbus's version is more simple and abstract; he makes no mention of cutting boughs or throwing sand, let alone constructing a house or gallows. There are no attempts in the initial landfall to inscribe the Spanish presence on the land, to leave even an ephemeral mark such as a gash in a tree or a cleared patch of grass.[14] His actions are performed entirely *for a world elsewhere.*

For Columbus taking possession is principally the performance of a set of linguistic acts: declaring, witnessing, recording. The acts are public and official: the admiral speaks as a representative of the king and queen, and his speech must be heard and understood by competent, named witnesses, witnesses who may subsequently be called upon to testify to the fact that the unfurling of the banner and the 'declarations that are required' took place as alleged. At issue is not only the crown's claim to sovereignty but Columbus's own status; after months of difficult negotiation, he had obtained, in the Capitulations of April 17, 1492, appointment as Admiral, Viceroy, and Governor-General over all islands and mainland 'which by his labor and industry shall be discovered or acquired.'[15] He was also granted one-tenth of all the treasure and merchandise produced or obtained in these domains, free of all taxes. In a further, extraordinary concession, the crown agreed that Columbus's title and prerogatives would be enjoyed by his heirs and successors 'perpetually.' On October 12 then Columbus is not only the medium through which the crown could claim possession; he also enacts the ritual of possession on his own behalf and on behalf of his descendants.

And because Columbus's culture does not entirely trust verbal testimony, because its judicial procedures require written proofs, he makes certain to perform his speech acts in the presence of the fleet's recorder (for a fleet which had no priest had a recorder), hence ensuring that everything would be written down and consequently have a greater authority. The papers are carefully sealed, preserved, carried back across thousands of leagues of ocean to officials who in turn countersign and process them according to the procedural rules; the notarized documents are a token of the truth of the encounter and hence of the legality of the claim. Or rather they help to produce 'truth' and 'legality,' ensuring that the words Columbus speaks do not disappear as soon as their sounds fade, ensuring that the memory of the encounter is fixed, ensuring that there are not competing versions of what happened on the beach on October 12th. A priest may be said to facilitate a transaction with eternity, but an *escrivano* facilitates a transaction with a more immediately useful form of temporality, the institutional form secured by writing.

A distinction between peoples who have writing and peoples who do not will, as we have seen, become crucial in the discourse of the New World, but in the initial moments with which we are concerned Columbus does not know enough about those he has encountered to make such a distinction. He evidently does not feel the need to know anything about them at this moment, and we should note that the instruction to De Solís similarly does not include any provision for recognition of the cultural level, rights, or even the existence of the natives. Columbus's journal mentions that naked people were sighted on shore before the Spanish landed, but it is not altogether clear that the ritual of possession took place within earshot of these people who subsequently approached in large numbers.[16] Ceremonies take the place of cultural contacts; rituals of possession stand in for negotiated contracts. Columbus acts entirely within what Michel de Certeau calls 'the scriptural operation'[17] of his own culture, an operation that leads him not simply to pronounce certain words or alternatively to write them down but rather to perform them orally in the presence of the fleet's named and officially sanctioned recorder. Writing here fixes a set of public linguistic acts, gives them official standing, makes them 'historical' events. But what are these linguistic acts? For whom and by what right are they being performed? Why are they assumed to be efficacious?

In part the answer may lie in the odd phrase in his letter to Santangel, 'y no me fué contradicho'—not, as the English translation renders it, 'and no opposition was offered to me,' but rather 'and I was not contradicted.' This presumably refers not to the Spanish—who were called upon to bear witness and who would scarcely object[18]—but to the natives. But what can such a phrase mean? It is possible, I suppose, to imagine it as either a cynical sneer or a skeptical joke. In the former case, Columbus would be laughing at the impossibility of the natives contradicting something they are deliberately kept from understanding or, alternatively, at their impotence to contradict a seizure of their lands even if they were to understand the proclamation perfectly. In the latter case, Columbus would be laughing at the natives' hopeless ignorance: 'if the horse had anything to say, he would speak up.' But rarely if ever in his writings does Columbus seem either cynical or skeptical, least of all here, when he is recounting the crucial event of the entire voyage. We must assume that he is writing in earnest and that he takes seriously the 'fact' that he was not contradicted.

The absence of 'contradiction' had a specific force: such a fact would be important in establishing for the Spanish crown a legal claim to the newly discovered lands by the 'voluntary choice' of the original inhabitants.[19] That is, if those inhabitants actually wished to transfer title to their lands and possessions to the Spanish, they should be allowed to do so. The legal basis for such a transaction is found in Roman law where, according to Justinian's *Institutes*, 'there is nothing so natural as that the intent of the owner to transfer his property to another should have effect given to it.'[20] In the *Digest* of Justinian Ulpian writes that 'We say that a person possesses by stealth who has entered into possession without the knowledge of him who, he suspects, would oppose his taking [*quem sibi controuersiam facturum suspicabatur*]. . . . No one acquires possession by stealth who takes possession with the knowledge or consent [*sciente aut uolente*] of the thing's owner.'[21] And in his important mid-thirteenth-century gloss on this passage, Accursius adds the phrase 'et non contradicente.'[22] From this phrase would seem to derive Columbus's declaration 'and I was not contradicted,' or in the Latin translation of his letter, 'contradicente nemine possessionem accepi.'[23]

But how should such a principle be thought to apply in this case? The problem is not simply opposing interests—the natives' desire to retain possession of their land against the Spanish desire to appropriate it—but incommensurable positions.[24] The Arawak are not simply denied the opportunity to dispute the Spanish claim; they are not in the same universe of discourse. Even if one discounts the incompatibility of a bureaucratic system based on legal title and a way of life that does not conceive of the land as alienable 'real estate,' the abyss between the two parties remains so overwhelming that Columbus's claim that he was not contradicted seems absurd.[25] Why should words spoken in a language the native inhabitants had obviously never before heard be thought to constitute a valid speech act, transferring their lands to those whose utterly incomprehensible visual signs—a cross, two crowns, the letters F and Y—were printed on the Spanish banners? Why should the natives be thought capable, under the circumstances, of assenting or offering a contradiction?[26]

The answer, I think, may lie in the extreme formalism of Columbus's linguistic acts. That is, Columbus is observing a form—the journal, let us recall, spoke of making the 'required declarations'—and that form evidently calls for the possibility of a contradiction, a counter-declaration to the one by which possession is claimed. It is this formal occasion that must be observed rather than the contingency for which the formal occasion must originally have been conceived. Fulfilling the forms is enough: what we would be tempted to dismiss as *mere* form is for Columbus and for the Spanish whom he serves the heart of the matter. Hence Columbus does not write, 'the natives did not contradict me,' but rather, 'I was not contradicted.' He is not concerned with a particular subjective consciousness responding to the proclamation and hence with consent as an inner act of volition but with the formal absence of an objection to his words. *Why* there was no objection is of no consequence; all that matters is that there was none. The formalism of Columbus's proclamation derives not only from the fact that it represents the scrupulous observance of a preconceived form (hence is not spontaneous or aleatory) but also from its complete indifference to the consciousness of the other. The words are a closed system, closed in such a way as to silence those whose objection might challenge or negate the proclamation which formally, but only formally, envisages the possibility of contradiction.

According to medieval concepts of natural law, uninhabited territories become the possession of the first to discover them.[27] We might say that Columbus's formalism tries to make the new lands uninhabited—*terrae nullius*—by emptying out the category of the other. The other exists only as an empty sign, a cipher. Hence there can be no contradiction to the proclamation from anyone on the islands themselves, because only linguistic competence, the ability to understand and to speak, would enable one to fill in the sign. There is, of course, a whole multinational culture—the Europe from which Columbus has come—that has this competence and could both understand and dispute the claimed possession, but then this culture is not in the right place at the right time. When the moment arrived to contradict the proclamation, those who could contradict it were absent, and all subsequent claims will be forever belated and thus invalid. When, almost immediately after his return, Columbus's letter is published in several languages all over Europe, in effect it promulgates the Spanish claim and affirms that the moment for contradiction has irrevocably passed. The ritual of possession, though it is apparently directed toward the natives, has its full meaning then in relation to other European powers when they come to hear of the discovery. It is as if from the instant of landfall Columbus imagines that everything he sees is already the possession of one of the monarchies he has offered to serve—Portuguese, English, Spanish—and he proceeds to establish the correct claim by the proper formal speech act. I said at the outset that Columbus's words—'And there I found very many islands filled with people innumerable, and of them all I have taken possession for their highnesses'—were empty place-holders for the unknown and unimaginable. We could call this quality of the words their *open formalism*, since it is precisely their formal vacancy (a set of blanks that have not yet been filled in) that makes possible the imperial indeterminacy of the claim to possession. But now we find that this openness is itself the effect of an underlying *closed formalism*, since the ritual of possession itself precludes the intervention (or even the understanding) of those who, the ceremony implicitly acknowledges, are most likely to object. Formalism then has the virtue of at once inviting and precluding contradiction both in the present and in the future: 'Speak now or forever hold your peace.'[28]

The formalism I have described is generally important in the functioning of legal and religious rituals, but it is by no means limited to these discourses. The letter to Santangel, after all, is not a legal document but a narrative.[29] Narrative is a comfortable home for the discursive strategy I have been describing because the pressure of linked events and the assumed coherence of the tale help to pull the reader past the awkwardness of incommensurable positions and silenced voices. It is one of the principal powers of narrative to gesture toward what is not in fact expressed, to create the illusion of presences that are in reality absent. For this reason, the formal acknowledgment of beings who are at the same time rendered silent is less discordant in Columbus's narrative, less obviously anomalous, than it is in juridical or theological discourse where it soon provoked eloquent and sustained protest.

If we recognize that formalism in the letter to Santangel functions as the discursive agent of Columbus's power, I think we should resist the notion that formalism has a necessary and inherent politics, and that this politics is colonialist. For in the next generation a comparable formalism led Francisco de Vitoria (*c.*1492–1546) to argue from the tenets of natural law that the indigenous peoples had not had their rights respected, and to challenge the basis for the whole Spanish claim to the Indies. Thus, for example, Vitoria quickly dispatches the claim to sovereignty through the right of discovery. There is a title, he writes in *De indiis*,

> which can be set up, namely, by right of discovery; and no other title was originally set up, and it was in virtue of this title alone that Columbus the Genoan first set sail. And this seems to be an adequate title because those regions which are deserted become, by the law of nations and the natural law, the property of the first occupant [*Inst.*, 2. 1. 12]. Therefore, as the Spaniards were the first to discover and occupy the provinces in question, they are in lawful possession thereof, just as if they had discovered some lonely and thitherto uninhabited region.
>
> Not much, however, need be said about this . . . title of ours, because, as proved above, the barbarians were true owners, both from the public and from the private standpoint. Now the rule of the law of nations is that what belongs to nobody is granted to the first occupant, as is expressly laid down in the aforementioned passage of the *Institutes*. And so, as the object in question was not without an owner, it does not fall under the title which we are discussing. . . . In and by itself [this title] gives no support to a seizure of the aborigines any more than if it had been they who had discovered us.[30]

It could be demonstrated then, on purely formal grounds, that Columbus's ritual of possession was not valid.[31] Conversely, a theoretical position quite opposed to formalism could be used to support the Spanish claim. Thus, from the perspective of an anti-formalist historicism, Gonzalo Fernandez de Oviedo, the official chronicler for Charles V, in effect discounts the paramount importance of Columbus's formal acts. To be sure, Oviedo celebrates the voyage for its visionary daring, its unprecedented use of navigational instruments, its geopolitical significance, but then he carefully collects stories designed to show that Columbus learned his route from a dying pilot, that others had been there before, that the alleged discovery is in reality a rediscovery. Above all, Oviedo proves to his own satisfaction at least that the Indies are identical to the Hesperides. And on the principle that 'provinces and kingdoms in olden days took the name of the princes or lords who founded, conquered, settled or fell heir to them,' he concludes that the Hesperides were named for Hesperus, twelfth king of Spain in descent from Tubal Cain, and hence that 'it has now been 3193 years that Spain and Hesperus, her king, have held dominion over these islands.' 'So, with such very ancient right,' he declares, 'God returned this domain to Spain after so many centuries.'[32]

Oviedo's argument was not a quaint expression of historical curiosity; it was a sophisticated intervention in the long legal battle, the *pleitos de Colón*, between the crown and Columbus's heirs over the latter's claim to hereditary rights in the New World. Those rights had been granted for any lands that Columbus had 'discovered or gained'; if there was no authentic discovery but only a restoration of rights, then the position of the heirs would be substantially weakened. A further function of Oviedo's historicizing claim was to weaken the link between Spanish sovereignty in the New World and the 'donation' of the Indies to Spain by Pope Alexander VI in 1493. Papal bulls granted to Ferdinand and Isabella dominion over all the lands inhabited by non-Christians that they might discover in the Atlantic. But, as Anthony Pagden notes, this donation 'rested on the two claims which Spanish jurists and theologians found hardest to accept: the claims that the papacy possessed temporal as well as spiritual authority and that it could exercise this authority over pagans as well as Christians.'[33] Moreover, when the Catholic Church began to play a more independent role in Spain's American possessions and to dispute certain of its policies, especially its treatment of the Indians, the crown sought to create some distance between the papal donation and its own 'right of possession,' now revealed to be of great antiquity. Hence a Spanish jurist of the late seventeenth century, Diego Andrés Rocha, maintains that from a theological perspective Spain's claim to the New World derives from God's providential design to propagate the true faith through the agency of the Spanish, but that from a juridical perspective it derives from the *derecho de reversion*, the right of restitution, whereby lands are returned to their legitimate possessors.[34] We should add that comparable 'historical' arguments—claims to prior migrations and possession by ancient rulers—were made for other European peoples, including the Portuguese, the Frisians, and the Welsh.[35] But obviously the further we get from actual power, the more idle (in a sense, the more 'merely formal') these claims become: even if all of Europe had freely granted that there was a strong resemblance between Nahuatl, the Aztec language, and Welsh, the Spanish crown was not about to cede its territorial claims in Mexico.

Should we not say then that the words do not matter, that the discursive tactics are interchangeable, that language is a mere screen for the brutal reality of power? There is a flood of words about the New World in the generations after Columbus, there are serious debates in Salamanca and elsewhere about the legitimacy of the Spanish rule, there are denunciations of atrocities and passionate defenses of the necessity of military sternness—but what difference does any of it make? Isn't the whole miserable story, the story of an absolute denial of consent, already written in the first Spanish sneeze, with its millions of invisible bullets? Isn't the fate of the natives sealed in the first innocently drawn blood: 'I showed them swords and they took them by the edge and through ignorance cut themselves' (*Diario*, 67). This 'ignorance'—the first glimpse of a decisive imbalance in military technology, carefully noted at the initial encounter—would, in conjunction with vulnerability to European disease, doom the natives of the Caribbean and fatally weaken the great Indian empires that the Spaniards were shortly to encounter. One should perhaps add another brute physical fact: the horrible misfortune that the earth of the New World harbored gold and that many of the native peoples worked this gold into ornaments and hence carried it on their bodies for the Spanish to see. No doubt the weapons and microbes would have reached the New World peoples anyway, but without the gold the destructive forces would have come more slowly, and there might have been time for a defense.

From this vantage-point, words seem like mere covers for Spanish actions and the physical consequences of those actions. The webs of discourse should be stripped away and discarded in order to face unflinchingly the terrible meaning of the 1492 and its aftermath: swords and bullets pierce naked flesh and microbes kill bodies that lack sufficient immunities. I am a teacher of literature, and so by training and impulse hostile to such an argument, but I find it very difficult to dismiss. Words in the New World seem always to be trailing after events that pursue a terrible logic quite other than the fragile meanings that they construct.

But if we are thus forced to abandon the dream of linguistic omnipotence, the fantasy that to understand the discourse is to understand the event, we are not at the same time compelled or even permitted to discard words altogether. For if microbes lie altogether beyond the grasp of Renaissance discourse, the other forces that we have cited as brute facts should under no circumstances be naturalized. The possession of weapons and the will to use them on defenseless people are cultural matters that are intimately bound up with discourse: with the stories that a culture tells itself, its conceptions of personal boundary and liability, its whole collective system of rules. And if gold is a natural phenomenon, the all-consuming craving for gold most assuredly is not.

The *unnaturalness* of the desire for gold is one of the great themes of the fifteenth and sixteenth centuries, a theme tirelessly rehearsed by poets, playwrights, and moralists and frequently illustrated by tales of European behavior in the New World. One of the most famous images of the Spanish in America depicts a group of Indians punishing a *conquistador* for his insatiable thirst for gold by pouring the molten metal down his throat.[36] In part such images, which drew upon ancient polemics against greed, reflected sectarian hostilities—here Protestant against Catholic—but in part they reflected a more ecumenical uneasiness in the face of the growth of a money economy and an uncertainty about the status of gold.

Moreover, if certain crucial aspects of the European encounter with the New World were beyond words (and beyond the comprehension of any of the participants), the Europeans themselves struggled to bring as much of their experience as possible under the control of discourse. How could they—or, for that matter, how could we—do otherwise?[37] And it is not only as a futile attempt to comprehend the unimaginable that this discourse may interest us but as both an instrument of empire and an expression, however constrained and half-hearted, of resistance.

Hence, to return to Columbus's initial proclamation, if the declaration that he was not contradicted is absurd, it is also a sign—one of the few signs that we have from this first voyage—of an ethical reservation, a sense that the wishes of the native inhabitants should be respected. The reservation is not direct, it may not have been conscious, and it was certainly not effective, but it nevertheless exists, so deeply entrenched in the language of the judicial procedure that it could not be simply forgotten or eliminated. The procedure was directed, I have observed, to other Europeans, in order to record and legitimate the Spanish claim, but legitimation necessarily included an acknowledgment of the existence of the natives and a recognition of values other than superior force. And though it is important to recognize the practical emptiness of this acknowledgment and to understand how it was emptied out, there seems to me nothing to be gained from a contemptuous dismissal of the discourse in which the acknowledgment is embedded. Where else do we get our own ragged sense that there is something other than force, our own craving for justice? In a dark time (or for that matter an expansive time filled with a sense of infinite possibility and an indifference to the human cost), the awareness of a 'contradiction' is carried precisely in the small textual resistances—a kind of imagined possibility, a dream of equity—that Columbus had to contrive to overcome.

The overcoming in this case is made possible by formalism. If there is no theoretical necessity to his formalism, no innate politics, and no determining power, there are none the less strategic reasons for its presence as a shaping force in his discourse. It enables him, as we have seen, to stage a legal ritual that depends upon the formal possibility of contradiction without actually permitting such contradiction; that is, it enables him to empty out the existence of the natives, while at the same time officially acknowledging that they exist. But does this paradox not simply empty out the legal ritual itself? Does it not make a mockery of the basis on which Columbus is grounding the Spanish claim to the Indies? Columbus's founding speech act in the New World is spectacularly 'infelicitous' in virtually every one of the senses detailed by Austin in *How To Do Things With Words*: it is a misfire, a misinvocation, a misapplication, and a misexecution.[38] And it is difficult to believe that Columbus is unaware of these infelicities, for he knows very well that these are *not* uninhabited territories; indeed he notes that they have an immense population—*gente sin número*. It might have been possible to argue that these numberless people were so barbarous that they had no rights—the argument was made repeatedly in the sixteenth century and beyond—but Columbus does not do so and would probably have resisted the suggestion, since he wishes to believe that he has arrived in the 'Indies' and hence he must assume that he is in the outlying regions of a great empire, ultimately under the control of the Grand Khan.[39] And he recognizes almost at once that even here, on these small islands with their naked inhabitants living in tiny hamlets and appearing to share everything, there is a political and social order of some kind.

Indeed in the log-book Columbus describes communities characterized not by savage confusion but by an admirable orderliness. He admires the 'wonderful dignity' of the native 'king' whose people 'all obey him so that it is a marvel.' 'All of these lords,' he goes on to note, 'are of few words and of very attractive customs; and their commands are for the most part carried out by hand signs so soon understood that it is a marvel' (*Diario*, 275). Columbus makes no mention of this indigenous social order in the opening sentences of the letter to Santangel—evidently he did not consider it relevant to the ceremony of possession—but he subsequently refers to their 'chief or king' who is given as many as twenty wives, while common men have only one.[40]

The recognition of a hierarchical society returns us to the question, how is it possible to 'take possession' of such a place in the presence of those who inhabit it? For Francisco de Vitoria, such a recognition should invalidate the Spanish claim; the Indians manifestly are rational human agents, 'because there is a certain method in their affairs, for they have polities which are orderly and arranged and they have definite marriage and magistrates, overlords, laws, and workshops, and a system of exchange, all of which call for the use of reason.'[41] The territory of people who live in such polities cannot justly be appropriated, even if the people are pagans and hence in a state of mortal sin. The juridical problem does not arise if the lands are uninhabited—for under the law of nations and natural law, deserted regions become the property of the first occupant—nor does it arise, at least in the same terms, if one is conquering a recognized enemy. In his account of the third voyage (1498–1500), Columbus, responding to attacks upon his conduct, attempts to recast his role. 'At home,' he writes to Doña Juana, governess to the Infante D. Juan, 'they judge me as a governor sent to Sicily or to a city or two under settled government, and where the laws can be fully maintained, without fear of all being lost.' Such a perspective on the situation, he argues, is wholly inappropriate: 'I ought to be judged as a captain who went from Spain to the Indies to conquer a people, warlike and numerous, and with customs and beliefs very different from ours, a people, living in highlands and mountains, having no settled dwellings, and apart from us; and where, by the will of God, I have brought under the dominion of the king and queen, our sovereigns, another world, whereby Spain, which was called poor, is now most rich.'[42]

The first letter is careful to indicate that the formal rites of legality had been observed; this letter by contrast insists that such observation would be wholly inappropriate, a kind of theoretical fastidiousness that ends by losing everything. By 1498 both Columbus's personal circumstances and the institutional context in which he was operating had changed profoundly. In 1493 Pope Alexander VI had issued the bull *Inter caetera*, donating the newly discovered lands, out of 'mere liberality, certain science, and apostolic authority,' to the sovereigns of Spain and Portugal.[43] The Indians in Columbus's account can now be assigned the marks of outlaws or rebels; they are people who live on the margins—'sierras y montes, syn pueblo asentado, ni nosotros'. This marginal existence, the lives of those who are 'not us,' marks their distance from civility. The 'infinity of small hamlets' mentioned in the first letter have disappeared,

Communication and cultural difference: the Tupinamba greeting ritual copied by a Frenchman. From Jean de Léry, *Histoire d'un voyage fait en la terre du Brésil, dite Amerique* (Geneva: Vignon, 1600). Bancroft Library, University of California, Berkeley.

and the Indians have been assimilated to a conception of nomadic barbarism as old as ancient Greece. They are the people who live outside of all just order, apart from settled human community and hence from the very condition of the virtuous life. 'He who is unable to live in society, or who has no need because he is sufficient for himself,' Aristotle wrote, 'must be either a beast or a god.'[44] The Indians were clearly not gods and hence could in this light be regarded as beasts.

Their unsettled life, in Columbus's self-justifying account, not only reveals their bestial nature but also marks the difficulty of pacifying or containing them. For European authority in the early modern period was the authority of the plain, of walled towns that could if necessary be besieged and starved into submission; the central authorities feared and hated the mountains. And, of course, for Columbus the natives of the New World are not merely like the untamed dwellers of the European wastelands; from the first days he suspects something worse, and the suspicion hardens into a certainty that many of the islands are inhabited by cannibals.[45]

But in 1492 Columbus goes out of his way to present a very different picture of all of the natives whom he actually encounters. These natives do not, to be sure, live in towns or villages, but they inhabit small hamlets (*pequeñas poblaciones*), and they are utterly harmless: 'They have no iron or steel or weapons, nor are they fitted to use them, not because they are not well-built men and of handsome stature, but because they are very marvellously timorous [*muy temerosos á maravilla*]' (i. 6). What makes their timorousness marvelous? They flee at the approach of the Spaniards, Columbus explains, 'even a father not waiting for his son' (i. 8). The example assumes a norm of natural courage, the courage that instinctively arises in all men to defend their offspring, or, more precisely, their male offspring. And this creatural instinct is inexplicably absent in the timorous natives, inexplicably not only in relation to a father's natural care for his son but in relation to the entirely friendly and generous deportment of the Spanish.

It is odd: Columbus has just unilaterally taken possession of everything he sees on behalf of the king and queen of Spain; he declares moreover that 'as soon as I arrived in the Indies, in the first island which I found, I took by force some of them, in order that they might learn and give me information' (i. 10).[46] Yet this armed invader who seizes lands and people regards his own intentions as impeccably generous: 'at every point where I have been and have been able to have speech, I have given to them of all that I had, such as cloth and many other things, without receiving anything for it' (i. 8). It is characteristic of Columbus's discourse that it

The go-between: Doña Marina interprets for Cortés. From *Lienzo de Tlaxcala* (original drawing by an Aztec artist). Photograph from Alfredo Chavero, *Antiqüedades Mexicanas,* 1892. Bancroft Library, University of California, Berkeley.

yokes together actions, attitudes, or perceptions that would seem ethically incompatible, here seizing everything on the one hand and giving everything on the other. The two are clearly related in some way, but they do not directly impinge on one another, just as there is an unexpressed, unacknowledged relation between the fact that the natives do not understand his language and the fact that no one contradicts his proclamation. It would, I suppose, be possible to term this hypocrisy, but the term suggests a staging of moral attitudes that are not actually felt in the deep recesses of the heart, a theatrical self-consciousness, that seems to me quite alien to Columbus's ardent faith. I think rather that we are encountering an important aspect of Columbus's discursive economy, a characteristic rhetorical feature of what we may call his Christian imperialism.

This discursive economy brings opposites into the closest conjunction with one another and yet leaves the heart of their relation a mystery. Columbus takes absolute possession on behalf of the Spanish crown in order to make an absolute gift; he seeks earthly gain in order to serve a divine purpose; the Indians must lose everything in order to receive everything; the innocent natives will give away their gold for trash, but they will receive a treasure far more precious than gold; the wicked natives (the 'cannibals') will be enslaved in order to be freed from their own bestiality. Empowering these paradoxes is an ancient Christian rhetoric that has its most famous Renaissance English expression in the Holy Sonnets of John Donne:

> That I may rise, and stand, o'erthrow mee, and bend
> Your force, to break, blowe, burn, and make me new . . .
> Take me to you, imprison me, for I
> Except you'enthrall mee, never shall be free,
> Nor ever chast, except you ravish me.

Columbus's version of this rhetoric is at once less histrionic and more paradoxical, since it is cast neither in a prayer nor in a poem but in a report establishing secular authority over newly discovered lands and peoples: imperialism is by no means the opposite of Christianity but neither is it simply identical with it. For like the legal formalism at which we have glanced, Christian faith could empower radically opposed positions: if in the name of Christianity, Queen Isabella could decree the use of force against the Indians 'whenever conversion to the holy Catholic Faith and allegiance to the Crown were not immediately forthcoming,'[47] so too in the name of Christianity, Bartolomé de Las Casas could bitterly condemn the entire Spanish enterprise.

From the first moments, the encounter with the New World mobilizes in Columbus cravings for power and status and wealth, cravings that sit in an uneasy relation to his Franciscan religiosity, his appetite to convert and save, his apocalyptic dreams. It would be a mistake to think of these simply as opposed desires—a spiritual side of Columbus at war with his carnal side—for the whole achievement of the discourse of Christian imperialism is to represent desires as *convertible* and in a constant process of exchange. Were these desires actually identical, Columbus would have no need to articulate all of the ways in which they are cross-coupled; were they actually opposed, he would not be able to exchange one for the other. The possibility of such an exchange, rooted perhaps in his experience of Italian merchant life, haunts his writing: 'Genoese, Venetians, and all who have pearls, precious stones, and other things of value, all carry them to the end of the world in order to exchange them, to turn [*convertir*] them into gold. Gold is most excellent. Gold constitutes treasure, and he who possesses it may do what he will in the world, and may so attain as to bring souls to Paradise' (ii. 102–4). In this rhapsodic moment, from his account of the fourth voyage, the conversion of commodities into gold slides liquidly into the conversion and hence salvation of souls. If it seems strange, we might recall that in the Spanish of the Middle Ages and Renaissance, the Crusade to the Holy Land was called not the *cruzada*—that word referred to the special papal concessions granted to the Spanish crown to fight against the infidel within its own territory—but rather the *empresa* or *negocio*, terms in which the mercantile and the religious are intertwined.[48]

The rhetorical task of Christian imperialism then is to bring together commodity conversion and spiritual conversion.[49] Most often these are simply juxtaposed by Columbus, as if the energies of the one would naturally spill over into the other but, on occasion, their interchange is articulated more directly: 'You shall say to their highnesses,' writes Columbus to his agent Antonio de Torres in 1494,

> that the welfare of the souls of the said cannibals [the natives whom the Spanish have enslaved and shipped back to Spain], and also of those here, has induced the idea that the more that may be sent over, the better it will be, and in this their highnesses may be served in the following way. That, having seen how necessary cattle and beasts of burden are here, for the support of the people who have to be here, and indeed for all these islands, their highnesses might give licence and a permit for a sufficient number of caravels to come here every year and to carry the said cattle and other supplies and things for the colonization of the country and the development of the land, and this at reasonable prices at the cost of those who transport them. Payment for these things could be made to them in slaves, from among these cannibals, a people very savage and suitable for the purpose, and well

made and of very good intelligence. We believe that they, having abandoned that inhumanity, will be better than any other slaves, and their inhumanity they will immediately lose when they are out of their own land. (i. 90–2)

Beasts of burden will be exchanged for beasts of burden: so many Indians for so many cattle. Columbus cannot be content, however, with a purely mercantile transaction, nor is this his overriding interest. He cannot allow himself, for reasons both tactical and more deeply spiritual, to say simply, 'We need cattle; we have slaves; let us trade one for the other.' The exchange must be presented as undertaken in the interests of the enslaved. We might call this enslavement with a human face, or rather, liberating enslavement. For the exchange Columbus envisions would put into practice the religious rhetoric that we glimpsed in Donne: at its core is not an economic transaction but a dream of marvelous transformation. Those Indians identified as cannibals will be hunted down, seized, torn from their lands and their culture, loaded onto ships still stinking of the animals for whom they are being exchanged, and sent into slavery. But the economic transaction as Columbus conceives it will be undertaken for the welfare of the souls of the enslaved: the Indians are exchanged for beasts in order to convert them into humans. This transformation will not enfranchise them; it will only make them into excellent slaves.[50] But they will have gained their spiritual freedom. At the heart of the transaction is not wealth or convenience, though these are welcome, but a metamorphosis from inhumanity into humanity. The Crown, we might note, evidently had doubts, on legal and religious grounds, about the legitimacy of the proposed exchange: Isabella intervened and stopped the sale of the slaves.[51]

The occult relation between apparent opposites in the Christian discourse of John Donne draws the reader toward contemplation of the mysterious nature of the Incarnation; the occult relation between apparent opposites in the Christian imperialist discourse of Columbus draws the reader toward contemplation of the 'marvelous' nature of the New World and its inhabitants. The wonder aroused by the cannibals is twofold; it lies in the uncanny conjunction of native intelligence and inhumanity, and again in the uncanny power of enslavement to humanize. But, as we have already observed, it is not only the warlike cannibals who awaken wonder. In the letter of 1500 Columbus wishes his readers to think of the Indians as warlike; in the letter of 1492 he wishes that they be thought timid, indeed marvelously timid.[52] The term 'marvelous,' which we have already seen Columbus use in the first sentence of the first letter, obviously appeals to readerly expectations about the genre of travel literature. But timidity in this context is a peculiar marvel, and Columbus intensifies its peculiarity by stressing that the natives are 'well-built men and of handsome stature.' We are not dealing here with a strange race of creatures that do not bear arms because they literally do not have arms, or legs, or heads on their shoulders. Columbus's readers would be well-prepared for the monstrous. What they might not expect to find is the marvelous in human timidity. In urging them to do so, and by thus relocating the marvelous from the grotesque to the ordinary, Columbus induces his readers to join him in what we may call an act of ideological forgetting. If one clearly remembered the actions Columbus has just described—the sudden arrival of armed and armored strangers, kidnapping, and expropriation of lands—it would be more difficult to find the natives' panic fear all that marvelous.

Columbus does not use the discourse of the marvelous in order to create a momentary amnesia about his actions; he induces a momentary amnesia about his actions in order to create the discourse of the marvelous. Indeed the production of a sense of the marvelous in the New World is at the very center of virtually all of Columbus's writings about his discoveries, though the meaning of that sense shifts over the years.[53] His constant insistence on the marvelous is generally treated as if it were a simple record of what he and his companions felt, as if Columbus's discourse were perfectly transparent and his feelings those 'naturally' evoked by his experiences. (Alternatively, it is possible to argue—incorrectly, I think—that Columbus had such an impoverished vocabulary that he could think of no other word to describe his experiences.)[54] But we may take Columbus himself in testimony to the special significance of the experience of wonder. In his official report to Ferdinand and Isabella on the third voyage, Columbus writes that in response to 'the defaming and disparagement of the undertaking that had been begun' in the New World, because he 'had not immediately sent caravels laden with gold,' he 'decided to come to Your Highnesses, and to cause you to wonder at everything, and to show you the reason that I had for all [*y maravillarme de todo, y mostrarles la razón que en todo avía*]' (ii. 4–6).[55] There is by the third voyage a specific political and rhetorical reason for the performance and production of wonder: the marvelous is precisely the sense that will confirm the power and validity of Columbus's claims against those cavilling skeptics who want more tangible signs of gain. Not to manifest and arouse wonder is to succumb to the attacks against him. The marvelous stands for the missing caravels laden with gold; it is—like the ritual of possession itself—a word pregnant with what is imagined, desired, promised.

The production of wonder then is not only an expression of the effect that the voyage had upon Columbus but a calculated rhetorical strategy, the evocation of an aesthetic response in the service of a legitimation process. It is possible that the *explicit* calculation marks the frustration of Columbus's early hopes and the darkening of his situation, and that his constant expressions of wonder in the earlier voyages are a more spontaneous response to the innocence, beauty, and freshness of the Caribbean islands and their peoples. But we should recall that Columbus's first use of the marvelous refers not to the land itself but to its possession—Columbus gives thanks to the 'Divine Majesty, Who has marvelously bestowed all this.' If the use of wonder as a rhetorical strategy becomes explicit in the third voyage, when an increasingly embattled Columbus is forced to articulate his purposes, its place in the legitimation process is already at work, as we have seen, in the first voyage.

Wonder, however, does not inherently legitimate a claim to possession. Indeed, as we have seen in *Mandeville's Travels*, in the Middle Ages the experience of marvels seems to lead precisely to a sense of dispossession, a disclaimer of dogmatic certainty, a self-estrangement in the face of the strangeness, diversity, and opacity of the world. The medieval sense of the marvelous, Jacques Le Goff has suggested, expressed perceptions of nature potentially or actually inimical to the transcendental being and providential authority of the Christian God and His servant the Church.[56] It stood then for all that could not be securely held, all that resisted appropriation. Why should Columbus, whose interests are diametrically opposed to dispossession and self-estrangement, continually invoke wonder? In part, he may do so because the marvelous is closely linked in classical and Christian rhetoric to heroic enterprise. The voyages of Odysseus in particular were for centuries the occasion for aesthetic and philosophical speculations on the relation between heroism and the arousal of wonder through a representation of marvels. In part, he may do so to associate his discoveries with a specifically 'Christian marvelous' that, in opposition to all that is irregular and heterodox in the experience of wonder, identifies spiritual authenticity with the proper evocation of marvels.[57] And, most simply and directly, Columbus may strive to arouse wonder because marvels are inseparably bound up in rhetorical and pictorial tradition with voyages to the Indies. To affirm the 'marvelous' nature of the discoveries is, even without the lucrative shipments yet on board, to make good on the claim to have reached the fabled realms of gold and spices. This is the significance, I think, of Columbus's mention in the first letter of a province in Cuba that the Indians call 'Avan' where 'the people are born with tails';[58] such prodigies were a virtual requirement for travelers to the Indies. That he singles out Cuba in particular as the probable site of the authenticating wonders of the East is probably a reflection of the hope Columbus recorded in the log-book that this island—toward which the natives seemed to be directing him—was Japan, or 'Cipango' as Marco Polo called it. 'And I believe so,' Columbus writes with a blind conviction born of wish-fulfillment, 'because I believe that it is so according to the signs that all the Indians of these islands and those that I have with me make (because I do not understand them through speech) [and] that it is the island of Cipango of which marvelous things [*cosas maravillosas*] are told' (*Diario*, 113).

Yet the observations that he records to create the effect of the marvelous are for the most part strikingly unlike the marvels conventionally recorded in travelers' tales. Once, off the coast of Haiti, Columbus sighted 'three mermaids [*serenas*] who came quite high out of the water,' but his log-book description of these prodigies—in all likelihood, Caribbean manatees or sea-cows—tellingly suggests a resistance to the traditional iconography: they 'were not as pretty as they are depicted, for somehow in the face they look like men' (*Diario*, 321).[59] In his log-book entry for November 4, 1492, Columbus notes apparent native confirmation of marvels about which he must have been inquiring: 'far from there,' the natives supposedly inform him, 'there were one-eyed men, and others, with snouts of dogs, who ate men, and that as soon as one was taken they cut his throat and drank his blood and cut off his genitals' (*Diario*, 133). (The display of signs that Columbus must have made to elicit this information may help to explain why the natives, as he notes in the same entry, were 'very timid.') But by the time he writes the first letter, he seems far more skeptical: 'In these islands I have so far found no human monstrosities, as many expected, but on the contrary the whole population is very well-formed' (i. 14). He appears to be distinguishing then between monstrosities and marvels: the former are vivid, physical violations of universal norms, the latter are physical impressions that arouse wonder. Columbus is not willing to rule out the possibility of the monstrous, but he is scrupulous in limiting his claims to have personally witnessed monstrosities; the marvelous, by contrast, he notes at first-hand again and again.

The marvelous functions for Columbus as the agent of conversion: a fluid mediator between outside and inside, spiritual and carnal, the realm of objects and the subjective impressions made by those objects, the recalcitrant otherness of a new world and the emotional effect aroused by that otherness. More precisely it registers the presence of Columbus's fears and desires in the very objects he perceives and conversely the presence in his discourse of a world of objects that exceed his understanding of the probable and the familiar. Hence, for example, he writes that he 'saw many trees very different from ours, and among them many which had branches of many kinds, and all on one trunk. And one little branch is of one kind, and another of another, and so different that it is the greatest wonder in the world [*la mayor maravilla del mundo*]' (*Diario*, 89). 'Here the fish are so different from ours,' he notes in the same log-book entry for October 16, 'that it is a marvel. There are some shaped like dories, of the finest colors in the world: blues, yellows, reds, and of all colors; and others colored in a thousand ways. And the colors are so fine that there is no man who would not marvel and take great delight in seeing them' (*Diario*, 89–91). As such passages suggest, it is not simply the recognition of the unusual that constitutes a marvel but a certain excess, a hyperbolic intensity, a sense of awed delight.[60]

The marvelous for Columbus usually involves then a surpassing of the measure but not in the direction of the monstrous or grotesque; rather, a heightening of impressions until they reach a kind of perfection. Española, he writes in the first letter, is 'very fertile to a limitless degree'; its harbors are 'beyond comparison with others which I know in Christendom,' it has many good and large rivers 'which is marvellous' (*que es maravilla*); and its mountains are 'beyond comparison with the island of Teneriffe' (i. 4).[61] These mountains, however, are not forbidding; 'all are most beautiful, of a thousand shapes, and all are accessible and filled with trees of a thousand kinds and tall, and they seem to touch the sky' (i. 4–6). The trees, Columbus is told, never lose their foliage, and he believes what is told, 'for I saw them as green and as lovely as they are in Spain in May. . . . And the nightingale was singing and other birds of a thousand kinds in the month of November' (i. 6). Large numbers, particularly 'a thousand,' are repeated as conventional talismans of wonder, though even much smaller figures will do: 'There are six or eight kinds of palm, which are a wonder to behold [*que es admiración verlas*] on account of their beautiful variety,' and there are 'marvellous pine groves [*pinares á maravilla*].' The marvelous, as can be seen here, has little or nothing to do with the grotesque or outlandish. It denotes, to be sure, some departure, displacement, or surpassing of the normal or the probable, but in the direction of delicious variety and loveliness.

This loveliness extends in the first letter to the natives. When they overcame their 'marvelous timorousness,' the natives 'all brought something to eat and drink, which they gave with extraordinary affection [*con un amor maravilloso*]' (i. 10). The log-book entries are even more explicit: 'they brought us all that they had in the world and knew that the Admiral wanted; and all so bigheartedly [*con vn Coraçon tan largo*] and so happily that it was a wonder [*maravilla*]' (*Diario*, 255).[62] Columbus's response to this marvelous generosity is revealing: 'The Admiral gave them glass beads and brass rings and bells: not because they asked for something, but because it seemed to him that it was right; and above all, says the Admiral, because he already considers them as Christians and as more the subjects of the sovereigns of Castile than the Castilians. And he says that nothing is lacking except to know the language and to give them orders, because everything they are ordered to do they will do without any opposition [*sin contradiçion algua*]' (*Diario*, 259). The spirit of the gift-giving, as Columbus understands it, is not reciprocal: the Indians give out of an unconstrained openness of heart that is a marvel; the Spanish in return give out of a sense of what is right, a sense of obligation bound up with the conviction that the Indians have *already* become the Christian subjects of the sovereigns of Castile.[63] They are easily imagined as subjects because they are so easily imagined as already subjected, inhabitants of lands appropriated without contradiction (*y no me fué contradicho*) on the day of the initial encounter. 'They should,' Columbus writes in the log-book entry for that day, 'be good and intelligent servants' (*Diario*, 67–9).

Columbus does not imagine that the Indians could have anything like a comparable thought about the Spanish. Their extraordinary affection, Columbus implies, is powered by their conviction that he, with his ships and men, have come from heaven;[64] that is, for the Indians who had never before seen large ships or clothed men the Spanish too are a marvel. But this recognition of a reverse wonderment does not qualify Columbus's own perceptions or render the marvelous a mere sign of unfamiliarity or *naïveté*. The natives do not make their mistake because they are stupid; they possess, he says, a very acute intelligence, 'so that it is amazing [*es maravilla*] how good an account they give of everything' (i. 10).[65] All of his delighted impressions cohere for Columbus in a single overwhelming perception: 'la Española es maravilla' (i. 7).[66]

In such a phrase the marvelous has been detached altogether from the enumeration of bizarre particulars and has been broadened in scope to characterize an entire place, a place of surprising and intense beauty. To look (*mirar*) at such a place is to wonder (*maravillar*). This characterization associates the discoveries with a long tradition of poems evoking the *locus amoenus*, the landscape of delight. Again and again Columbus's log-book records the intense pleasure of looking:

> [October 14:] And later [I noticed], near the said islet, groves of trees, the most beautiful that I saw and with their leaves as green as those of Castile in the months of April and May. (*Diario*, 75–7)

[October 17:] In this time I also walked among those trees, which were more beautiful to see than any other thing that has ever been seen, seeing as much verdure and in such degree as in the month of May in Adalusia. (*Diario*, 93)

[October 19:] [T]he island [is] the most beautiful thing that I have seen. For if the others are very beautiful this one is more so. It is an island of many very green and very large trees. . . . I do not know where to go first; nor do my eyes grow tired of seeing such beautiful verdure and so different from ours. (*Diario*, 99–101)

[October 21:] [If the other islands] already seen are very beautiful and green and fertile, this one is much more so and with large and very green groves of trees. Here there are some big lakes and over and around them the groves are marvelous. And here and in all of the island the groves are all green and the verdure like that in April in Andalusia. And the singing of the small birds [is so marvelous] that it seems that a man would never want to leave this place. And [there are] flocks of parrots that obscure the sun; and birds of so many kinds and sizes, and so different from ours, that it is a marvel. (*Diario*, 105)

'It seems that a man would never want to leave this place.' If the dream of marvelous possession in such passages is tinged with an undertone of loss, it is not only because Columbus feels the urgent compulsion to pass on to other islands—'I am not taking pains to see much in detail because I could not do it in 50 years and because I want to see and explore as much as I can so I can return to Your Highnesses in April' (*Diario*, 103)—but also because in Christian poetry the *locus amoenus* at its most intense is always touched with remembrance of paradise lost. In the years that follow, the location of the Earthly Paradise interests Columbus with increasing intensity and becomes intertwined with other dreams: the discourse of enraptured looking is shaped by a longing at once erotic and infantile, by the gaze, marveling and forever unsatisfied, of love poetry.

The world is not perfectly round, he writes in a letter sent from Hispaniola in 1498, during his third voyage, but rather has the shape of a pear or of a ball on which is placed 'something like a woman's nipple' (ii. 30). The nipple of the world is the newly discovered land and all signs point to the location at its center of the Earthly Paradise.[67] And if these signs—above all the great streams of fresh water that emanate from the land—do not point to Eden, if the water does not come from paradise, it seems, Columbus writes, 'to be a still greater marvel (*pareçe aun mayor maravilla*), for I do not believe that there is known in the world a river so great and so deep' (ii. 38). The notion of a marvel greater than paradise is startling, but it arises from the only other hypothesis Columbus can posit for his observations: 'And I say that if it be not from the earthly paradise that this river comes, it originates from a vast land, lying to the south, of which hitherto no knowledge has been obtained' (ii. 42). Faced with such a staggering thought—the idea, in effect, of South America—Columbus retreats to the safer ground of the land of Eden: 'But I am much more convinced in my own mind that there where I have said is the earthly paradise.'

An actual recovery of the earthly paradise would partake of the miraculous, but Columbus stops short of such a claim, as he does throughout most of his writings.[68] In effect, the marvelous takes the place of the miraculous, absorbing some of its force but avoiding the theological and evidentiary problems inherent in directly asserting a miracle. Instead of a theological claim, the term *maravilla* as Columbus uses it makes a different kind of claim, one that combines religious and erotic longings in a vision of surpassing beauty. That marvelous vision had since late antiquity played a crucial role in European aesthetics, a role that intensified in the Middle Ages and was exhaustively theorized in the generations after Columbus. 'No one can be called a poet,' writes the influential Italian critic Minturno in the 1550s, 'who does not excel in the power of arousing wonder.'[69] For Aristotelians wonder is associated with pleasure as the end of poetry; in the *Poetics* Aristotle examines the strategies by which tragedians and epic poets employ the marvelous to arouse pleasurable wonder. For the Platonists too wonder is an essential element in art, for it is one of the principal effects of beauty. In the words of Plotinus, 'This is the effect that Beauty must ever induce, wonderment and a pleasant astonishment, longing and love and a dread that is pleasurable.'[70] In the sixteenth century, the Neoplatonist Francesco Patrizi defines the poet as a 'maker of the marvelous,' and the marvelous is found, as he puts it, when men 'are astounded, ravished in ecstasy.' Patrizi goes so far as to posit marveling as a special faculty of the mind, a faculty which in effect mediates between the capacity to think and the capacity to feel.[71]

The aesthetic theory of the marvelous sidesteps the miraculous but does not altogether resolve questions of credibility. Indeed for the Aristotelian Francesco Robortelli, the marvelous and the credible are in conflict, a conflict that may be masked by a variety of poetic devices but cannot be altogether eliminated.[72] But other poets and theorists saw the two as working in conjunction to produce pleasure. Lodovico Castelvetro wrote that the poet 'must above all seek credibility or verisimilitude in combination with the marvelous: credibility so that the unimaginative audience will believe, the marvelous so that it will find pleasure in the uncommon and the extraordinary';[73] 'we find some true things more marvelous than the false,' argued Jacopo Mazzoni, 'not merely in natural things . . . but also in human history';[74] and Tasso elaborated a theory of the Christian marvelous in which verisimilitude is conferred by faith: 'One and the same action may therefore be both marvelous and verisimilar: marvelous if one consider it in itself and hemmed in by natural limitations, verisimilar if one consider it separated from such limitations with respect to its cause, which is a supernatural force capable of and accustomed to producing such marvels.'[75]

In Renaissance aesthetic theory wonder is associated with the overcoming of great difficulties and with a strange blend of chance and human intention (Castelvetro); or with the spectacle of the unexpected and the extraordinary (Robortelli); or with passions, reversals, and discoveries (Vettori); or with the reconciliation of unity and variety (Tasso); or with novel and surprising twists of narrative (Denores, Talentoni), or with the effects of awe and wonder associated with religious feelings and hence with sublimity and high gravity (Patrizi).[76] Virtually all of these aesthetic categories are implicit in Columbus's insistent use of the marvelous, not, of course, because he is deliberately alluding to them—they are, for the most part, fully articulated only after his time—but because they emerged from the same cultural matrix that shaped his language and perceptions.

We are now perhaps in a position to understand why the term is so important to him and how it bears on the formal legal ritual by which he claims Spanish possession of the Indies.[77] That ritual had at its center, as we have seen, a defect, an absurdity, a tragicomic invocation of the possibility of a refusal that could not in fact conceivably occur: *y no me fué contradicho*. The legal declaration could take place in the spirit of a radical formalism, but that formalism leaves in its wake an emotional and intellectual vacancy, a hole, that threatens to draw the reader of Columbus's discourse toward laughter or tears and toward a questioning of the legitimacy of the Spanish claim.[78] Columbus tries to draw the reader toward wonder, a sense of the marvelous that in effect fills up the emptiness at the center of the maimed rite of possession. Immediately after describing that rite, let us recall, Columbus declares that 'To the first island which I found, I gave the name *San Salvador*, in remembrance of the Divine Majesty, Who has marvelously bestowed all this.' The marvel of the divine gift here is at once a legitimation and a transcendence of the legal act. Roman law procedures dictate the principal gesture of appropriation, but they are supplemented by an incommensurable and marvelous assurance, the assurance in effect of the Biblical promise: 'If you diligently keep all these commandments that I now charge you to observe, by loving the Lord your God, by conforming to his ways and by holding fast to him, the Lord will drive out all these nations before you and you shall occupy the territory of nations greater and more powerful than you. Every place where you set the soles of your feet shall be yours' (Deut. 11: 22–4).

By itself a sense of the marvelous cannot confer title; on the contrary, it is associated with longing, and you long precisely for what you do not have. Columbus's whole life is marked by a craving for something that continually eluded him, for the kingdom or the paradise or the Jerusalem that he could not reach, and his expressions of the marvelous, insofar as they articulate this craving, continue the medieval sense that wonder and secure temporal possession are mutually exclusive. But something happens to the discourse of the marvelous when it is linked to the discourse of the law: the inadequacy of the legal ritual to confer title and the incapacity of the marvelous to confer possession cancel each other out, and both the claim and the emotion are intensified by the conjunction. Neither discourse is freestanding and autonomous; on the contrary, each—like individual words themselves—takes its meaning from its conjunction with other motifs, tropes, and speech acts, and from the situation in which it is inserted. And there is a further motive for the conjunction: under the actual circumstances of the first encounter, there was no discourse adequate to the occasion. In the unprecedented, volatile state of emergence and emergency in which Columbus finds himself, anything he says or does will be defective. His response is to conjoin the most resonant legal ritual he can summon up with the most resonant emotion.

In a remarkable passage to which I have already alluded, Aquinas's teacher, Albertus Magnus, attempts in his *Commentary on the Metaphysics of Aristotle* to provide a convincing account of the internal dynamics of wonder:

> wonder is defined as a constriction and suspension of the heart caused by amazement at the sensible appearance of something so portentous, great, and unusual, that the heart suffers a systole. Hence wonder is something like fear in its effect on the heart. This effect of wonder, then, this constriction and systole of the heart, springs from an unfulfilled but felt desire to know the cause of that which appears portentous and unusual: so it was in the beginning when men, up to that time unskilled, began to philosophize. . . . Now the man who is puzzled and wonders apparently does not know. Hence wonder is the movement of the man who does not know on his way to finding out, to get at the bottom of that at which he wonders and to determine its cause. . . . Such is the origin of philosophy.[79]

Wonder here is not a steady state; it is inherently unstable, a shifter, not only the sign but the principal instigator of movement. For Albertus Magnus the movement driven by the marvelous is from the blankness of ignorance to the fullness of philosophical understanding.[80] Obviously, wonder does not lead Columbus toward philosophy, but it does, in response to God's portentous and unusual gift, lead him toward an act that is closely linked in the Middle Ages and Renaissance to philosophy: the act of naming. That naming, to be sure, has much to do with the manifestation of power through eponymous titles—hence Fernandina, Isabella, and Isla Juana (for Prince Juan, islands traditionally having feminine endings). Moreover, the legal act of possession customarily involved naming, since crown lawyers 'believed that no one could well lay claim to a nameless city, and that a province without a name was hardly a province at all.'[81] But more than legal formality is involved here. The first two names—San Salvador and Isla de Santa María de Concepcíon—suggest once again that the assertion of possession is bound up for Christian imperialism with the giving of a precious gift. And the giving of the gift is in turn bound up with superior knowledge, the knowledge of the truth.

When in Genesis 2: 19 Adam names the animals, medieval commentators understood this to be an act of marvelous *understanding*. Martin Luther is following a long exegetical tradition when he glosses the verse as follows:

> Here again we are reminded of the superior knowledge and wisdom of Adam, who was created in innocence and righteousness. Without any new enlightenment, solely because of the excellence of his nature, he views all the animals and thus arrives at such a knowledge of their nature that he can give each one a suitable name that harmonizes with its nature.[82]

Such understanding, Luther continues, is linked with power: 'From this enlightenment there also followed, of course, the rule over all the animals, something which is also pointed out here, since they were named in accordance with Adam's will. Therefore by one single word he was able to compel lions, bears, boars, tigers, and whatever else there is among the most outstanding animals to carry out whatever suited their nature' (pp. 119–20). As Francis Bacon puts it, when man 'shall be able to call the creatures by their true names he shall again command them.'[83]

Columbus may have thought that he was near to Paradise, but he also knew that he was the inheritor of Adam's sin through which, as Luther remarks, we lost Paradise as well as this power to bestow primal names and to compel through naming. In his letter, moreover, Columbus makes it clear that he is encountering not a world that has never before been named but rather a world of alien names: 'the Indians call it "Guanahaní." ' His act then is a cancellation of an existing name.[84] But why should Columbus, unlike Marco Polo or Mandeville, think to rename the lands he has encountered? Why should he confer on each island 'una nombre nuevo'?

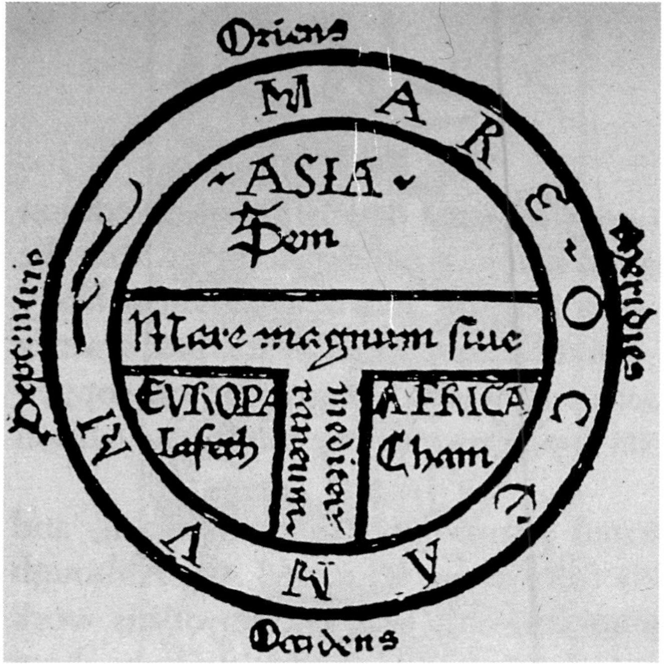

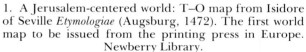

1. A Jerusalem-centered world: T–O map from Isidore of Seville *Etymologiae* (Augsburg, 1472). The first world map to be issued from the printing press in Europe. Newberry Library.

2. The marvels of the East: from a Spanish edition of *Mandeville's Travels* (*Libro de las Maravillas del mundo llamado Selva deleytosa* [Alcala, 1547]). Houghton Library, Harvard University.

Columnam à Præfecto prima navigatione locatam VIII.
venerantur Floridenses.
8

3. Signs of possession: Athore shows Laudonnière the marker-column set up by Ribault and now worshipped by the Indians. From Theodor de Bry, *America*, Part I (1591), pl. VIII. Bancroft Library, University of California, Berkeley.

4. The Spanish 'thirst' for gold quenched: Indians pouring molten gold in the mouth of a captive. From Theodor de Bry, *America*, Part IV (1592), pl. XX. Bancroft Library, University of California, Berkeley.

5. The gift of trifles: Algonquian child holding an English doll. Watercolor by John White. British Library.

6. The gift of necessities: Inhabitants of Guiana bringing food to Sir Walter Ralegh. From Theodor de Bry, *America*, Part VII/VIII (1599). Bancroft Library, University of California, Berkeley.

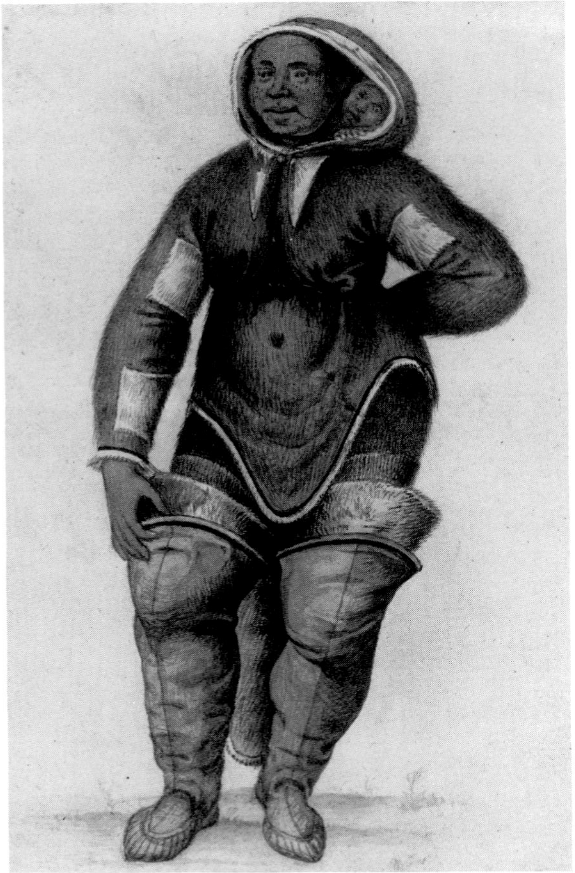

7. & 8. The European display of the natives: Eskimo man, woman, and baby. Copy after drawings by John White, 1577. Trustees of the British Museum.

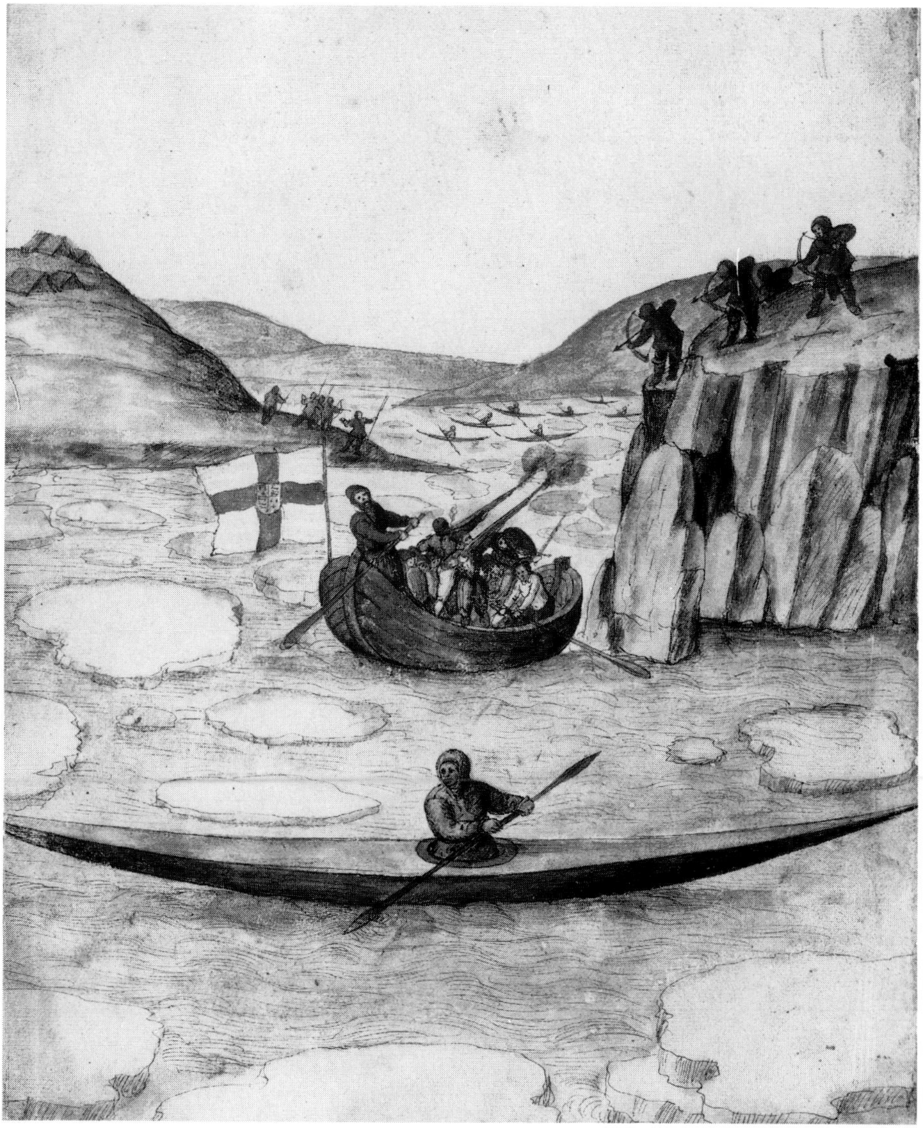

9. Skirmish between Englishmen and Eskimos. Copy after drawing by John White. Trustees of the British Museum.

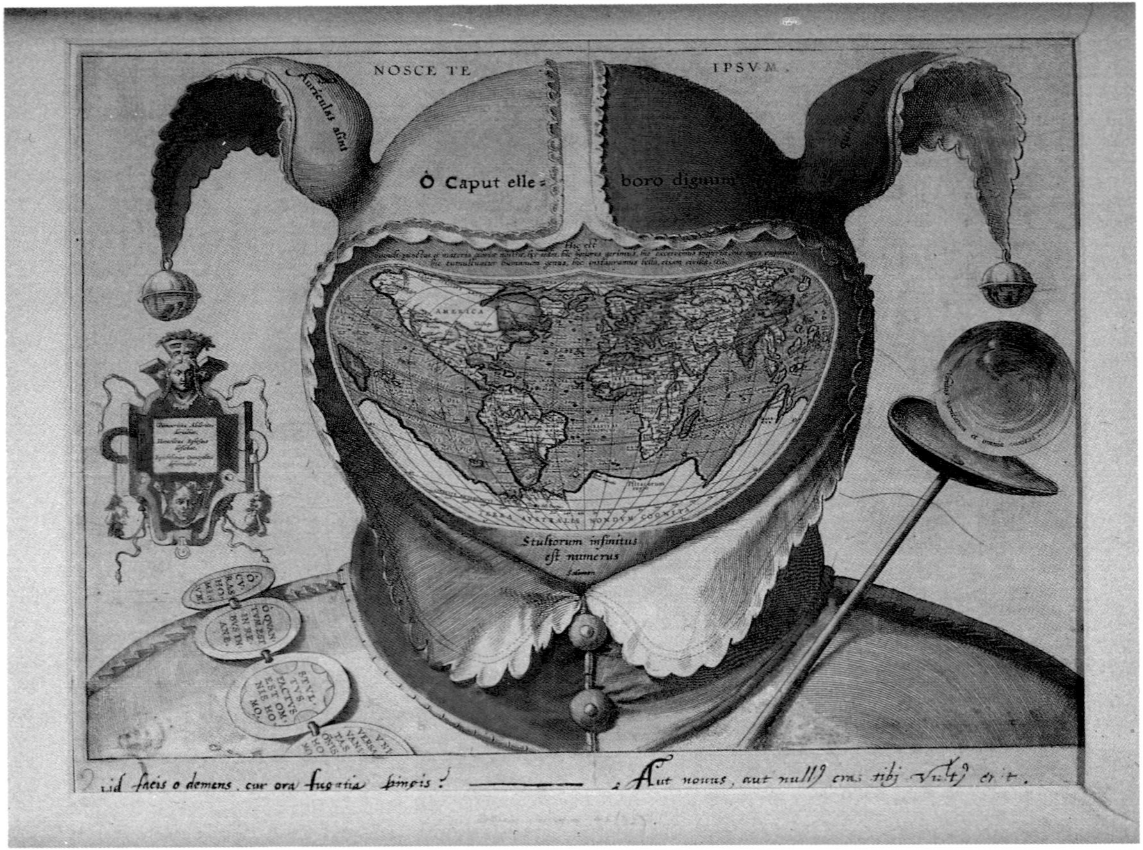

10. Travel as folly. Anonymous map based on one by Ortelius, enclosed within the visor of a fool's cap, *c.*1600. Douce Portfolio 142 (92). Bodleian Library, Oxford.

In order, he says, to commemorate the Savior's marvelous gift. The founding action of Christian imperialism is a christening.[85] Such a christening entails the cancellation of the native name—the erasure of the alien, perhaps demonic, identity—and hence a kind of making new; it is at once an exorcism, an appropriation, and a gift. Christening then is the culminating instance of the marvelous speech act: in the wonder of the proper name, the movement from ignorance to knowledge, the taking of possession, the conferral of identity are fused in a moment of pure linguistic formalism.

In the first encounter, Columbus had seized several of the natives to use them as informants and interpreters. Six of these survived the voyage back to Spain and in a remarkable ceremony, with Ferdinand, Isabella, and the Infante acting as godparents, were baptized.[86] The cleverest of the natives, the one most serviceable to the Spanish, was given Columbus's own surname and the Christian name of his first-born child: he was christened Don Diego Colón. The magic of renaming extended to Columbus himself: after the Discovery, in place of Cristóbal, he began to sign his letters Christoferens, the Christ-bearer.[87] And according to the cosmographer Sebastian Münster, the king of Spain said that Columbus should be called not *Almirante*, the admiral, but *Admirans*, the one who wonders.[88] This playful christening conveys in tiny compass the trajectory we have been following: from legal ritual through the experience of the marvelous to the mystical understanding and appropriative power of naming. The claim of possession is grounded in the power of wonder.

As Columbus's vision darkened over the years, he seems to have invested more and more of his hopes for possession in the marvelous power of the name. Looking back on his years of fruitless searching for royal support, he declares that he never gave up hope, because God 'spake so clearly of these lands by the mouth of Isaiah, in many places of his Book, affirming that from Spain His holy name should be proclaimed to them' (ii. 4). Columbus's first act of naming then—San Salvador for Guanahaní—is the fulfillment of a Biblical prophecy.[89] Making new is paradoxically the realization of the old. If the act of naming makes the world conform to the word, Columbus believes at the same time that the word is conforming at last to the world.[90] In the words of Scripture, 'As his name is, so is he' (1 Samuel 25: 25).

On his last voyage to the New World, in despair, surrounded by hostile natives, 'utterly alone, in a high fever and in a state of great exhaustion,' Columbus falls alseep and hears a 'compassionate voice' that speaks to him about his own name:

A very early German woodcut (Augsburg or Nuremburg *c.*1505), ostensibly illustrating the Tupinambas of coastal Brazil. Note the conjunction of domesticity and horror. The Spencer Collection, New York Public Library, Astor, Lenox, and Tilden Foundations.

O fool and slow to believe and to serve thy God, the God of all! What more did He for Moses or for His servant David? Since thou wast born, ever has He had thee in His most watchful care. When He saw thee of an age with which He was content, He caused thy name to sound marvellously in the land [*maravillosamente hizo sonar tu nombre en la tierra*].

Now it is not the divine name but Columbus's own that is the heart of the wonder. And now, in Columbus's mind and in his text, the conjunction of the land, the marvelous, and the name produces an absolute possession, not for the king and queen of Spain but for himself alone. 'The Indies, which are so rich a part of the world,' the mysterious voice continues,

He gave thee for thine own; thou hast divided them as it pleased thee, and He enabled thee to do this. Of the barriers of the Ocean sea, which were closed with such mighty chains, He gave thee the keys; and thou wast obeyed in many lands and among Christians thou hast gained an honourable fame. What did He more for the people of Israel when He brought them out of Egypt? Or for David, whom from a shepherd He made to be king in Judaea?[91]

For a moment at least—a moment at once of perfect wonder and of possessive madness—Columbus has become king of the Promised Land.

CHAPTER FOUR

Kidnapping Language

ON his third voyage to the New World, Columbus found himself anchored off the coast of an island he named Trinidad.[1] A large canoe with twenty-four men, armed with bows and arrows and wooden shields, approached his ship. The sight impressed Columbus; the Indians, he writes, were 'well-proportioned and not negroes, but whiter than the others who have been seen in the Indies, and very graceful and with handsome bodies, and hair long and smooth, cut in the manner of Castile' (ii. 14). He noticed something else: 'They had their heads wrapped in scarves of cotton, worked elaborately and in colours, which, I believe, were *almaizares*.' *Almaizares* were veils or scarves worn by the Moors in Spain, most often as head coverings, and they resembled the East Indian turbans depicted in illuminations of Mandeville and Marco Polo. The natives of Trinidad made a further use of them as well: 'They wore another of these scarves round the body and covered themselves with them in place of drawers.'

As Tzvetan Todorov has shrewdly remarked, Columbus was less an intense observer than an intense reader of signs, and the details that he notes here as elsewhere are not attempts to record the world as it presented itself to his eyes but compilations of significant markers.[2] The idea of discovery as entailing an act of sustained, highly particularized narrative representation of differences was quite alien to him; he had little or no interest in bringing back a rich, circumstantial description of the lands he had found. He had spent years before his embarkation in 1492 collecting signs, and this activity basically set the pattern of his observations thereafter.

Thus, for example, we find him noting in the margins of his books that in the Azores the sea had carried to shore the bodies of two dead men 'who seemed very broad in the face and of an appearance different from that of Christians'; or again that 'in Galway in Ireland, a man and a woman, of extraordinary appearance, have come to land on two tree trunks'; or again that 450 leagues west of Cape St Vincent a Portuguese pilot had hauled aboard his ship a 'piece of wood artificially worked, and, as he judged, not by means of an iron tool.'[3] Columbus's log-book for the outbound voyage in 1492 suggests a kind of obsession with these signs, an obsession quite understandable under the circumstances:

> [September 17:] They saw much weed and very often and it was vegetation from rocks and it came from a westerly direction; they judged themselves to be near land. . . . [T]hey saw much more vegetation and what seemed to be river weed, in which they found a live crab that the Admiral kept; and he says that those were sure signs of land. . . . They saw many dolphins and the men of the *Niña* killed one. The Admiral says here that those signs were from the west where I hope that in mighty God in Whose hands are all victories that very soon He will give us land. (*Diario*, 33–5)
>
> [September 18:] There appeared in the north a large cloud mass, which is a sign of being near land. (*Diario*, 35)
>
> [September 19:] Some drizzles of rain came without wind, which is a sure sign of land. (*Diario*, 37)
>
> [September 20:] Two boobies came to the ship and later another, which is a sign of being near land. (*Diario*, 37)

Three weeks later Columbus and his men are still noting the signs:

> [October 11:] They saw petrels and a green bulrush near the ship. The men of the caravel *Pinta* saw a cane and a stick and took on board another small stick that appeared to have been worked with iron, and a piece of cane, and other vegetation originating on land, and a small plank. The men of the caravel *Niña* also saw signs of land and a small stick loaded with barnacles. With these signs everyone breathed more easily and cheered up. (*Diario*, 57–9)[4]

These signs, the last collected quite literally on the eve of the discovery, serve as confirmation and promise: confirmation of a theory, promise of the fulfillment of a desire. We can detect in each of the notations the trace of a pause, a caesura, that marks a tension between the visual and the verbal, seeing and reading. The visual seems inherently particularizing: *this* patch of seaweed, *that* bird; the verbal inherently generalizing and abstracting:

seaweed and bird are written down as signs of a still invisible and featureless, but theoretically necessary, land. The tension does not disclose a stable or absolute difference here between vision as the particular and language as the general: not only are Columbus's observations known to us entirely through writing, but his act of writing them—and perhaps of seeing them in the first place—depends upon a structure of expectation and perception in which the word is at least as fully implicated as the eye. Still, the form of the journal entry characteristically registers first the material sighting and then its significance; the space between the two—what I have called the caesura—is the place of discovery where the explanatory power of writing repeatedly tames the opacity of the eye's objects by rendering them transparent signs.

That is, the sightings are important only in relation to what Columbus already knows and what he can write about them on the basis of that knowledge. If they fail in their promise, they will be demoted from the status of signs and not noticed any longer. It was, after all, the *known* world that Columbus had set out to discover, if by an unknown route: that was the point of reading Marco Polo and Mandeville. As Todorov writes, Columbus 'knows in advance what he will find; the concrete experience is there to illustrate a truth already possessed, not to be interrogated according to preestablished rules in order to seek the truth.'[5]

The paradox of the meaningful—or perhaps we can simply say the full—sign is that it is empty in the sense of hollow or transparent: a glass through which Columbus looks to find what he expects to find, or, more accurately perhaps, a foreign word he expects to construe and to incorporate into his own language. In the late sixteenth century Richard Mulcaster wittily called this incorporation—the process of making the 'stranger denisons' of other tongues 'bond to the rules of our writing'—*enfranchisement*.[6] The sign that Columbus cannot enfranchise, that is irreducibly strange or opaque, is *en route* to losing its status as a sign. For opacity here can only signal an obstacle standing in the way of the desired access to the known.

In a sense then the best voyage will be one in which one learns next to nothing; most of the signs will simply confirm what one already knows.[7] Columbus wrote, to be sure, that 'the further one goes, the more one learns' (*andando más, más se sabe*) (ii. 43). But the context in which he advances this perfectly banal proverb is revealing: he is arguing that the earth's surface has much more dry land than either the 'vulgar' or certain learned Greek and Arab geographers believe. Columbus's appeal to experience merely confirms the book of Esdras and a host of authorities who claim that 'of the seven parts of the world, six are uncovered and the one remaining is covered by water' (ii. 40–2). The experience is a sign that Columbus—and Petrus Comestor and Nicolaus of Lyra and St Augustine and St Ambrose and Cardinal Pedro de Aliaco and many others—were right all along. The important point is not that this view in fact turned out to be hopelessly wrong but that practical knowledge, the actual observations and recorded events, serve to confirm what Columbus already believes. If they do not, they are not made to serve as the bases for new, radically different hypotheses; they are for the most part simply demoted from signification. Only when these demotions become constant and when the pressure of articulating the known on the site of geographical or cultural difference becomes overwhelming does the representational system itself significantly change. And Columbus himself was strongly resistant to such change.

There is another sense too in which Columbus's reading of the signs tends to confirm what he already knows. In his log-book entry for October 12, 1492, he turns his attention to the naked bodies of the natives and tries to decipher what he sees:

> I saw some who had marks of wounds on their bodies and I made signs to them asking what they were; and they showed me how the people from other islands nearby came there and tried to take them, and how they defended themselves; and I believed and believe that they come here from *tierra firme* to take them captive [*por captivos*]. (*Diario*, 67)[8]

This is, let us remember, the first day of contact between Europeans and natives, and we would do well to be skeptical about the exchange of signs that Columbus reports. I suppose that we are meant to imagine Columbus touching or pointing to the wounds and then miming the question 'why?' or 'who did this?'; the natives in return would gesture toward one of the other islands visible in the distance and then act out invasion, resistance, capture. But charades or pantomimes depend upon a shared gestural language that can take the place of speech; as anyone knows who has tried to ask the simplest of questions in a culture with a different gestural language, exchanges of the kind Columbus describes are fraught with difficulties. And Columbus, of course, takes a step beyond the exchange itself, declaring that he believes (*yo crey, e creo*) that the invaders do not come from the islands toward which the natives appear to be gesturing but from the mainland he has not yet seen and further that the purpose of these invasions is to take captives.

If we ask why he believes this on the basis of scars and a few gestures—why his discourse (anticipating much colonial discourse to follow) is a fantasmatic representation of authoritative certainty in the face of spectacular ignorance—the answer lies in part in his conviction that he is near the mainland of China. But beyond this conviction there is perhaps a deeper source of certainty: when he looks at the bodies of the natives, he sees their literal vulnerability (something that would have been largely hidden beneath the Europeans' armor). Immediately after he has recorded his belief that the inhabitants of the mainland come to take these natives as captives, he continues,

> They should be good and intelligent servants for I see that they say very quickly everything that is said to them; and I believe that they would become Christians very easily, for it seemed to me that they had no religion. Our Lord pleasing, at the time of my departure I will take six of them from here to Your Highnesses in order that they may learn to speak. No animals did I see on this island except parrots. (*Diario*, 67–9)

It is Columbus then who has come from the mainland and intends to take captives. The people he observes before him and whom he admires for skills similar to those of the parrots in the trees have almost no opacity. What he sees when he reads the signs and looks off toward China is himself.

Let us return now to Trinidad and to Columbus's attempt to read the signs. In search of the mainland, he encounters people who look different from the islanders he had been encountering; those have been naked and relatively dark-skinned; these are lighter in color and are wearing, if not clothes, then at least elaborately worked cotton scarves. The scarves must be read: they are, he says, *almaizares*, Moorish veils. This suggests to him that he is at last encountering not virtually transparent members of simple, backward tribes but a different civilization—closer to the culture of the East for which he had been so long searching—and he naturally wishes to make contact with them.[9]

The Indians themselves appeared at first to share this desire. They shouted something to the Europeans which neither Columbus nor anyone else could understand; Columbus, for his part, ordered signs to be made that they should approach. But this initial attempt at communication was a failure; two hours passed, and the Indians kept their distance. Columbus ordered that pans and other bright objects be displayed, but though the Indians drew slightly closer, they did not come up to his ship where he waited eager, as he says, to have speech with them. He then had a remarkable idea: 'I caused to be brought up to the castle of the poop a tambourine, that they might play it, and some young men to dance, believing that they would draw near to see the festivity.' He hoped to coax the natives into contact not by addressing them or by offering objects—

both of these time-honored expedients seemed to have failed—but by displaying an art form, staging a cultural event, representing a fiesta.[10] The effect was immediate but not quite what he had in mind: 'As soon as they observed the playing and dancing, they all dropped their oars and laid hand on their bows and strung them, and each one of them took up his shield, and they began to shoot arrows.' The dancing that was for Columbus's culture a token of peace—one thinks of the graceful dancers in Lorenzetti's 'Buon Governo'—was evidently for the natives of Trinidad an unambiguous declaration of war. Columbus ordered the fiesta to stop and the cross-bows to fire: 'I never saw any more of them or of the other inhabitants of this island' (ii. 14–16).

This small fiasco may be taken as an introduction to a set of questions that greatly concerned both the Europeans and the natives of the New World: How does one read the signs of the other? How does one make signs to the other? How does one reconcile the desire for transparent signs with the opacity of an unknown culture? How does one move from mute wonder to communication? These questions will lead us from the display and interpretation of signs to the exchange of gifts and the bartering of goods, for the hand gestures and facial expressions and mutually incomprehensible speeches made at the first moments of contact almost immediately give way to the profferring of material objects: food, articles of clothing, crafted pieces of metal, stone or glass, animal skins. And barter and gift-giving in turn will lead us to the learning of language. The three modes of communication—mute signs, material exchange, and language—are in turn bound up in a larger question: how is it possible for one system of representation to establish contact with a different system? And this question will lead us to reflect on certain characteristics of the European system of representation in the early modern period—its mobility, its dependence on improvisation, and above all its paradoxical yoking of empty and full, worthless and valuable, counterfeit and real.

It is characteristic of Mandeville that he never registers the problem of cross-cultural communication. He claims to speak with Saracens, Jews, Armenians, Copts, Chaldeans, Indians, Tibetans, and the like with unmediated fluency. He acknowledges linguistic difference but only at the level of the alphabets that he reproduces in the spirit with which he records strange customs and beliefs. These alphabets—colorful, spectacularly inaccurate, and useless—are supremely unattached signifiers, material tokens of pretended travel and dispossession. But Mandeville's dialogues are only possible with imaginary others; in the early years of contact with the natives of the New World, voyagers frequently express frustration at the difficulty of understanding the other, and the sense of difficulty intensifies rather than lessens over time. 'Both parties were grieved that they did not understand one another,' writes Columbus in 1500, 'they in order to ask the others of our country, and our men in order to learn about their land' (ii. 22).

On his first voyage, provoked perhaps by the uniform nakedness of the peoples he encountered, Columbus had concluded that there was no substantial diversity of languages in the lands he had found; this apparent uniformity surprised and pleased him, for it would make the task of conversion much simpler: 'In all these islands, I saw no great diversity in the appearance of the people or in their manners and language. On the contrary, they all understand one another, which is a very curious thing, on account of which I hope that their highnesses will determine upon their conversion to our holy faith, towards which they are very inclined' (i. 10–12).[11] By the second voyage, he acknowledged that there was greater linguistic diversity than he had at first thought: 'It is the truth that, as among these people those of one island have little intercourse with those of another, in languages there is some difference between them' (i. 88). And by the fourth voyage, the differences have multiplied and hardened into a serious obstacle: 'Of all these lands and of that which there is in them, owing to the lack of an interpreter, they could not learn very much. The villages, although they are very close together, have each a different language, and it is so much so that they do not understand one another any more than we understand the Arabs' (ii. 102).

The early discourse of the New World then is full of questions that cannot be asked or answers that cannot be understood. 'Due to the lack of language,' complains Verrazzano, 'we were unable to find out by signs or gestures how much religious faith these people we found possessed.'[12] Canoes of Indians, Cartier writes, 'came after our long-boat dancing and showing many signs of joy, and of their desire to be friends, saying to us in their language: *Napou tou daman asurtat*, and other words, we did not understand. . . . And seeing that no matter how much we signed to them, they would not go back, we shot off over their heads two small cannon.'[13] Dionise Settle writes glumly of the desolate northern islands to which the English had come, 'I have . . . left the names of the Countreys . . . untouched, for lacke of understanding the peoples language.'[14] And Sir Richard Hawkins reports an encounter with two or three naked Indians who 'spake unto us, and made diverse signs; now pointing to the Harbour, out of which we were come; and then to the mouth of the Straites: but we understood nothing of their meaning. Yet they left us with many imaginations.' What the English did not imagine, until they thought about the encounter later, was that the Indians were probably warning them of an approaching storm, 'for they have great insight in the change of weather,' Hawkins notes, 'and besides have secret dealing with the Prince of Darknesse, who many times declareth unto them things to come.'[15]

In the absence of a common language both Europeans and natives attempted, as we have seen several times now, to communicate with signs. Despite Columbus's experience off Trinidad, most of the early voyagers seem at least fitfully to share Augustine's conviction that there is 'a kind of universal language, consisting of expressions of the face and eyes, gestures and tones of voice, which can show whether a person means to ask for something and get it, or refuse it and have nothing to do with it.'[16] Augustine is articulating assumptions that are bound up with the rhetorical culture of late antiquity. Quintillian had written of a 'law of gesture'—a *chironomia*—and sketched the range of bodily motions and expressions that could be used with powerful effect 'even without the aid of words.' For 'not only a movement of the hand, but even a nod, may express our meaning,' he observed, 'and such gestures are to the dumb instead of speech' (*Inst.* 11. 3. 65–6). Quintillian took special note of the expressive power of dancing—a distant foreshadowing of Columbus's communicative experiment—but it was above all the hands that seemed to him eloquent, 'for other parts of the body assist the speaker, but these, I may almost say, speak themselves. . . . So that amidst the great diversity of tongues pervading all nations and people, the language of the hands appears to be a language common to all men' (*Inst.* 11. 3. 85–7).[17]

Certain Indian gestures—above all, perhaps, the tearful greeting widespread in South America and among some North American tribes—seemed irreducibly strange to most Europeans, but what is more striking is how confident the early voyagers were, despite their disappointments and frustrations, in their ability to make themselves understood and to comprehend unfamiliar signs.[18] So, for example, Amadas and Barlowe report that on the first English voyage to Virginia in 1584 they made initial contact with a man who spoke 'of many things not understood by us.' Shortly thereafter they were greeted by an important personage—'the Kings brother'—who 'beckoned us to come and sit by him, which we performed: and being set hee made all signes of joy and welcome, striking on his head and his breast and afterwardes on ours, to shewe wee were all one, smiling and making shewe the best he could of all love, and familiaritie.' He then 'made a long speech to us.'[19] When the English responded by presenting gifts to the chief and to those around him, the chief gave in signs what the English construed as a brief lesson about the local social structure: 'presently he arose and tooke all from them and put it into his owne basket, making signes and tokens, that all things ought to bee delivered unto him, and the rest were but his servants, and followers.'[20] That this 'nobleman's' smile denotes 'all love, and familiaritie' seems a barely plausible if exceedingly optimistic reading; that his gestures are intended to show that 'wee were all one' seems a more daring interpretive leap; that his way of receiving gifts discloses a set of social relationships (including a 'king,' 'servants, and followers') seems a rash presumption, dependent on the uncritical application of a European model.

Amadas and Barlowe have been sent by Sir Walter Ralegh to locate a promising territory for an English colony. Without understanding a word that has been said to them, they believe (or at least profess to believe) that the country they have 'discovered'—a country called 'Wingandacoa, and now by her Majestie Virginia'—is inhabited by 'people most gentle, loving, and faithfull, voide of all guile and treason, and such as live after the maner of the golden age' (p. 305). Accordingly, all signs are read in the most favorable light, a light that discloses at once a reassuring confirmation of the familiar hierarchical social structure and a radical innocence. The gratifying consequence of this somewhat paradoxical combination of qualities is revealed by the favorable exchange rate: 'we exchanged our tinne dish for twentie skinnes, woorth twentie Crownes, or twentie Nobles: and a copper kettle for fiftie skins woorth fifty Crownes. They offered us good exchange for our hatchets, and axes, and for knives, and would have given any thing for swordes: but wee would not depart with any' (p. 302). A lively interest in swords sits strangely with life in the manner of the Golden Age. But then it is already an odd Golden Age that has kings and servants. In Shakespeare's *Tempest* old Gonzalo is ridiculed for category confusions of this kind: 'The latter end of his commonwealth forgets the beginning' (II. i. 158). It is not clear if such contradictions troubled Amadas and Barlowe—or if they even noticed them. There was little reason for them to construct a coherent, internally consistent account of Virginia; their report is a prospectus for potential investors in future voyages, and consequently they assemble an inventory of hopeful signs.

We should not underestimate the cynical calculation with which the early travel texts were often put together, but calculation cannot adequately explain the reckless optimism—epistemological as well as strategic—that they frequently express. It is not only rudimentary understanding that must be painstakingly learned but also an acknowledgment of opacity:

Europeans found it extremely difficult to recognize just how difficult, distorted, and uneven were these first, tentative attempts at cross-cultural communication. As we have already seen in the case of Columbus, the great temptation was to assume transparency, to rush from wonder—the experience of stunned surprise—to possession or at least the illusion of possession. And hence the moments of blankness—'we could not understand. . . ,' 'we do not know. . . ,' 'we could not explain. . . ,'—are intertwined strangely with the confident assumption that there was no significant barrier to communication or appropriation: 'We passed through many and dissimilar tongues. Our Lord granted us favor with the people who spoke them for they always understood us, and we them. We questioned them, and received their answers by signs, just as if they spoke our language and we theirs.'[21]

This assumption is fueled in part by a recurrent failure to comprehend the resistant cultural otherness of New World peoples. On the one hand, there is a tendency to imagine the Indians as virtual blanks—wild, unformed creatures, as naked in culture as they are in body. On the other hand, there is a tendency to imagine the Indians as virtual doubles, fully conversant with the language and culture of the Europeans. These tendencies seem like opposites, but they are in fact versions of one another, as we can glimpse in a remark by the chronicler Peter Martyr: 'For lyke as rased or vnpaynted tables, are apte to receaue what formes soo euer are fyrst drawne theron by the hande of the paynter, euen soo these naked and simple people, doo soone receaue the customes of owre Religion, and by conuersation with owre men, shake of[f] theyr fierce and natiue barbarousnes.'[22] One moment the Indians have no culture; the next moment they have ours.

The assumption of cultural transparency was alluring but, as at least a few Europeans recognized, it was also dangerous and potentially unjust. Las Casas angrily attacks the pretense that complex negotiations could be conducted through interpreters who in reality 'communicate with a few phrases like "Gimme bread," "Gimme food," "Take this, gimme that," and otherwise carry on with gestures.'[23] Narratives that represent Indians and Spaniards in sophisticated dialogue are, he suggests, most often intentional falsifications, designed to make the arbitrary and violent actions of the conquistadors appear more just than they actually were. No doubt Las Casas was right—the official reports bespeak a fathomless cynicism—but there also seems to have been a great deal of what we may call 'filling in the blanks.' The Europeans and the interpreters themselves translated such fragments as they understood or thought they understood into a coherent story, and they came to believe that the story was what they had actually heard. It was all too easy to conclude that apparent incomprehension was willful non-compliance; there could be, and according to Las Casas there were, murderous results.[24]

It is a source of mordant satisfaction—and a sign of the inescapable mutuality of language—that the assumption of cultural transparency was not limited to the Europeans and consequently that the danger was not limited to the natives. Consider the testimony of Hernando de Escalante Fontaneda who was shipwrecked in Florida and held captive by the Carlos (Calusa) Indians for some seventeen years. Escalante, who spoke four languages, occasionally served as interpreter for other shipwrecked Spaniards and helped to save their lives. 'For the natives who took them,' he reports in a 'memorial' transcribed around 1575, 'would order them to dance and sing; and as they were not understood, and the Indians themselves are very artful, (for the most so of any are the people of Florida,) they thought the Christians were obstinate, and unwilling to do so. And so they would kill them, and report to their cacique that for their craft and disobedience they had been slain, because they would not do as they were told.'[25]

In a weird revision of the story with which we began, Spanish sailors are once again commanded to stage a fiesta, but now the command comes from their native captors in a language they do not understand. And, disastrously, the Spanish cannot communicate their failure to understand. Did such scenes actually take place? It is impossible to know—Escalante has a personal interest in emphasizing the importance of his unusual mastery of languages—but in his account at least the principal issue is a recognition of the existence of linguistic opacity. To survive, the Spanish must somehow prove that they cannot understand the words that are being spoken to them, and, in the face of their captors' presumption that they are both devious and disobedient, the proof requires some ingenuity. Hence Escalante describes a strange occasion in which he, in the company of a black captive, tried to demonstrate to a powerful cacique that it was language difference and not obstinacy that was the problem. The cacique is puzzled by the strange behavior of his captives and turns to Escalante for an explanation:

> 'Escalante, tell us the truth, for you well know that I like you much: When we require these, your companions, to dance and sing, and do other things, why are they so dissembling and obstinate that they will not? or is it that they do not fear death, or will not yield to a people unlike them in their customs? Answer me; and if you do not know the reason, ask it of those newly taken, who for their own fault are

prisoners now, a people whom once we held to be gods come down from the sky.' And I, answering my lord and master, told him the truth: 'Sir, as I understand it, they are not contrary, nor do they behave badly on purpose but it is because they cannot comprehend you, which they earnestly strive to do.' He said it was not true; that often he would command them to do things, and sometimes they would obey him, and at others they would not, however much they might be told. I said to him: 'With all that, my lord, they do not intentionally behave amiss, nor for perversity, but from not understanding. Speak to them, that I may be a witness, and likewise this your freedman.' And the cacique, laughing, said: 'Se-le-te-ga,' to the new comers; and they asked what it was he said to them. The negro, who was near to them, laughed, and said to the cacique: 'Master, I will tell you the truth; they have not understood, and they ask Escalante what it is you say, and he does not wish to tell them until you command him.' Then the cacique believed the truth, and said to me: 'Declare it to them, Escalante; for now do I really believe you.' I made known to them the meaning of Se-le-tega, which is, 'Run to the look-out, see if there be any people coming;' they of Florida abbreviate their words more than we. The cacique, discovering the truth, said to his vassals, that when they should find Christians thus cast away, and take them, they must require them to do nothing without giving notice, that one might go to them who should understand their language. (p. 12)

Escalante is recounting a kind of primal language lesson: not the learning of a new language but the acknowledgment of linguistic difference that must precede such learning. Without this acknowledgment, one's own language would seem as natural and inevitable as breathing, and in the face of strangers one would simply begin to speak (and, in the case of a chief, to issue commands). This, as Escalante conceives it, has been the problem in Florida: he depicts the cacique not as a malevolent brute but as a genially ignorant sovereign, a powerful liege lord accustomed to obedience. With Escalante's help, the cacique discovers the truth of difference—his Christian captives are not wicked but simply other—and he establishes regulations that ensure fair treatment. The language lesson then is the precondition for the invention of procedural justice.

Let us recall that Columbus took possession of the New World with a legal ritual performed in Spanish and that, after 1513, *conquistadores* were supposed to read to all newly encountered peoples the *Requerimiento*, a document in Spanish that informed these peoples of their rights and obligations as vassals of the king and queen of Spain. Prompt obedience, the text declares, will be rewarded; refusal or malicious delay will be harshly punished:

And we protest that the deaths and losses which shall accrue from this are your fault, and not that of their Highnesses, or ours, nor of these cavaliers who come with us. And that we have said this to you and made this Requisition, we request the notary here present to give us his testimony in writing, and we ask the rest who are present that they should be witnesses of this Requisition.[26]

A strange blend of ritual, cynicism, legal fiction, and perverse idealism, the *Requerimiento* contains at its core the conviction that there is no serious language barrier between the Indians and the Europeans. And to a thoughtful and informed observer like Las Casas, the dangerous absurdity of this conviction was fully apparent: Las Casas writes that he doesn't know 'whether to laugh or cry' at the *Requerimiento*.[27]

From the perspective provided by Las Casas, Escalante's story would seem to be a sly, displaced critique of Spanish linguistic colonialism, a critique made possible by his long years living with the natives of Florida. The cacique's rule—that all requirements must be made in the language of the other—is set over against an injustice that began on October 12, 1492 and was given full institutional confirmation after 1513. And yet, though everything in Escalante's account would seem to call out for such a critique, it does not seem to have occurred to him. On the contrary, in his memorial he counsels the Spanish not to seek peace with the natives who are, he writes, 'very faithless.' Therefore, 'let the Indians be taken in hand gently, inviting them to peace; then putting them under deck, husbands and wives together, sell them among the Islands, and even upon Terra-Firma for money, as some old nobles of Spain buy vassals of the king. In this way, there could be management of them, and their number become thinned' (p. 12).[28] A process of mimetic doubling and projection—a representation of the natives as a displaced European self-representation—does not lead to identification with the other but to a ruthless will to possess.

The shipwrecked Spaniards, in Escalante's account, try to obey the commands of their captors, even without understanding them, but their efforts only make matters worse, for their moments of accidental or inspired compliance simply persuade the cacique that they are perversely obstinate at other moments. They are, in effect, discovering the limits of improvisation, the ability to insert the self in the sign systems of others. It is unusual to encounter an acknowledgment of its limits; more often the discourse of the New World celebrates the power not only to survive through improvisation but to profit hugely from the adroit manipulation of alien signs. Even the tearful greeting was not beyond imitation: Jean de Léry describes the Brazilian ceremony of welcome—'Then the women come and surround the bed, crouching with their buttocks against the ground and with both hands over their eyes; in this manner, weeping their welcome to the visitor, they will say a thousand things in his praise'—and he notes that the French accommodated themselves to it: 'If the newly arrived guest who is seated in the bed wants in turn to please them, he must assume the appropriate expression, and if he doesn't quite get to the point of tears (I have seen some of our nation, who, upon hearing the bleating of these women next to them, were such babies as to be reduced to tears themselves), at least when he answers them he must heave a few sighs and pretend to weep.'[29] The untheatrical Calvinist Léry is made uneasy by the more flamboyant improvisers, weeping with their Brazilian hosts, but he grasps the essential principle: to 'assume the appropriate expression.' And this principle is repeatedly found as well among the natives.

Tzvetan Todorov has argued that the Indians were incapable of the improvisatory consciousness so marked in the Europeans, but the argument seems to me difficult to sustain in the face of the substantial evidence of the native mastery of European signs (a mastery confirmed even in the Europeans' contemptuous dismissal of the natives as 'parrots').[30] Such improvisation on the part of either Europeans or natives should not be construed as the equivalent of sympathetic understanding; it is rather what we can call appropriative mimesis, imitation in the interest of acquisition. As such it need not have entailed any grasp of the cultural reality of the other, only a willingness to make contact and to effect some kind of exchange. But the very existence of such exchanges—and they began in the very first moments of encounter, in situations of extraordinary cultural distance and mutual strangeness—is itself remarkable. We cannot make a universal principle out of this desire to possess a token of otherness, for there were peoples who resisted all contact and showed no interest in economic exchange,[31] but it is sufficiently widespread to warrant a presumption about the behavior of most human beings (exactly the presumption that Columbus, setting out pots and pans on his deck, was displaying). And it is in these early exchanges that we can glimpse most clearly some of the founding acts of practical imagination in the European apprehension of the New World.

An early seventeenth-century report of an English expedition to Newfoundland, under the leadership of the Bristol merchant John Guy, gives us an unusually detailed (and impressively modest) account of the tentative establishment of trading relations through the manipulation and interpretation of signs. In November, 1612, a small party of Englishmen came at night to a few uninhabited Beothuck Indian houses on a lake (the Indian inhabitants had gone to a nearby island): 'We fownd theare a copper kettle

Indians fleeing the approach of Columbus's ships: from *De insulis inventis epistola Cristoferi Colom* (Basel, 1493). British Library.

kepte very brighte, a furre gowne, some seale skinnes, ane old sayle, & a fishing reele. Order was taken that nothing should be diminished, & because the savages should know that some had bin theare, everything was removed out of his place, & broughte into one of the cabins, and laid orderlie one upon the other, & the kettle hanged over them, wheearin thear was put some bisket, & three or fower amber beades. This was done to beginne to winne them by fayre meanes.'[32] 'To win them'—the purpose here is not military victory or the establishment of sovereignty but the establishment of trading relations; what is to be won is confidence and trust. Accordingly, the English make explicit signs of their presence: it would presumably have been detected in any case, but by carefully moving the inhabitants' belongings and by leaving small gifts of food and beads, the English indicate both that they *wish* their presence known and that they come in friendship. Their act entails an imagining of the Beothuck response when they return to the village, a calculation of their probable interpretation of the signs—and the manifest fact that the intruders have so carefully imagined the villagers' response is implicitly one of the signs that they have left.

These initial gestures are rewarded:

Presentlie two canoaes appeared, & one man alone comming towards us with a flag in his hand of a wolfskinne, shaking yt, & making a lowde noice, which we tooke to be for a parlie, wheareupon a white flag was put out & the barke & shallope rowed towards them: which the savages did not like of, & soe tooke them to theire canoaes againe, & weare goeing away. Wheareopon the barke wheared onto them & flourished the flag of truce, & came to anker, which pleased them, & then they stayed.

A key interpretive move is made when the English construe the wolfskin 'flag' and the loud noise as requests for a 'parley' (as opposed, for example, to construing them as a menace),[33] and in a further act of interpretive sensitivity they grasp, after a small misstep, that they should not give the appearance of pursuit but rather come to anchor. At this point the two sides can actually make contact:

Presentlie after, the shalloppe landed Mr. Whittington with the flag of truce, who went towards them. Then they rowed into the shoare with one canoa, thother standing aloofe of, & landed two men, one of them having the white skinne in his hand, & comming towards Mr. Whittington, the savage made a loude speeche, & shaked the skinne, which was awnsweared by Mr. Whittington in like manner & as the savage drew neere he threw downe the whitte skinne into the grownde. The like was done by Mr. Whittington. Wheareupon both the savages passed over a little water streame towards Mr. Whittington daunsing, leaping, & singing, &

coming togeather, the foremost of them, presented unto him a chaine of leather full of small perwincle shelles, a spilting knife, & a feather that stucke in his heare. The other gave him ane arrow without a head, & the former was requited with a linnen cap, & a hand towell, who put presentlie the linnen cap upon his head, and to the other he gave a knife. And after hand in hand they all three did sing, & daunce. Upon this one of our companie called Fraunces Tipton went a shoare, unto whom one of the savages came running: & gave him a chaine such as is before spoaken of, who was gratefied by Fraunces Tipton with a knife, & a small piece of brasse. Then all fower togeather daunced, laughing, & makeing signes of ioy, & gladnes, sometimes strikeing the breastes of our companie & sometymes theyre owne. (pp. 57–8)

For a simple moment—two Indians and two Europeans imitating each other, exchanging small gifts and dancing together on the shore—there is something like a secular communion.

John Guy is principally interested in barter, and through patience and cautious deduction—the essential elements in the mode of 'silent trade' that is recorded as early as Herodotus[34]—he manages to effect some exchange. The Indians go off but they leave some skins hanging on poles; when these are left in place for several days, the English conclude that they were goods intended for trade:

we remayned satisffied fullie that they weare broughte theather of purpose to barter with us, & that they would stand to our curtesie to leave for yt what we should thinke good. Because we weare not furnished with fit things for to trucke, we tooke onlie a beaver skinne, a sable skinne, & a bird skinne, leaving for them, a hatchet, a knife & fower needles threaded. Mr. Whittington had a paire of sezers which he lefte theare for a small beaver skinne, all the reste we theare untouched and came that nighte to the harbour that we weare in at our entring, which we call Flagstaffe Harbour, because we fownd theare the flagstaffe throwen by the savages away. (pp. 60–1)[35]

The English merchant's account is unusual for making no great claims—no glimpse of vast riches, no promise of easy conversion, no elaborate deductions about religious belief or social order. But for this reason his account provides a useful elementary model—initial contact, material exchange, and naming—for the hundreds and even thousands of more complex encounters that have survived in the travel discourse of the period. Consider, for example, the testimony of Jacques Cartier. When Cartier sees the Indians holding up furs on sticks, he assumes that they are proposing to engage in barter, though he does not immediately 'care to trust to their signs.'[36] On the next day he ventures to make some signals in return—'we . . . made signs to them that we wished them no harm'—and then sends two men on shore 'to offer them some knives and other iron goods, and a red cap to give to their chief.' The initial, tentative gestures then have materialized, as it were, into gifts, and the gifts lead to further signs: 'The savages showed a marvellously great pleasure in possessing and obtaining these iron wares and other commodities, dancing and going through many ceremonies, and throwing salt water over their heads with their hands.' And these signs of extreme joy lead in turn to what we may call an extreme exchange: 'They bartered all they had to such an extent that all went back naked without anything on them' (i. 300).

When the scene is repeated a few days later, with still more intense manifestations of delight, Cartier ventures a further reading of the signs. The natives have once again 'offered everything that they owned' so that 'nothing was left to them but their naked bodies.' From this the Frenchman concludes that 'they are people who would be easy to convert.' This conclusion would seem to be based on their ease in the presence of the Europeans and on their apparent willingness to strip themselves bare, as if he saw them joyfully divesting themselves of their beliefs as well as their belongings. Cartier describes their evident delight as if it were already an act of homage to the Christian god: 'Then they joined their hands together and raised them to heaven, exhibiting many signs of joy.' As he looks around the Gulf of St Lawrence on a warm July day, Cartier draws similarly optimistic conclusions about the land he has discovered: 'Their country is more temperate than Spain and the finest it is possible to see.' After taking inventory of its resources, he returns to its inhabitants and pursues the reading of signs still further: 'I am more than ever of opinion that these people would be easy to convert to our holy faith. They call a hatchet in their language, cochy, and a knife, bacan. We named this bay, Chaleur Bay' (i. 300).

These three sentences manifest the blank refusal of logical connectives characteristic of much of early travel writing, but there is a hidden logic: Cartier's reading of the natives' response to barter has led him to the conclusion that they would be easy to convert; the task of conversion will necessitate the learning of their language, which here begins with the notation of their words for two of the European articles in which they take such delight; and the inscription of Indian words in European letters is paradoxically a step toward the renaming, the linguistic appropriation, of the land. Perhaps we should call it the *misnaming* of the land, since the conviction that Canada had the climate of the Costa del Sol led to fatal blunders. (The inlet off the Gaspee Peninsula is, however, still called Chaleur Bay.)

In Cartier, as in almost all early European accounts, the language of the Indians is noted not in order to register cultural specificity but in order to facilitate barter, movement, and assimilation through conversion. And though, as we have seen, the explorers often expressed frustration at their inability to understand the natives, they did not, as a rule, make any serious attempt to overcome the language barrier by actually learning Indian tongues. This is not only because explorers, by training and inclination, are not easily confused with linguists (or, more relevantly, with missionaries), but also because they had little practical interest in immersing themselves in native culture and no desire to do so. To learn a language may be a step toward mastery, but to *study* a language is to place oneself in a situation of dependency, to submit.[37] Moreover, not understanding Indian speech allowed a certain agreeable latitude in construing the signs of the other. 'When the Spaniards discovered this land,' writes Antonio de Ciudad Real in 1588, 'their leader asked the Indians how it was called; as they did not understand him, they said *uic athan*, which means, what do you say or what do you speak, that we do not understand you. And then the Spaniard ordered it set down that it be called *Yucatan*.'[38] The Maya expression of incomprehension becomes the colonial name of the land that is wrested from them.

I have already quoted Verrazzano's admission that 'due to the lack of language, we were unable to find out by signs or gestures how much religious faith these people we found possess.' But the passage then continues:

> We think they have neither religion nor laws, that they do not know of a First Cause or Author, that they do not worship the sky, the stars, the sun, the moon, or other planets, nor do they even practice any kind of idolatry; we do not know whether they offer any sacrifices or other prayers, nor are there any temples or churches of prayer among their peoples. We consider that they have no religion and that they live in absolute freedom, and that everything they do proceeds from Ignorance; for they are very easily persuaded, and they imitated everything that they saw us Christians do with regard to divine worship, with the same fervor and enthusiasm that we had. (i. 287)

It is, of course, Verrazzano who is proceeding from an ignorance that he freely acknowledges, but this ignorance does not prevent him from constructing a promising model of the other. The model resembles that sketched by Columbus on the first day; it construes the Indian as a screen or a vacancy—a state of 'absolute freedom'—and imagines that this vacancy will be filled by imitation.

Such a conception of the Indians assimilates them in part to children, and we may relate this assimilation to the sense of infantilization that many people experience when they find themselves in a country where they do not speak the language. That this sense is not an exclusively modern one is confirmed by Mowbray's extravagant response in Shakespeare's *Richard II*, to his sentence of exile in France:

> I am too old to fawn upon a nurse,
> Too far in years to be a pupil now.
> (I. iii. 170–1)

In the case of the New World voyagers, of course, what is striking is that, though they are on foreign shores, the Europeans do not feel themselves infantilized; it is rather the natives whom they see as children in relation to European languages.

It is perhaps because of this reversal that the European explorers and conquerors allow themselves on the whole to admire Indian facility in learning their tongues. We have already seen Columbus's comment on the Indians' ability to mimic. Similarly, the Earl of Cumberland reports that the natives of Dominica have 'great desire to understand the English tongue; for some of them will point to most parts of the body, and having told the name of it in the language of Dominica, he would not rest till he were told the name of it in English, which having once told he would repeate till he could either name it right, or at least till he thought it was right, and so commonly it should be, saving that to all words ending in a consonant they alwayes set the second vowall, as for chinne, they say chin-ne, so making most of the monasillables, dissillables.'[39] Or again John Brereton in 1602 writes that the Indians 'pronounce our Language with great facilitie; for one of them one day sitting by mee, upon occasion I spake smiling to him these words: how now, sirrha, are you so sawcy with my Tobacco? which words (without any further repetition) he suddenly spake so plaine and distinctly, as if hee had beene long Scholar in the Language.'[40]

It is tempting to find in such moments of genial admiration relief from the miserable chronicles of colonial exploitation and violence, and those Europeans who regarded the Indians as able children certainly seem preferable to those who treated them as demonic beasts. But we must at least remark the eerie subtext of the exchange between John Brereton and his Indian interlocutor: the politics of domination and appropriation, the gross inequalities of economic, status, and power relations, are rehearsed—mimicked—in so reduced a form that the colonizer does not even notice them, any more perhaps than does the colonized, as he repeats the words, 'how now, sirrha, are you so sawcy with my Tobacco?'

The radically unequal distribution of power that lies at the heart of almost all language learning in the New World is most perfectly realized in the explorers' preferred method for dealing with the language problem, an expedient that maximizes rapidity of access and eschews an acknowledgment of the obstructive constraints of otherness. From the very first day in 1492, the principal means chosen by the Europeans to establish linguistic contact was kidnapping—or perhaps, after Mulcaster, we should call the act 'enfranchisement.' I have already cited Columbus's log-book entry, announcing his intention to seize several of the natives who have come to greet him and to take them back to Spain 'so that they can learn to speak.' On October 15, only three days after landfall, Columbus reports the escape of two of these captives: one seems to have jumped overboard and swum to shore, the other managed to flee in one of the native 'dugouts' that Columbus had earlier admired—they 'go marvelously,' he wrote on October 13th (*Diario*, 69).[41] Now the marvel of the canoe's speed (for 'there were never ship's launch that could overtake it even if we had a big head start' [*Diario*, 81]) is disclosed as a strategic edge, one of the few technological advantages that the natives enjoy. Hence flight which Columbus sees as shameful—when the Spanish went in pursuit of the escapees, he writes, 'they all fled like chickens' (*Diario*, 81)—is in fact a form of politics, under the circumstances almost the only rational politics available to the natives.[42]

Even Columbus seems to recognize that there is a strategic dimension to the flight of his captives, a dimension that requires a response beyond pursuit. Shortly after the escape an Indian paddles toward the ship in the hope of trading a ball of cotton and is seized by the Spanish sailors. Columbus writes that he sent for the Indian, gave him some small gifts—a red bonnet, small green glass beads, and two bells—and ordered that he be released:

> And later I saw, on land, at the time of the arrival of the other man—[the man] to whom I had given the things aforesaid and whose ball of cotton I had not wanted to take from him, although he wanted to give it to me—that all the others went up to him. He considered it a great marvel, and indeed it seemed to him that we were good people and that the other man who had fled had done us some harm and that for this we were taking him with us. And the reason that I behaved in this way toward him, ordering him set free and giving him the things mentioned, was in order that they would hold us in this esteem so that, when Your Highnesses some other time again send people here, the natives will receive them well. And everything that I gave him was not worth four *maravedís*. (*Diario*, 81–3)

We must recognize, I think, that this is largely a fantasy of astute improvisation: how could Columbus know what the man thought about the Spanish or about the captive who had escaped? But the fantasy is highly significant. It indicates that Columbus regards his gift-giving not only in terms of the politics of conversion but also in terms of the politics of empire. He wishes to make the escaped captive's story—that without warning the strangers seized him and took him from his island by force—seem a lie. Through unrequited generosity, Columbus wishes to create—he imagines that he has created—a sense of wonder in the natives that will put the escaped captive's story in doubt. And Columbus notes that this generosity is not even expensive: less than four *maravedís*'s worth. As early as October 15, 1492, then, wonder functions in Columbus as a strategy—here a strategy of deliberate deception, an opportunistic distortion of the awkward and potentially damaging reality of kidnapping natives to serve as interpreters.

On his second voyage, Columbus seized more natives—cannibals, as he thought, 'men and women and boys and girls.' He suggests to the Spanish king and queen that they be 'placed in charge of persons so that they may be able better to learn the language, employing them in forms of service, and ordering that gradually greater care be given to them than to other slaves, so that some may learn from others.' The crucial step, as he understands it, is to remove them as completely as possible from their own linguistic culture—if possible, by sending them to Castile or at the least by isolating them from one another on board ship. And in Castile too, he advises, it is important that they be isolated from their fellows: 'If they do not speak to each other or see each other until much later, they will learn more quickly there than here, and they will be better interpreters, although here there has been no failure to do what could be done.'[43]

Columbus's ultimate hope is that Spanish language will, as it were, carry with it Spanish religion: 'there in Castile, learning the language, they will much more readily receive baptism and secure the welfare of their souls' (i. 88). But this is the view of an explorer, not a missionary; the friars who came in the wake of the discovery and conquest painstakingly studied the native tongues, and, as Inga Clendinnen observes, they 'showed little enthusiasm for teaching their charges Spanish, for knowledge of Spanish would open the way to corrupting influences by challenging their own role as mediators between Spaniard and Indian.'[44] Discoverers like Columbus face an immediate need for interpreters, and the way in which he and almost every other European thinks to get them is through capture. The act is described with extraordinary frequency and casualness. An Indian was taken, notes Ponce de León, 'so that he might learn the language' (*New American World*, i. 236). When his Indian ally Taignoagny asks Cartier to kidnap and take back to France one of his enemies, Cartier refuses, saying that the king, 'his master, had forbidden him to carry off to France any man or woman but only two or three boys to learn the language' (*New American World*, i. 325). In the event, Cartier carries off the chief, Donnacona, and nine others. Charles V instructs Narvaéz in Florida that he is not to seize anyone 'except one or two people, no more, on each voyage of discovery, for interpreters, and other matters necessary to these voyages' (*New American World*, ii. 9). De Soto captures a hundred Indians and takes them:

> in chains with collars about their necks and they were used for carrying the baggage and grinding the maize and for other services which so fastened in this manner they could perform. . . . As soon as the women and young children were a hundred leagues from their land, having become unmindful, they were taken along unbound, and served in that way, and in a very short time learned the language of the Christians. (*New American World*, ii. 109)

Indians who learned the language served as intermediaries, informants, and guides, but they could not always be counted upon to serve the colonists' interests. For there was always the possibility—already glimpsed in the moment when the Indian simply repeats the Englishman's 'how now, sirrha, are you so sawcy with my Tobacco?'—that language learning will undermine the exploitative relation. At what point will the native, initiated into the European language and system of exchange, begin to realize that his people are being robbed? When will he counsel them to demand more for their goods and services? When will he cease to marvel and begin to curse? Cartier had seized two Indians, taken them to France, and then carried them back to Canada the next year to serve as interpreters. At first their presence was extremely useful, not only because they translated well but because they told their chief that they had been well treated in France. But it soon became clear to Cartier that his interpreters were not wedded to his own interests. When Indians came to the ships to exchange food for 'knives, awls, beads and other trinkets . . . we perceived,' the French recorder writes, 'that the two rogues whom we had brought with us, were telling them and giving them to understand that what we bartered to them was of no value, and that for what they brought us, they could as easily get hatchets as knives' (*New American World*, 310). Thereafter, relations with the natives rapidly deteriorated.[45]

The Europeans then queasily oscillate between the motives of exploitation and conversion: they have a simultaneous interest in preserving difference—hence maintaining the possibility of grossly unfair economic exchange—and in erasing difference—hence both Christianizing the natives and obtaining competent interpreters. They want the natives to be at once different and the same, others and brothers. Though far more difficult to come by, the most reliable interpreter, under these circumstances, was one of the Europeans' own, either an unfortunate who had been kidnapped by the Indians and then recovered or, much less frequently, someone of low status who had been deliberately left for months or years to live with the Indians. In the midst of a difficult voyage of De Soto, Juan Ortiz, a Spaniard who had been captured by the Indians and had learned their language, died, and his absence was sorely felt:

> After that, a youth who had been seized in Cutifachiqui and who now knew something of the language of the Christians, served as interpreter. So great a misfortune was the death of Juan Ortiz, with regard to the explorer trying to leave the land, that to learn from the Indians what he stated in four words, with the youth the whole day was needed; and most of the time he understood just the opposite of what was asked, so that many times it came about that the road they took one day, and at times, two or three days, they would return on, and they would wander about lost from one side of those woods to the other. (*New American World*, ii. 137)

Conversely, to have a reliable, resourceful interpreter was an inestimable advantage; it is quite possible that Cortés would have failed to conquer the Aztec empire had he not had the astonishing services of the formidable Doña Marina.

I will return in the next chapter to these crucial and often poignant figures, caught between mutually uncomprehending worlds, but I want now to draw together the issues of representation, exchange, and captivity by looking at a single, rather marginal enterprise: the three attempts in the 1570s by Martin Frobisher to locate the Northwest Passage. The initial encounter between the English and the inhabitants of the large island they discovered (now known as Baffin Island) was marked by mutual caution: a single Eskimo came on board the English ship, the *Gabriel*, while a single Englishman ventured on land. The Eskimo made what appeared to be signs of 'great wondering at all things': the ship itself must have seemed unimaginably strange to him, and he was presented with some 'trifles' with which he seemed very pleased.[46] (Only the English food that he was given to taste appeared to leave him unimpressed.) After this brief mutual reconnaissance, the men were returned to their respective peoples, but Frobisher himself evidently remained suspicious. The natives made what the English construed as signs of friendship—'laying their head in their hands'—but the English refused to land more men. Instead they once again took an Eskimo on board and presented him with trifles, evidently pieces of cloth.

The repeated use of the term 'trifles' is worth remarking, since it signals not only the modest value of the English gifts, as they perceive them, but the entrancing prospect of a quick, easy profit. The European dream, endlessly reiterated in the literature of exploration, is of the grossly unequal gift exchange: I give you a glass bead and you give me a pearl worth half your tribe.[47] The concept of relative economic value—the notion that a glass bead or hawk's bell would be a precious rarity in the New World—is alien to most Europeans; they think that the savages simply do not understand the natural worth of things and hence can be tricked into exchanging treasure for trifles, full signs for empty signs.[48] Where they might then have imagined mutual gift-giving or, alternatively, a mutually satisfactory economic transaction, the Europeans instead tended to imagine an exchange of empty signs, of alluring counterfeits, for overwhelming abundance. Objects of little value provide access to objects of immense value; indeed the more worthless and hollow the trifle, the more value is gained in the exchange.

The inhabitants of the New World are particularly vulnerable, early voyagers report, to the allure of bright surfaces, as if their inward blankness compelled them to respond only to outward appearances.[49] Europeans by contrast congratulate themselves for their greater perspicacity, but at the same time their accounts of the unequal exchanges frequently imply a sense of bad faith, a sense—reflected in the very term 'trifle'—that they are taking advantage of native innocence. Of course, this bad faith is part of the pleasure of the profitable transaction, but it is a distinctly uneasy pleasure, and the anxiety it aroused may be reflected in the frequency with which the early narratives associate unequal exchange with subsequent disaster.

The Eskimos did not wear gold ornaments, but they did have some objects of value: 'they exchanged coats of seales, and beares skinnes, and such like, with our men,' writes one of the participants in Frobisher's first voyage, 'and received belles, looking glasses, and other toyes, in recompense.'[50] It was evidently the lure of such bargains that drew five English sailors who were carrying an Eskimo back to shore to attempt, against Frobisher's orders, to have some further 'traffic' with a group of the natives; the five were immediately seized and carried off. Now the usual situation—Europeans safely in possession of both natives and their valuables—was reversed, and the English feared the worst. The fear, shaped by a powerful cultural fantasy operative in virtually all early encounters, was of cannibalism, a supposition strengthened by what the English had already seen of Eskimo eating habits: 'considering, also, their ravenesse and bloudy disposition in eating anye kinde of rawe flesh or carrion, howsoever stinking,' writes George Best, it seemed likely that the English prisoners would be viewed as quite good meat.[51] The English later learned that the Eskimos, perhaps with a comparable opinion of English food, regarded the strangers as likely to be cannibals.[52]

Frustrated in his attempts to recover his men, Frobisher determined at least, as Best puts it, 'to bring some token from thence of his being there' (Collinson, 74). The token was a native lured into English hands with trifles:

> for knowing well how they greatly delighted in our toyes, and specially in belles, he rang a pretie lowbel, making wise that he would give him the same that would come and fetch it. And bycause they would not come within his daunger for feare, he flung one bell unto them, which of purpose he threw short, that it might fal into the sea and be lost. And to make them more greedie of the matter he rang a lowder bell, so that in the ende one of them came neare the ship side to receive the bell, which, when he thought to take at the captaine's hand he was thereby taken himself; for the captain being redily provided, let the bel fal and cought the man fast, and plucked him with maine force boate and al into his bark out of the sea. (Collinson, 74)

If Frobisher hoped to extract information from his prisoner about the kidnapped Englishmen, he was quickly disappointed: when the Eskimo found himself in captivity, Best writes, 'for very choller and disdain, he bit his tong in twayne within his mouth.' Nevertheless, he survived the voyage and made a sensation upon the *Gabriel*'s return to England, a living 'witnesse,' in Best's words, 'of the captaines farre and tedious travell towards the unknowne parts of the worlde, as did well appeare by this strange Infidel, whose like was never seen, red, nor harde of before, and whose language was neyther knowne nor understoode of anye' (Collinson, 74).[53] The native was of particular interest to the public because his Tartar features were construed as a sign that Frobisher had indeed found the elusive passage to the East, but the display was soon cut short in the usual way by the captive's death. For reasons I do not understand it was first decided to embalm the corpse and send it back to the island, but the plan was abandoned. Instead Frobisher's partner and chief financial backer, Michael Lok, hired a Dutch engraver, William Cure, to make a death-mask and a Dutch painter, Cornelius Ketel, to make a series of portraits.

The Eskimo is taken as a 'token'—even without learning English, even with a language 'neyther knowne nor understoode of anye,' he is a valuable sign—and transformed into a 'witness' of otherness. When alive, he is displayed, with his boat, as a marvel, 'such a wonder onto the whole city and to the rest of the realm that heard of yt as seemed never to have happened the like great matter to any man's knowledge' (Lok, in Collinson, 87). When dead, he is first set to be transformed into a frozen image of himself and then, when this expedient fails, his appearance is registered in a set of pictorial images that supplement the verbal descriptions that are already in circulation.[54] The captive then is caught up in a kind of representational machine that, at a minimum, produced the following images: numerous word 'pictures,' as Lok put it, 'in ink and paper,' the death-mask, two full-size portraits with boat and native dress (one painted for the queen and the other for the Muscovy Company), another depicting him in English dress, and yet another depicting him naked, along with two small pictures of his head.

The small pictures presumably direct attention specifically to his Tartar-like features, but the full-size portraits appear to reflect a set of larger competing hypotheses about the meaning of Frobisher's savage. Depiction in native dress bespeaks an interest in the strangeness of distant peoples, in facial features, clothing, and tribal insignia that bear witness to difference, while the inclusion of the kayak suggests an interest in adaptive technology as well as appearance. In this representation the captive serves as a token of cultural otherness. The portrait in English dress by contrast appears to cancel difference and bears witness to the metamorphic power of clothing.[55] It suggests that there is nothing ineradicable about the Eskimo's strangeness, that his savagery is an effect produced by appearances that can be altered. In this representation the captive serves as a token of assimilable otherness.

One portrait then implies an art that is the register of difference, a mimetic technique that enables its master to exchange trifles for treasure; the other portrait, converting the alien into a European, implies an art that is the register of equivalence, a mimetic technique that enables its master to transform others into brothers. Finally, the third portrait, the portrait of the Eskimo stripped of his clothing, suggests at once a resistant and absolute nakedness, specific, unique, and untranslatable *and* a bare, forked animality that is the common condition of all men and women. In this ambivalent representation the captive serves as an opaque, unreadable body and as a token of unaccommodated, universal humanity.[56]

Frobisher had brought another kind of token back from his island, an ore sample that proved similarly open to competing interpretations. The first three assayers thought it worthless, but failure—an empty sign—was not acceptable, and an assayer was eventually found who declared that it was rich in gold. The report enabled Lok to raise enough capital to send Frobisher out on a second voyage, no longer principally to search for the Northwest Passage but to mine the ore and, if possible, to recover the five lost men. Frobisher was also instructed to bring back to England 'iii or iiii or 8 or tenne' of the natives, including some children, and he planned to take at least one captive immediately to serve as an interpreter. When uneasy gift and trading relations had once again been established with the natives, he saw his chance. After Frobisher presented some 'pinnes and pointes, and such trifles' to an Eskimo, 'one of the salvages for lacke of better marchandise, cutte off the tayle of his coate (which is a chiefe ornament among them) and gave it unto oure general for a present)' (Collinson, 130–1). At that moment of mutual exchange, the Englishman attempted to seize his prey; the native managed to resist, wounding Frobisher in the buttock, but he was eventually taken.

The English apparently never learned, or at least never bothered to record, their captive's name; he is called this 'straunge and newe praye,' 'our savage captive,' or simply one of the 'country people' (Collinson, 131, 145). And he does not appear to have learned English or to have taught his captors his own language. But in a limited way he did serve as a useful interpreter and native informant. Best reports that in response to English questions asked in sign language, he denied that his people were anthropophagi: the bones that the English found were not, the captive indicated, the sign of a cannibal feast but the remains of a man slain by wolves. And when the English found a cache of objects—'sleddes, bridles, kettels of fishe skinnes, knives of bone, and such other like'—'our savage declared unto us the use of all those things' by acting out native practices: 'And taking in his hand one of those countrey brydels, he caughte one of our dogges, and hampred him handsomely therein, as we do our horses, and with a whip in his hande, he taught the dogge to drawe in a sledde as we doe horses in a coatche, setting himself thereuppon like a guide: so that we might see, they use dogges for that purpose, as we doe our horses' (Collinson, 136–7).

What does it mean for the Eskimo to perform his own culture as a kind of theatrical demonstration for the gaze of his captors? It means making the opaque signs of an alien world comprehensible, suggesting to the English certain parallels between what they regard as a strange, savage culture and their own. It means attempting to lay to rest his captors' worst fears, above all the fear of cannibalism, by emptying certain signs of their apparent meaning. It involves a co-operation that is also co-optation, since the co-operation has nothing reciprocal about it, and the captive remains just that, a prisoner on his own shores, miming his culture's survival skills for people who speak an unknown language, who come from an unknown place, who have already seized another of his tribe and who show no interest whatever in his own survival.

On one of the occasions on which the English had brought 'the savage captive' on shore 'to declare ye use of such things as we saw,' there was a strange occurrence. The native withdrew somewhat from the company of his captors—he was evidently not being held in close restraint—and, in Best's words, 'set up five small stickes round in a circle, one by another, with one smal bone placed just in ye middst of all' (Collinson, 138). The action was clearly purposive, but it was not an attempt to communicate, declare, or explain anything to the English. The man who first spotted it thought that it must be a charm or act of witchcraft—a possibility that was not for the English a quaint instance of native superstition, since sixteenth-century Europeans did not at all feel invulnerable to such charms.[57] But after some discussion, the English came to the conclusion that the Eskimo was fashioning a symbolic representation, a sign, for his own people: 'ye best conjecture we could make thereof, was, that he would thereby his countreymen should understand y^{t} for our five men which they betrayed the last yeare (whom he signified by ye five sticks) he was taken and kept prisoner, which he signified by ye bone in ye midst.'

But how is this conjecture to be validated? How can the English know that they are not being bewitched or that the representation does not mean something else? After all, the sign is highly abstract; it does not readily suggest its own interpretation, and, if the sticks are indeed symbols of Englishmen, it certainly could as easily mean that the Eskimo is being held prisoner not *in exchange for* but more simply *by* a group of Englishmen.[58] The English hypothesis is confirmed to their own satisfaction when the captive apparently confesses that he knows something about the five kidnapped Englishmen, though what he knows is by no means clear.

The 'confession,' or what the English imagined to be a confession, is not spontaneous; it is provoked by an English sign, a counter-representation, displayed to the native. Here is Best's account, following directly upon his conjecture about the meaning of the sticks and bone:

For afterwardes, when we shewed him the picture of his countreyman, which ye last yeare was brought into England. . . he was upon the suddayne muche amazed thereat, and beholding advisedly the same with silence a good while, as though he would streyne courtesie whether shoulde begin ye speech (for he thoughte him no doubte a lively creature) at length, began to question with him, as with his companion, and finding him dumme and mute, seemed to suspect him, as one disdaynful, and would with a little help have growen into choller at the matter, until at last by feeling and handling, he founde him but a deceiving picture. And then with great noyse and cryes, ceased not wondering, thinking that we coulde make menne live or die at our pleasure.

And thereuppon calling the matter to hys remembrance, he gave us plainely to understande by signes, that he had knowledge of the taking of our five men the last yeare, and confessing the manner of eche thing, numbred the five men upon his five fingers, and poynted unto a boate in our ship, which was like unto that wherein our men were betrayed: And when we made him signes that they were slaine and eaten, he earnestly denied, and made signes to the contrarie. (Collinson, 138–9)[59]

The Eskimo's initial response to the picture of his countryman, we are told, is governed by a code of manners—Best calls it 'courtesy'; as in the story of the tar baby, he becomes enraged when his companion remains 'dumb and mute.' He thinks that he is receiving a social affront, until he realizes 'by feeling and handling' that he is not dealing with a 'lively creature' but rather with a 'deceiving picture.' In an effort comparable to the English effort to understand the sticks and the bone, the captive then would appear to be moving from naïve literalism—mistaking the picture for a real person—toward a grasp of symbolic representation. And the crucial stage in this movement is a recognition of deceit, a perception of the counterfeiting or emptiness that is ambivalently intertwined with the mimetic power of Western painting. This painting, unlike the non-naturalistic sticks and bones, looks like it will speak, but it remains 'dumb and mute.'

But just at the point in Best's account in which the native grasps that he is dealing with an empty sign, a trifle, a counterfeit, there is a shift in the opposite direction: from the disillusionment that comes with understanding that European representation is based upon empty signs to a radical subjection to the magical power revealed by the emptiness: 'And then with great noise and cryes, ceased not wondring, thinking that we could make men live or die at our pleasure.' The English have passed from the fear of native witchcraft to a conjectural understanding of native representation; the captive has passed from a sense of English representation to a conjectural fear of English witchcraft.

Why does the native move from credulity (the painting as living person) to disillusionment (the painting as counterfeit) to wonder (the English as magically powerful)? Two kinds of answers suggest themselves: the first is that the captive is constructing a conjecture about his experience. At first he thinks that the companion is alive, then he thinks that he has been turned into something 'dumb and mute'—that is, dead—then he concludes that the English have produced both of these experiences: hence they 'could make men live or die' at their pleasure. We cannot know, of course, if the Eskimo thought any such thing: what we are given are not his words—the English, you may recall, did not learn his language—but rather an English interpretation of the meaning of his 'noyse and cryes.' And when we grasp that we are dealing less with native experience than with English conjectures, we move to the second kind of answer: George Best is projecting onto the captive a characteristic English conception of their own powers of representation, and above all, of aesthetic representation. In this conception the artist is at once the bestower of life and the master of deception, art is that which resurrects the dead and art is a cunning counterfeit, the sign is full and the sign is empty. We sometimes treat these as alternative positions, but, as we have now seen again and again, they are inextricably bound together. In Renaissance English literature the paradox is perhaps most exquisitely realized in Prospero's double fantasy: art as absolute illusion ('the baseless fabric of this vision') and art as absolute power ('graves at my command|Have wak'd their sleepers, op'd and let 'em forth|By my so potent Art'). Best produces both fantasies, attributing them in immediate sequence to the savage who now knows that the painting is not his companion but a counterfeit and hence a demonstration of the power of the English to give life or to kill.

According to Best, it is at the moment of this paradoxical recognition that the captive makes signs that 'plainely' show that he 'had knowledge of the taking of our five men'—that is, under the pressure of the painting, with its manifestation of English power, the Eskimo confesses his guilt and at the same time allays the worst of the English suspicions, the fear that their kidnapped countrymen have been eaten. The reassuring confession is a tribute to the power of art, art that can, as Hamlet said of the theater, compel the guilty to proclaim their malefactions.

But if the English infuse into their strange encounter their powerful confidence in the system of symbolic representation that they carried with them, their dream of the executive power of signs, their fantasy of plenitude and control, they continue to be haunted by the sense of emptiness that is paradoxically bound up with the imagined potency of their art. For the empty results, frustrations, and hardships of the Frobisher voyages suggest how fragile this potency is, how much it depends upon wish-fulfillment, how tenuously it clings to the actual experiences of otherness. The great English artists of the Renaissance all grasp this terrible vulnerability: when they appropriate the imaginative energies of the New World discoveries, they carefully transform them into self-consciously fictive, deliberately ambivalent images of Noplace, Faery Land, and a mysterious island in a Virgilian sea.[60]

In the trifling islands of art brutal power can be transformed into just authority, emptiness can be absorbed into desire, and loss can undergo a magical sea-change into infinite riches. But in the bleak tundra of Frobisher's island, craft and kidnapping, scanning the signs and scrabbling for gold, lead only to failure. The painting of a dead native cannot restore the lost Englishmen, imprisoned or buried somewhere in the cold, barren, nameless island; access to the Northwest Passage is blocked by ice; and instead of the spices and gold of Cathay, there is only the enigmatic black rock.

In the absence of any secure grasp of the native language or culture, the little that the English learn from their captive seems overwhelmed by all that they do not understand, and when they do not understand, they can only continue to entrap, kidnap, and project vain fantasies. Hence later in the second voyage they surprise and seize two women. One of them, Best writes, was old and ugly, and 'our men thought she had bin a divell or some witch, and therefore let her go' (Collinson, 142–3). The other was young and nursing a child whom the English had inadvertently wounded. They took these back to the ship and with great excitement brought the female and male captive together in what the English seem to have regarded as a theatrical spectacle: 'every man with silence desired to beholde the manner of their meeting and entertainment' (Collinson, 144). But the spectacle was incomprehensible: at first the captives were silent, then the woman turned away and began to sing, and then, when they were brought together again, the man 'with sterne and stayed countenance beganne to tell a long solemne tale.' The English, of course, could not understand any of it, and since the man and woman were strictly modest in each other's presence, there was little else to see. The reciprocal kidnapping has led then to an almost complete blankness.

On Frobisher's return, Queen Elizabeth finally gave the discovery a name, but it is one that encapsulates the whole problem of the voyage: she called the island 'Meta Incognita,' the unknown mark or boundary, the empty sign (Collinson, 226). The captives quickly died. The black rock still aroused enough hope, however, to fund yet a third voyage. This time the Eskimos altogether eluded capture, and the English worked in an eerie solitude to mine and load the ore. They had thought to leave some men behind, but the weather was miserable, and the plan was abandoned. Before they left, however, they built a house out of lime and stone.

Frobisher thought perhaps that the structure, like the crosses and coats of arms left on other shores, would serve as a sign of English occupation and hence possession. In order 'to allure those brutish and uncivill people to courtesie,' writes Best, the house was filled with trifles: toys, bells, knives, pictures of men and women etched in lead, models of men on horseback, looking-glasses, whistles, and pipes. The Englishmen then built an oven, baked bread in it, closed the door and left the island.

There was no fourth voyage. The 1,296 tons of ore that Frobisher brought back from Meta Incognita was fool's gold.

CHAPTER FIVE

The Go-Between

THE native seized as a token and then displayed, sketched, painted, described, and embalmed is quite literally captured by and for European representation. He is caught up in a complex system of mimetic circulation that also includes the pictures etched in lead, the models of men on horseback, the mirrors, and even the representative loaf of bread left behind in the representative house designed to lure the so-called brutes to a so-called courtesy. Everywhere we look in the encounter of the Old World and the New—in Protestant voyages and Catholic, in the squares of Aztec cities and in European palaces—we find an intensive deployment of representations, from the canoeing exhibitions on the Thames in the early seventeenth century to the doll of an English gentlewoman clutched by the Algonquian child in one of John White's drawings, from the Aztec gold sun admired by Dürer in Brussels to the innumerable crosses erected by Europeans in the harbor mouths and high places of America, from the Tupi featherwork carried back to France to the sixpence nailed by Drake to a post in California. European contact with the New World natives is continually mediated by representations; indeed contact itself, at least where it does not consist entirely of acts of wounding and killing, is very often contact between representatives bearing representations. And even the wounding and killing is often bound up with an attack on representations, as the smashing of a 'brutish idol' and the smashing of a 'brutish' human are easily confounded with one another. For throughout the discourse of travel there is very little distance between a representation and a representative: Columbus, with his banners and his cross, stands for something beyond himself, as, in his eyes, do the natives before him.[1]

Mimetic circulation—the movement and uses of the representational machinery deployed in such voyages as Frobisher's—is double: first, representations and the particular technologies that generate them are carried from place to place, most often moving according to the logic of conquest and of trade though occasionally swerving in unforeseen directions, propelled by perversity or accident; second, those who receive representations from elsewhere themselves move, with greater or lesser freedom, among a range of images and techniques simultaneously available in their culture. The Balinese anecdote with which I began this book—the crowd moving among the various screens in a festive, unconstrained enjoyment of radically divergent representational modes—is obviously a utopian reverie at the furthest extreme from Frobisher's captive forced to contemplate the painting of a dead brother. Utopian but not *altogether* removed from a lived reality: I, Stephen Greenblatt, saw it with my own eyes. And what I witnessed in Bali, as I have remarked, is a reflection of what we can witness every day at home.

I do not wish to underestimate the forces of domination, constriction, and repression at work in contemporary representational practices, let alone in the practices of the intolerant, aggressive, and rigidly hierarchical cultures of the late fifteenth and sixteenth centuries. Even in highly mobile cultures such as our own, there are constraints and coded limits on what may be represented and on access to the means of representation; how much more so in the texts and pictures produced in late medieval and early modern Europe? Nor do I mean to suggest that the two forms of circulation, external (as when the Eskimo's picture is carried out of England to Meta Incognita) and internal (as when the captive turns from his culture's way of representing in sticks and bones to the Europeans' paint and canvas), are always compatible. Judaism, Christianity, and Islam all have spectacular legacies of what the Hebrew Bible calls God's 'jealousy,' which has on occasion taken the form of an ardent enthusiasm for external circulation coupled with a violent hostility toward internal. That is, Western religions have often embraced the idea of a spreading of their representations while resisting the possibility of free movement of alternative symbolic systems within the already-established spheres of their influence.[2] There is almost no authentic reciprocity in the exchange of representations between Europeans and the peoples of the New World, no equality of giving and receiving. The whole experience of Europeans in America was shaped, I have argued, by a particularly intense dream of possession, and though Christian missionaries obviously intended to *give* a great gift, it is difficult to avoid a sense that this gift too was a kind of taking possession. Still, there is always some degree of mimetic circulation both within and without a given culture, and for the Europeans in America this circulation was the very condition for the dream of possession.

But what does the phrase 'a given culture' mean? Who 'gives' it? What is the origin of the boundaries that enable us to speak of 'within' and 'without'? Cultures are inherently unstable, mediatory modes of fashioning experience. Only as a result of the social imposition of an imaginary order of exclusion—through the operation of what in the discussion that follows I will call 'blockage'—can culture be invoked as a stable entity within which there are characteristic representations that are ordered, exported, accommodated. Such blockage occurs constantly—an infinite, unrestricted, undifferentiated circulation would lead to the collapse of cultural identity altogether—but it is never absolute. The rhetoric of absolute blockage is everywhere in the discourse of early modern Europe, but the reality is more porous, more open, more unsettled than it first appears. Any element in the structure of a culture is potentially up for grabs. Any idea, however orthodox, can be challenged. Any representation can be circulated. And it is the character of this circulation—secret or open, rapid or sluggish, violently imposed or freely embraced, constrained by guilt and anxiety or experienced as pleasure—that regulates the accommodation, assimilation, and representation of the culture of the other.

This representation is never quite synonymous with direct possession of a social reality which is always mobile and elusive, though the discourse of travel is saturated with the glittering promise of such possession and records extraordinary steps taken to secure it. As we have seen, European voyagers crate up artifacts that they have purchased or stolen or received as gifts, and they take unsuspecting or undefended natives captive, not only in order to serve as interpreters but in order to ship them back for display at home. Such displays—Columbus's Arawaks or Frobisher's Eskimos—appear to have been immensely popular, and by the early seventeenth century could figure as sources of income. Hence Shakespeare's Trinculo dreams about getting the savage Caliban back to England.

'Holiday fools,' he is sure, will pay handsomely to see the monster: 'When they will not give a doit to relieve a lame beggar, they will lay out ten to see a dead Indian' (*The Tempest*, II. ii. 30–2).

What the spectators get for their money is the experience of wonder in the presence of the alien: they see and perhaps touch (or, we are told in the case of Caliban, smell) a fragment of a world elsewhere, a world of difference. But, of course, that world is not present; only a sliver of it, an anecdote in the form of a dead or dying captive, has crossed the immense distance. And, as the very name Indian suggests, even this sliver of otherness is not accessible to direct apprehension; the viewers carry with them to the exhibits, as to the lands from which the exhibits have been seized, a powerful set of mediating conceptions by which they assimilate exotic representations to their own culture.[3] These conceptions are at once agents and obstacles in the drive to possess a secure knowledge of the alien; they are bound up with the primal act of witnessing around which virtually the entire discourse of travel is constructed.

Everything in the European dream of possession rests on witnessing, a witnessing understood as a form of significant and representative seeing. To see is to secure the truth of what might otherwise be deemed incredible: 'I might not this believe,' as Horatio says of the ghost of old Hamlet, 'Without the sensible and true avouch|Of mine own eyes' (I. I. 56–8). But, though it is essential, 'the sensible and true avouch' of the eyewitness is almost always insufficient, for there is no time, as Columbus remarked from the beginning, actually to see all that has been 'discovered.' The discoverer sees only a fragment and then imagines the rest in the act of appropriation. The supplement that imagination brings to vision expands the perceptual field, encompassing the distant hills and valleys or the whole of an island or an entire continent, and the bit that has actually been seen becomes by metonymy a representation of the whole. That representation is in turn conveyed, reported to an audience elsewhere, and seeing turns into witnessing. The person who witnesses becomes the point of contact, the mediator between 'ourselves' and what is out there beyond our sight. But how can such mediation meaningfully occur? What perceptions should count as significant enough to represent the unseen as well as the seen? Why should any eyewitnessing be trusted? The answers to these questions have a long history, for the problem of mediation in the act of eyewitnessing is already fully present in the first great Western representation of otherness, Herodotus' *Histories*.

Herodotus is at once a decisive shaping force and a very marginal figure in our inquiry. His was not a text that Columbus or the other early voyagers to the New World took with them.[4] But Herodotus' *Histories* had instituted certain key discursive principles that the many subsequent attacks on his veracity and the ensuing oblivion did not displace. Above all, his great work insisted upon the crucial importance of travel for an understanding of the world. Travel enables one to collect information, to verify rumors, to witness marvels, to distinguish between fables and truth. It represents a willingness to escape from the cultural narrowness that attends knowing only one's own people. It enables one to place familiar customs in relation to the customs of others and hence to view the ordinary and everyday in a revealing new light. It offers the dream of what Christian Meier calls 'a multi-subjective, contingency-oriented account.'[5] This perspective does not necessarily entail the suspension of cultural judgments. Herodotus is not committed to relativism; he holds firmly to Greek language and culture as the model against which non-Greek practices are interpreted.[6] But for him historical authority is linked to mobility; it cannot be achieved by remaining within the metropolitan bounds.

There is a type of historical authority that draws its strength and coherence from its massive centeredness, its ability to situate itself at the institutional and moral core of its particular culture. From this stable, well-defended position the possessors of such authority pass judgment on what is brought before them, and they are suspicious of whatever resists the great centrifugal pull toward the center. Herodotus by contrast views history as necessarily decentered; his authority is bound up with an appeal to what he has personally seen and heard outside the city limits.[7] He was the product of the culture of walled cities, but his work derives its force and conviction from passing beyond the walls, from entering into circulation.

Travel in Herodotus is linked with the insistent claim to personal experience, the authority of the eyewitness. It is possible to imagine a history based upon extensive travel that does not overtly make this claim but rather suppresses it in the name of an alternative conception of history, such as that articulated brilliantly by Thucidydes. That is, we have to understand Herodotus' references to his travels less as an autobiographical fact than as a discursive choice. We have, after all, no way of verifying Herodotus' travels, any more than we do Mandeville's; we are dealing rather with what Michel de Certeau calls the text's utterative markings and modalities. The most characteristic of the markings is an appeal to the narrator's own presence: 'I have heard,' 'I say,' 'I write,' and above all 'I have seen.'

To understand the central historical achievement of his own culture, as he conceives it, Herodotus must understand alien cultures. There is in his writing then a continual driving out to the boundaries, an interest in reaching the farthest point to which one can travel—the limit-point of eyewitness—and an interest too in what lies beyond even this boundary, the point at which eyewitness must inevitably give way to hearsay.[8] For by the other he means not only the great historical antagonist of the Greek city-states, the Persian empire, but those who function as the other's other: Lydians, Babylonians, Massagetae, Egyptians, Libyans, and, above all, Scythians.

In a brilliant, book-length analysis of Herodotus' representation of the Scythians, François Hartog suggests that the Athenian claim to be of autochthonous birth called forth the inverse fantasy: in the Scythians, the Athenian imagination figured a people who had absolutely no attachment to any place, who were always somewhere else, who were *aporoi*. For the urban Greeks nomadism was the indelible mark of the Scythians' distance from civility, the sign and substance of an alien existence, the quintessence of otherness.

But if nomads are always elsewhere—people, as Columbus said of the Indians, 'living in highlands and mountains, having no settled dwellings, and apart from us'—how can the historian know anything about them? The problem is raised directly when Herodotus tries to calculate how many Scythians there are, for questions of scale and measurement are close to the center of his conception of historical understanding.[9] It is important to know the size of the people whom one is encountering—otherwise, one is tempted to say (with a glance ahead), it would be possible to confuse a tiny Caribbean island with the empire of the Great Khan. But how to gauge the numbers of a nomadic people?

The numbers of the Scythians I was not able to learn with accuracy. I heard, indeed, different accounts of how many they are, some saying they are very many and some few—few, that is, as far as they are true Scythians. But they showed me something that I could actually see in this matter. There is between the river Borysthenes and the river Hypanis a place, Exampaeus. I mentioned it a little while ago when I said that there was a brackish spring there and that the water flowing from it renders the river Hypanis undrinkable. In this place is set a bronze bowl that in size is some six times larger than the bowl at the mouth of the Pontus that Pausanias, son of Cleombrotus, dedicated. For anyone who has not yet seen Pausanius' bowl, I will show the size of the other this way: the Scythian bowl contains easily 5,400 gallons and in thickness is about four inches. This vessel, the natives say, was made out of arrowheads. For, they say, their king, Ariantas, wanted to know the number of the Scythians, and he had them all bring, each one, an arrowhead. He threatened with death whoever failed to bring the arrowheads. Thus was collected a huge mass of arrowheads, and then he resolved to make and leave after him a memorial made of them. So he made this bowl from the arrowheads and dedicated it in this place, Exampaeus. So much have I heard of the number of the Scythians. (4. 81. 310–11)

How many Scythians are there then? The testimony of the ear is unreliable—evidently, even King Ariantas was unable to depend on mere reports—but the eye offers something more, a direct witnessing of the material evidence. Herodotus then sets what he has heard against what he has personally seen, the artifact carefully situated in the landscape. But what does this witnessing actually tell us? The eye is apparently more reliable than the ear, but the object of the eye's attention is only meaningful in the context of a story told to the historian by 'the natives.' Herodotus does not identify these people, nor does he mention the interpreter who presumably acted as go-between. If we knew when King Ariantas lived, and if we knew how large the average Scythian arrowhead was at that time, and if we knew how scrupulously observed was the king's command,[10] and if we knew the exact dimensions of the bronze bowl, and if we knew that the tale of its origin and purpose was any more reliable than the reports Herodotus has rejected, then we might be able to calculate the approximate population of Scythia for that particular period. But, of course, we know none of these things.

To his own question—how large is the population of Scythia?—Herodotus clearly wishes to give the answer 'enormous.' The bowl, a poetic image cleverly disguised as a piece of hard historical evidence, is part of a strategy of authentication: the reader is invited to accept Herodotus' view (invited in this case to register woolly vagueness as impressive cliometrical precision) because Herodotus himself witnessed the truth, or rather because the historian has deduced the truth from the cultural artifact and has initiated the reader into his deductive method. Moreover, Herodotus gives the reader who cannot, of course, personally view the evidence two ways to orient himself in relation to that strange artifact: by comparison with a familiar Greek artifact and by figures for the capacity and the reported thickness of the Scythian bowl. The latter orientation evidently assumes the Greek reader's familiarity with techniques of mathematical calculation that would make it possible roughly to estimate the number of arrowheads needed to fashion a four-inch-thick bowl able to hold 5,400 gallons. It is not the calculation but the calculation-effect that Herodotus offers, the promise of a mental activity that would measure and hence master an alien object. The former orientation—the comparison of the Scythian bowl with the bowl at the mouth of the Pontus dedicated by a Spartan king—also offers the comfort of placing the unfamiliar in a familiar context, though the calculation here (the one bowl six times larger than the other) suggests at the same time the marvelous, disturbing immensity of the nomadic horde.

The Scythian bowl, the 'memorial' of the impermanent and elusive, utterly unreliable and yet tantalizingly concrete, the talisman of eyewitness and the visible trace of an old story, is in effect an emblem of historiographical curiosity within the large landscape of Herodotus' own text. The bowl is the concrete image of an anecdote—an anecdote of an anecdote, at once its reification and its explanation. It is constructed out of objects that have been removed from practical circulation and use in the flux of nomadic existence and gathered together by powerful command. These objects are not numbered—that is, not turned into a sum for rational calculation—nor are they left in their original state from which they could easily be returned to circulation and use. Instead, they are melted into lastingness. Their evidentiary value is at once destroyed and enhanced: an actual number that would at least tell us how many Scythians existed at a particular time is replaced by a visible testimony to the idea of great size. The object exists to arouse wonder; it is itself a wonder that may be witnessed and recorded in a text.

The 'I have seen' then functions not only in the representation of the other but in what de Certeau calls the 'fabrication and accreditation of the *text as a witness of the other*.'[11] In this example, the text has become a place by virtue of Herodotus' pointing to locations within it, just as he points to particular landmarks that he has personally witnessed: 'Exampaeus, which I mentioned a little further back . . .' At a particular point in both the textual and physical landscape there is an artifact that is the sign of history. But ultimately the sign—the Scythian bowl, the textual history—only calls attention to the elusiveness, the indeterminacy, of what it is meant to signify.

Herodotus is no sentimental celebrant of elusiveness—the difficulty of knowing anything about the Scythians does not attract him at all—but paradoxically it is in nomadism, generated in diacritical opposition to Greek civilization, that he finds the Scythians' uniquely admirable positive accomplishment: 'The Scythian nation has made the most clever discovery among all the people we know, and of the one thing that is greatest in human affairs—though for the rest I do not admire them much.' The secret of this remarkable discovery—invincibility—is nomadic indeterminacy: 'This greatest thing that they have discovered is how no invader who comes against them can ever escape and how none can catch them if they do not wish to be caught.' For the Scythians survival depends upon the absence of those things that elsewhere promise self-preservation: fortifications, specialized armies, impressive military equipment, substantial stockpiles of food from the orderly, well-tilled fields. Each of these talismans of security would, in the Scythian context, be not only irrelevant but dangerous; survival lies precisely in the opposite direction: 'For this people has no cities or settled forts; they carry their houses with them and shoot with bows from horseback; they live off herds of cattle, not from tillage, and their dwellings are on their wagons. How then can they fail to be invincible and inaccessible for others?' (4. 46. 298)

Aporia, Hartog suggests, has here been decisively reconceived: it is no longer an absence, a lack, a negation; it is a positive strategy. Nomadism 'is not a way of life and in addition a strategy, rather, a strategy which is in addition a way of life—a strategy which imposes a way of life.'[12]

One might think that Herodotus achieves this highly original refiguration of nomadism by breaking away from Greek ethnocentric evaluation of the other and hence discovering in an alien way of life an internal logic and justification. Hartog persuasively argues, however, that Herodotus interprets the Scythian way of life in the context of what he regards as the crucial decision that saved Athens and the whole of Greece: the Athenian decision to abandon their city to the invaders and to commit themselves to the 'wooden walls' of their fleet. What made Herodotus' conceptual breakthrough possible was the structural parallel between the Scythians' strategic nomadism against Darius and the Athenians' strategy of taking to the ships against Xerxes.[13]

Herodotus' interpretation of Scythian nomadism is a distorted reflection of the mobility that lies at the heart of the historian's method. Herodotus had raised to an epistemological principle and a crucial rhetorical device the refusal to be bound within the walls of the city. Knowledge depends upon travel, upon a refusal to respect boundaries, upon a restless drive toward the margins. Scythian nomadism is an anamorphic representation of this principle or rather a mimetic circulation, a rapid movement between two apparently opposed systematic cultural constructions of reality. The effect of the circulation is to create a legitimating place for the historian's eye in the zone of *aporia*, to suggest that the historian's apparently aimless wandering is strategic, to celebrate the historian's blend of ideological engagement and elusiveness.

This discovery of the self in the other and the other in the self confers upon Herodotus' voice a special authority, for it deepens the power and authenticity of the eyewitness, but it does not render that authority secure.

If the historian's strategic discursive mobility mediates between the savage Scythians and the civilized Athenians, it does so by sacrificing domestic security, unsettling cultural identity with a set of subversive resemblances that anticipate Mandeville's antipodean logic. It is not surprising that one of the charges brought against Herodotus was that he was *philo-barbaros*, 'pro-Barbarian.'[14] He has succeeded in comprehending the alien by injecting its wildness into the victory celebration of the polis. And in the grain of his own voice, the historian has made it possible to hear echoes of the nomad. To use Walter Benjamin's great epigram in a way he had not intended, 'There is no document of civilization which is not at the same time a document of barbarism.'[15]

I want to return now to the European encounter with the New World. There is no easy transition from the Classical representation of the barbarian to the Christian representation of the savage, and there is no Renaissance Herodotus.[16] We are dealing not with the history of a great culture's salvation but with the chronicle of a great culture's destruction, a chronicle written for the most part by cruel and intolerant victors, often quite ignorant of the peoples they had conquered. Most Europeans turned upon the natives of America the indifferent gaze of men who do not care whether the beings before them live or die. Not only do the Renaissance chronicles lack the intelligence and range of Herodotus' *Histories*, but there is something inherently debased about their accounts of glorious conquests.

But what we may call Herodotus' sense of resonance, his awareness that a momentous military encounter was also an encounter between distinct yet strangely linked cultural worlds, finds partial parallels in at least several sixteenth-century accounts. Among the most interesting of these is Bernal Díaz del Castillo's *Conquest of New Spain* (*Historia Verdadera de la Conquista de la Nueva España*). Bernal Díaz had served under Cortés in the campaign against the Aztecs; many years later, an old and (by his account) poor man, he wrote a lengthy narrative of the astonishing events in which he had participated. He presents himself as a humble observer, a simple and straightforward man who transcribes an undistorted version of the facts. He can produce a 'historia verdadera' because he does not aspire to a mastery of the arts of rhetoric and because he directly participated in the actions. Indeed one of his aims, he claims, is to counter the lies and distortions disseminated in a work written by Francisco Lopez de Gómara, a man who had not seen the New World for himself and who prefers 'retórica muy subida' to the simple truth. Bernal Díaz, by contrast, proposes to describe what actually happened, without recourse to the 'lofty rhetoric' with which others attempt 'to give lustre and repute to their statements.'[17] His success in achieving an apparently transparent reportorial mode is suggested by the judgment of the great nineteenth-century historian Prescott: 'Bernal Díaz, the untutored child of nature, is a most true and literal copyist of nature. He transfers the scenes of real life by a sort of *daguerreotype* process, if I may say so, to his pages.'[18]

'That which I have myself seen and the fighting I have gone through, with the help of God I will describe, quite simply, as a fair eyewitness [*como buen testigo de vista*] without twisting events one way or another' (i. 3). 'A fair eyewitness'—this is the central rhetorical principle of Bernal Díaz's text, a principle that extends even to events that he did not personally witness.[19] As in Herodotus, the experiential core becomes not so much the text's subject as its representational mode, its guarantee of authenticity and accuracy. The narrator is not interested in registering the nuances of his own personal situation, his particular shaping of the events he describes—hence the ease with which Prescott can transform him into 'the untutored child of nature,' a phrase more often reserved for the 'savages' encountered by the Europeans. Bernal Díaz has witnessed for himself, and therefore he possesses the truth. He possesses it directly, without interpretive mediation, and his text is that possession—his narrative is, he says, all that he has personally gained from those terrible struggles. For Prescott such a narrative is the equivalent of a photographic record of the way things actually happened in 'real life.'

The eyewitness directly possesses the truth and can simply present it; he who has not seen for himself must persuade. Thus, for example, the Dominican Las Casas can condemn the behavior of the Spanish at Cholula, where they and their allies committed large-scale unprovoked massacres, but Bernal Díaz, as a man of action, knows the truth from personal experience and therefore can dismiss the charges. Las Casas writes 'so artfully' that he would persuade those who had not seen the event themselves, but our narrator has witnessed it, indeed has participated in it, and can decisively say that the massacres were absolutely necessary: 'If perchance we had not inflicted that punishment, our lives would have been in great danger' (ii. 21).

For this principle of eyewitness to be effective, Bernal Díaz must situate himself at the center of events; for a start, he claims, against all probability, to have participated in all three Yucatán voyages—the expedition under Francisco Hernández de Córdova in 1517, under Juan de Grijalva in 1518, and under Cortés in 1519. He further claims fantastic powers of direct recollection: writing some fifty years after the events, he professes to recall precise details in proper narrative order—casual conversations, local strategies, false starts, passing impressions, as well as grand events and major battles. And he gives himself a significant presence to these events—how else could he claim to be a reliable eyewitness? By his own account, he is continually at Cortés's side; he is directly involved in all the major struggles; he has a personal stake in the purposes—gold, imperial power, religion—of the enterprise. At the same time he must insinuate a partial detachment, so that his acts of witnessing do not seem to be merely self-serving justifications. This detachment Bernal Díaz establishes by suggesting that he always remained something of an outsider, a modest failure. His position at the edges of the great events and personalities allows him to criticize certain decisions by Cortés and certain Spanish excesses. Indeed there is a sense of irony that pervades much of the text, even when the author is not directly questioning something that has been done. Thus, for example, after he discovers a conspiracy against his leadership, Cortés orders that several of the conspirators be hanged, that another have his feet cut off, that others be lashed. 'I remember,' Bernal Díaz writes, 'that when Cortés signed that sentence, he said with great grief and sighs: "Would that I did not know how to write, so as not to have to sign away men's lives!"—and it seems to me that that saying is common among judges who have to sentence men to death, and is a quotation taken from that cruel Nero at the time when he showed signs of being a good Emperor' (i. 207). Where is Bernal Díaz here? He is not quite questioning Cortés's sincerity or challenging his authority, but he is allowing himself a sardonic, knowing smile, a local irony.

The irony, sharp as it is, is less a sign of doubt than a principle of authentication, a mark of the narrator's honesty and independence of spirit. At any moment this independence can call into question the claims of authority: Cortés can be made to seem arbitrary, grasping, and unfair; orthodox enunciations of religious purpose can be revealed to be *post hoc* justifications for actions already taken for quite different reasons. But the criticisms always remain local; in Bernal Díaz, unlike Herodotus, ironies are not allowed to extend to the entire enterprise. The containment of skepticism is linked to what I have called a strategy of mimetic blockage or exclusion.

The Conquest of New Spain depends upon a radical distinction between Spanish practices and Aztec practices that are disturbingly homologous. That the kingdom Bernal Díaz serves was militarily aggressive and expansionary does not inhibit his characterization of Aztec society as militarily aggressive and expansionary. That the captain he serves was systematically duplicitous does not inhibit his condemnation of Aztec duplicity. That the church he serves was ruthlessly persecuting heretics, Jews, and Moors does not inhibit his intense horror at the inhumanity of Aztec and Mayan priests. But how can absolute difference be maintained in the face of the strong affinities, echoes, structural parallels? It is not that Bernal Díaz is unaware of a network of resemblances. On the island they name San Juan de Ulúa the Spanish find a temple whose priests, he notes, wore 'very large black cloaks and hoods, such as the Dominicans or canons wear' (i. 55); similarly, the priests in Cempoala 'wore black cloaks like cassocks and long gowns reaching to their feet' (i. 189); and near the great temple of Tlaltelolco was 'a sort of nunnery where many of the daughters of the inhabitants of Mexico were sheltered like nuns' (ii. 82). The priests evidently are part of a clerical hierarchy, for in the city of Cholula, Bernal Díaz writes, the Spanish encounter a 'very important personage . . . who had charge of or command over all the Cues [temples] in the City, and was a sort of Bishop among the priests' (ii. 6). The priests—called *papas*, as Bernal Díaz repeatedly notes—preside over a cult centered on impressive buildings housing images and on solemn rituals of prayer and sacrifice. 'Much in the same way as we in Castile have in every city our holy churches and parish churches and hermitages and wayside chapels, so in this country of New Spain they have their Idol houses' (v. 263). As in Spain, some of the images are regarded as holier and more efficacious than others, so that, for example, to the 'great oratory' of Cholula worshipers went 'on pilgrimages from all parts of New Spain to obtain absolution' (ii. 82).

We have then in *The Conquest of New Spain* an accumulation of the kind of resemblances that led Herodotus to intuit a hidden relation between the apparently opposite cultures of Greece and Scythia, and led Mandeville to extend an imaginative embrace to the idolatrous rituals of the East. How does Bernal Díaz resist this intuition? How does he maintain the sharp edge of loathing that characterizes his description of native religion and subtends his justification of the destruction of native culture? And how does he keep this loathing from infecting his account of his own religion and culture? There are vices to which Bernal Díaz sees the Indians as particularly prone—drunkenness, fornication, and sodomy—but these are vices so frequently denounced in his own culture that they hardly constitute a point of absolute difference. Rather, the key to the exclusion or blockage is a native practice that does not fall in the category of familiar European vices, a practice that is not part of the European repertory of moral disasters such as extreme cruelty or lust or blasphemy, a practice that seems to Bernal Díaz an unmitigated horror marking an absolute difference between his culture and the culture of the other: the Mayan and Aztec practice of human sacrifice and ritual cannibalism.[20]

According to Bernal Díaz, the Spanish come across the first signs of this practice early in their initial reconnaissance of the Yucatán and are utterly astonished by what they see in the temple or *cue*:

> They led us to some large houses very well built of masonry which were the Temples of their Idols, and on the walls were figured the bodies of many great serpents and snakes and other pictures of evil-looking Idols. These walls surrounded a sort of Altar covered with clotted blood. On the other side of the Idols were symbols like crosses, and all were coloured. At all this we stood wondering, as they were things never seen or heard of before. (i. 19)

It is important to remind ourselves once again that such a passage is not a neutral transcription of reality, that the details are not accidentally recorded, and that the mode of eyewitness reportage is a rhetorical device. His description of his first encounter with the religion of Mexico—what 'we' saw and felt in the presence of the horrifying idols—must be understood in the context of the European discourse of wonder; its articulations, both of its objects of vision and its emotions, are shaped, through the complex, indirect processes by which discursive traditions do their work, by those moments in William of Rubruck or Odoric of Pordenone or Mandeville or Columbus in which the voyager describes in awe-struck fascination 'things never seen or heard of before.'

Throughout *The Conquest of New Spain*, carefully set in the midst of the tough, practical, more or less familiar details of a military expedition, there are such expressions of absolute wonder, expressions of the unique and unprecedented that can only be articulated in the recycled language of other texts. Next to the first glimpse of the native temple, we can set Bernal Díaz's description of the first glimpse of the Aztec capital:

> When we saw so many cities and villages built in the water and other great towns on dry land and that straight and level causeway going towards Mexico, we were amazed and said that it was like the enchantments they tell of in the legend of Amadis, on account of the great towers and cues and buildings rising from the water, and all built of masonry. And some of our soldiers even asked whether the things that we saw were not a dream? It is not to be wondered at that I here write it down in this manner, for there is so much to think over that I do not know how to describe it, seeing things as we did that had never been heard of or seen before, not even dreamed about. (ii. 37)

'We cannot conceive of the undreamed,' writes Richard Wilbur. In the face of the undreamed, and consequently in a crisis of representation, Bernal Díaz turns to the language of medieval romance, with its dream images, its magical castles and temples, its rhetoric of amazement. The reference to *Amadis of Gaul* stands in place of an eyewitness description that is at once imperative and impossible. The absolutely other cannot be conveyed at all, cannot perhaps be even perceived, but the romance can at least gesture toward this other, marked with the signs of fantasy, unreality, enchantment. The enchanted city rising from the water provokes wonder by its entirely unexpected grandeur, wealth, and solidity, a solidity ('all built of masonry') that paradoxically contributes to the sense of dreamlike unreality. For in a romance what seems most palpable and secure can in an instant vanish without a trace. Bernal Díaz infuses some such feeling of mysterious loss into this first vision of the great City of Mexico, for he describes the marvelous palaces and gardens and lakes only to conclude that these objects of the wondering gaze have disappeared:

> I say again that I stood looking at it and thought that never in the world would there be discovered other lands such as these, for at that time there was no Peru, nor any thought of it. [Of all these wonders that I then beheld] to-day all is overthrown and lost, nothing left standing. (ii. 38)

Temporarily unspoken at this moment is the Spanish role in destroying the great city. Bernal Díaz is not ashamed of that role—in some sense he glories in it and therefore significantly downplays the crucial participation of the tens of thousands of Indian allies—but he wishes here to concentrate on the stupefaction of the Spanish: 'Gazing on such wonderful sights, we did not know what to say, or whether what appeared before us was real' (ii. 39). Something strange has happened to the principle of eyewitness throughout this passage. At the very moment that it is called upon to do its crucial work—to testify to the radically new, to record what had never before been seen and has now been forever lost—the conjoined powers of sight and description are immobilized by wonder. To wonder is to experience both the failure of words—the stumbling recourse to the old chivalric fables—and the failure of vision, since seeing brings no assurance that the objects of sight actually exist. The assurance comes rather from violence: the still moment of admiration gives way to the Spanish penetration of the city and the horrifying chain of events that leads to its destruction. 'Let us make no words about it,' writes Bernal Díaz, 'for deeds are the best witnesses to what I say here and elsewhere' (ii. 43).

But why should deeds—pulling down the towers, defiling the palaces, killing thousands of people, filling the canals and lakes with rubble and corpses—be a suitable witness? Why should a sense of reality that eluded sight and words be given by acts of violence? The answer is twofold. First, it is destruction that gives the Spanish *possession* of the empire. When the land and its people are intact, when the cities are whole, the markets flourishing, the warriors and priests and aristocrats and administrators performing their functions, then the Spanish are radically excluded: the Mexico first glimpsed is not only strange but ungraspable, its capital not only exotic but in effect imaginary. Only when it is violated, turned into a charnel house, can it be taken as a reality and appropriated. Second, it is destruction that gives the Spanish presence its *purpose*. To be sure, the amassing of vast wealth and territory and vassals would seem like purpose enough, and yet this acquisition—which cannot, in any case, be accomplished without destruction on a massive scale—is not in Bernal Díaz's narrative a sufficient ideological motive. That motive is given by a transcendent design, a design revealed (at least in retrospect) at the moment that wonder gave way to act, the act of marching along the causeway and into the surreal city: 'Coming to think it over,' Bernal Díaz writes, 'it seems to me a great mercy that our Lord Jesus Christ was pleased to give us grace and courage to dare to enter into such a city' (ii. 42–3).

The invocation of Jesus Christ returns us to Bernal Díaz's 'eyewitness' account of the interior of the native temple and of the religious practices glimpsed there for the first time. That account centered, as we have seen, on wonder, but the emphasis on things hitherto unseen and unheard is at once powerful and misleading: powerful because it insists, in ways we have now explored at some length, on the absolutely unprecedented nature of the encounter; misleading because it covers over a deeply disturbing resemblance. For what Bernal Díaz actually describes is not the unimaginably alien—how could such a thing ever be described?—but a displaced version of his own system of belief: temple, high altar, cult of holy blood, statues before which offerings are made, 'symbols like crosses.' This is the very center of the homologies that link the invaders and those they come to enslave and destroy, and hence this is the place at which what I have called blockage must be most powerfully effective. That his own religion centered on expiatory sacrifice and upon the symbolic eating and drinking of his god's body and blood does not inhibit Bernal Díaz's horrified response to what his culture construed as the weirdly literal Aztec equivalents. The parallels are largely the product of his culture's own projections, ways of bearing witness to the indescribable through a description of what is already known, but insofar as they are registered at all, they only intensify his revulsion. What emotion is powerful enough to cut the complex mimetic knot that links the eyewitness and the world he describes? What function of the imagination can erect absolute difference at the point of deepest resemblance? The answer is wonder.

Wonder effects the crucial break with an other that can only be described, only witnessed, in the language and images of sameness. It erects an obstacle that is at the same time an agent of arousal. For the blockage that constitutes a recognition of distance excites a desire to cross the threshold, break through the barrier, enter the space of the alien. The greatest scene of wonder in *The Conquest of New Spain* takes place on the straight and level causeway leading into the city, in the immobilized moment before the Spanish embark on the path of penetration. But the path that leads from wonder back out to the web of connections—connections that make descriptions, judgments, and actions possible—branches in two sharply opposed directions. One path leads to the discursive strategies that we have analyzed in Herodotus or Mandeville: that is, to articulations of the hidden links between the radically opposed ways of being and hence to some form of acceptance of the other in the self and the self in the other. The movement is from radical alterity—you have nothing in common with the other—to a self-recognition that is also a mode of self-estrangement: you *are* the other and the other is you. The alternative path leads to the discursive strategies that we have analyzed in Columbus and now in Bernal Díaz: that is, to articulations of the radical differences that make renaming, transformation, and appropriation possible. The movement here must pass through identification to complete estrangement: for a moment you see yourself confounded with the other, but then you make the other become an alien object, a thing, that you can destroy or incorporate at will.

It is, I have argued throughout this book, the dream of possession that is the key to this latter path. With a deep emblematic appropriateness, when Cortés and his men had entered the city, they were housed in palaces where Montezuma had 'the great oratories for his idols, and a secret chamber where he kept bars and jewels of gold, which was the treasure that he had inherited from his father' (ii. 43). For the Aztecs, at least as Bernal Díaz understands it, the Spanish and the 'idols' were virtually identical: 'They took us to lodge in that house, because they called us Teules, and took us for such, so that we should be with the Idols or Teules which were kept there' (ii. 43). But out of this momentary identification of self and other would come both absolute difference and absolute possession: the Spanish would destroy the Teules and would break through the walls into the secret treasure chamber. At the first sight of that treasure, Cortés and his captains are 'carried away' (*elevados*) and speechless; Bernal Díaz too is lost in wonder. But the wonder—and the strategic decision not to touch or speak of what they had found—is a prelude to appropriation: when the time is ripe, the Spanish seize the treasure, melt it down, and ship it back to Spain. 'Since the wise King Solomon built . . . the Holy Temple of Jerusalem with the gold and silver which they brought him from the Islands of Tarsis, Ophir, and Saba,' Bernal Díaz writes, 'there has never been reported in any ancient writings more gold and silver and riches than what has gone daily to Castile from these lands' (v. 271).[21] The possession need not be personal—Bernal Díaz professes to have acquired very little for himself from his adventures[22]—but the enterprise in which he serves is fanatically dedicated to swallowing the whole vast land mass and all of its peoples. Theirs was the greatest experiment in political, economic, and cultural cannibalism in the history of the Western world.

The Spaniards' greatest fear was that they would be assimilated, literally absorbed, by being eaten.[23] It is hardly surprising that they should have been horrified by the signs of Indian cannibalism. Given who they were and where they found themselves, what else could they have felt? What is the point of pretending that they should have had a more detached, as it were anthropological, appreciation of the practice? A hostile army in a vast, menacing land, how could they have entertained the odd relation between Aztec cannibalism (as they understood it) and the Eucharist? The Spanish saw themselves, not without reason, as threatened, and they would have been horrified even without the direct threat to their own lives, for Europeans had long identified cannibalism as an emblem of extreme horror.

Under the circumstances—the circumstances of Aztec military and religious ferocity and of Spanish greed, fear, and aggression—Bernal Díaz understandably does not indulge in that sense of mimetic circulation, secret-sharing with the alien, that characterized Herodotus' history and Mandeville's travelogue.[24] Moreover, for a Spanish Catholic to recognize such a connection might have seemed to acknowledge the force of the heretical Protestant attack on the mass as cannibalism, an acknowledgment both unacceptable and, in this period, quite possibly dangerous.[25] But it is significant that in Bernal Díaz absolute difference is established at the site of the most intimate and uncanny parallel, the site where the secret sharing would under different circumstances have occurred: in the temple, where high altar, holy blood, and the mysterious signs of the cross produce wonder and revulsion.

The creation of blockage at this site is directly linked to the repeated occasions in *The Conquest of New Spain* in which the Spanish attack the

Mexican idols and substitute their own symbolic representations of the deity. When *The Conquest of New Spain* was first printed in 1632 under the direction of the Mercedarian Fray Alonso de Remón, the frontispiece reflected an attempt to match the military conquests of Cortés with the spiritual conquests attributed to the Mercedarian friar who accompanied him, Fray Bartolomé Olmedo. But it is actually Cortés in Bernal Díaz's text who is shown repeatedly preaching the immediate substitution of the Christian cult of sacrifice for the Indian cult.[26] Thus, for example, on the island of Cozumel, the Spanish encounter an 'oratory' (*adoratorio*) to which Indians come in pilgrimage to offer sacrifices to their 'Idols.' The Spanish are fascinated to see in the crowded courtyard that many of the pilgrims 'were burning a resin like our incense': 'as this was a new sight to us we stood round watching it with attention [*paramos a mirar en ello con atención*]' (i. 97). Their attention intensifies as one of the priests or *papas* climbs to the top of the oratory and begins to preach a 'black sermon' to the people assembled below. At this point Cortés decides to intervene:

He sent for the Cacique and all the principal chiefs and the priest himself, and, as well as he could through the aid of our interpreter, he told them that if we were to be brothers they must cast those most evil Idols out of their temple, for they were not gods at all but very evil things which led them astray and could lead their souls to hell. Then he spoke to them about good and holy things, and told them to set up in the place of their Idols an image of Our Lady which he gave them, and a cross, which would always aid them and bring good harvests and would save their souls. And he told them in a very excellent way other things about our holy faith. (i. 97)

The Indians respond 'that their forefathers had worshipped those Idols because they were good,' whereupon Cortés decides to solve the problem of religious otherness by direct action:

Then Cortés ordered us to break the Idols to pieces and roll them down the steps, and this we did; then he ordered lime to be brought, of which there was a good store in the town, and Indian masons, and he set up a very fair altar on which we placed the figure of Our Lady; and he ordered two of our party named Alonzo Yáñez and Alvaro López who were carpenters and joiners to make a cross of some rough timber which was there, and it was placed in a small chapel near the altar and the priest named Juan Díaz said mass there, and the Cacique and the heathen priest and all the Indians stood watching us with attention (*todos los indios estaban mirando con atención*). (ii. 98)

How is it possible for Cortés to imagine that his culture's symbols can simply replace the symbols of an entirely different culture? What does it mean to speak and to act across such a cultural abyss? To an experience of absolute difference must be conjoined a perception of identity, identity marked for the *conquistadores* at once by the uncanny mirroring of religious practices (pilgrimage, incense, sermon) and by the promise of a 'brotherhood' that can be earned by substituting one set of figures for another. The scene that begins with the Spanish absorbed in watching the Indian worship ends with the Indians absorbed in watching the Spanish worship, the symmetrical moments linked by the act of violent substitution. For the Spanish the dream is not simply to worship their god in a strange land but to capture for their own symbols—symbols of the one truth—the devotional energies of the Indians. In one of his letters, Cortés calls for the conversion of the Indians to the Holy Catholic faith, so that 'the devotion, trust and hope which they have in these their idols' would be 'transferred to the divine power of God; for it is certain that if they were to worship the true God with such fervor, faith and diligence, they would perform many miracles.'[27]

The idea of brotherhood that we glimpse briefly here returns in a more powerful form later in *The Conquest of New Spain*. In Tenochtitlán, according to Bernal Díaz, 'through our interpreters Doña Marina and Aguilar,' Cortés explains to Montezuma 'how we are all brothers, sons of one father and one mother who were called Adam and Eve, and how such a brother as our great Emperor, grieving for the perdition of so many souls, such as those which their idols were leading to Hell, where they burn in living flames, had sent us, so that after what he [Montezuma] had now heard he would put a stop to it and they would no longer adore these Idols or sacrifice Indian men and women to them, for we were all brethren, nor should they commit sodomy or thefts' (ii. 57). The cynicism and mendacity of this moment—Cortés had not been sent by his 'emperor' at all, let alone for the purpose of saving souls, and in a just universe the pious admonition against theft would have stuck in the hypocrite's throat—should not lead us simply to discard the myth of brotherhood, for the oscillation between brother and other under the sign of wonder is one of the principal tactics in Cortés's strategy of conquest and the principal representational device in Bernal Díaz's account of the peoples of Mexico. A primordial brotherhood ('sons of one father and one mother') seems to be confirmed by deep homologies of worship (oratories, priests, sermons) and at the same time blocked by demonic practices, practices that make the Indians radically alien.

The reply Bernal Díaz attributes to Montezuma marks not a failure of comprehension but a refusal of the principal of blockage, the principal by which homologies are resolved into antitheses, brothers into others:

'Señor Malinche, I have understood your words and arguments very well before now, from what you said to my servants at the sand dunes, this about three Gods and the Cross, and all those things that you have preached in the towns through which you have come. We have not made any answer to it because here throughout all time we have worshipped our own gods, and thought they were good, as no doubt yours are, so do not trouble to speak to us any more about them at present.' (ii. 57)

At least as Bernal Díaz represents this exchange, it is this tolerant acceptance of more than one order of things—'we have worshipped our own gods, and thought they were good, as no doubt yours are'—that marks the distance between the Indians and the Spanish. For Christian imperialism there can be only one order of truth, an order whose universality paradoxically enables the strategy of exclusion I have called blockage: the belief that 'all men are brothers,' as Marc Shell has observed, is quickly transformed into the belief that 'only my brothers are men.'

But if for the Spanish an absolute cultural blockage occurs around the images of cannibalism and idolatry, there still has to be some point of contact for understanding to occur, some basis for communication and negotiation. Otherwise the encounter would be a complete blank, a brute clash of bodies in which the invaders, hopelessly outnumbered, would certainly be destroyed. The Spanish need to facilitate the improvisational manipulation of the other. They cannot completely dispense with mimetic circulation, a sense of the underlying strategic intersection of representational forms, while at the same time they are committed to a mimetic blockage, a radical differentiation that is a constitutive feature of the destructive enterprise and of the text that records and apologizes for the enterprise. One consequence is that sympathetic feelings for the other can only occur under the sign of death. There is a powerful current of nostalgia in *The Conquest of New Spain* for what has been destroyed, but only because it has been destroyed, just as Bernal Díaz claims that Cortés and his men wept for Montezuma after he had been killed. The nostalgia is a sign of an anecdote already told, a sign linked to Bernal Díaz's age and his sense of himself as almost dead. A further and more important consequence is that the circulation that is the condition of knowledge in Herodotus can now only take place through the mediation of another. It is not Bernal Díaz (or Cortés) who passes from one representational form to another, who mediates between systems, who inhabits the inbetween. It is rather a figure absent from Herodotus, the figure of the interpreter, the translator, the go-between.

There are several such figures in *The Conquest of New Spain*. At the 'oratory' on Cozumel, Cortés's interpreter was a baptized Indian whom the Spanish called Melchior or Melchorejo. Melchior had been taken captive during the first Spanish expedition to the Yucatán under Francisco Hernández de Córdoba, brought to Cuba where he learned some Spanish, and sent back to the Yucatán to serve as an interpreter for Grijalva's expedition. The Spanish evidently did not trust Melchior's acculturation, since at one point Grijalva decided not to use him to deliver a message, for fear the interpreter would desert and return to his own people.[28] Melchior survived this voyage and returned to the Yucatán yet again, this time with Cortés. In Cozumel he would have been very close to the place where he had been kidnapped years before, and Bernal Díaz notes that he understood the local dialect very well: hence, perhaps, Cortés's decision to accompany his destruction of the 'idols' with a sermon on brotherhood and Christianity, a sermon supposedly translated by Melchior.

Perhaps we should wonder what the interpreter actually said; the Spanish, after all, had no way of knowing for sure, and Melchior's subsequent actions license a certain skepticism. For shortly after his service at the 'oratory,' he fled: 'he had run off with the people of Tabasco, and it appears that the day before he had left the Spanish clothes that had been given to him hung up in the palm grove' (i. 113). With the clothes, Melchior had, Cortés feared, put off any vestige of loyalty to his Christian 'brothers'—'Cortés was much annoyed at his flight,' Bernal Díaz writes, 'fearing that he would tell things to his fellow countrymen to our disadvantage.' In the event, the fears proved justified, for when Cortés asked the caciques of Tabasco why they had ferociously attacked the Spanish, they replied that 'the Indian whom we had brought as an Interpreter, who escaped in the night, had advised them to attack us both by day and night' (i. 127). Kidnapped, baptized, dressed in Spanish clothes, used as an interpreter—Melchior's strange life, or more accurately the narrative of that life, is an artifact of the encounter between alien peoples, an anecdote of the nervous oscillation between self and other. And what was his fate after his escape? The Indians, Bernal Díaz believes, 'had offered him as a sacrifice because his counsel had cost them so dear.'

Melchior was not the only failure in Cortés's search for a reliable intermediary. Through Melchior, he had learned from the caciques of Cozumel that two Spaniards had been shipwrecked on an earlier expedition and had lived as slaves for eight years in the Yucatán. Cortés sent a letter to the men, along with beads for ransom. One of them, Jeronimo de Aguilar, embraced his liberation, but the other, Gonzalo Guerrero, refused: 'Brother Aguilar, I am married and have three children and the Indians look on me as a Cacique and captain in wartime,—You go and God be with you, but I have my face tattooed and my ears pierced, what would the Spaniards say should they see me in this guise? and look how handsome these boys of mine are . . .' (i. 95). Guerrero is for Bernal Díaz a disastrous instance of the failure of blockage. The self had collapsed into the other: as the Spanish put it in a report to the king, Guerrero had been made an Indian [*estar ya hecho indio*].[29]

Jeronimo de Aguilar too initially seemed close to complete absorption: the first Spaniards to see him 'could not distinguish him from the Indian as he was naturally brown and he had his hair shorn like an Indian slave' (i. 101). But there was a sign that Aguilar, who had taken holy orders, was not altogether transformed: 'he had on a ragged old cloak, and a worse loin cloth with which he covered his nakedness, and he had tied up, in a bundle in his cloak, a Book of Hours, old and worn.' When Cortés glimpsed this living emblem of cultural hybridity, he asked 'Where is the Spaniard,' whereupon 'the Spaniard squatted down on his haunches as the Indians do and said "I am he."' Cortés ordered that he be given proper Spanish clothing and immediately began to use him as an interpreter. But there were limitations to Aguilar's usefulness: in the first place, when Cortés asked him about the country, Aguilar replied 'that, having been a slave, he only knew about hewing wood and drawing water and working in the maize-fields' (i. 65); in the second place, while he knew the principal language of the Yucatán, he was completely ignorant of the language of Mexico itself. This was a serious problem because it soon became evident that Spanish hopes for conquest rested on their ability to enlist the military and logistical support of the Indian peoples who had been conquered by the Aztecs. Cortés desperately needed a reliable, knowledgeable informant and interpreter, someone who could translate the Mexican language, Nahuatl, into the Yucatec language, Maya, which Aguilar could then translate into Castillian, someone who could take Cortés's threats and promises, translated by Aguilar, and communicate them accurately to the Mexicans, someone who could do so without revealing Spanish weakness or duplicity.

Such was the difficult role of the most important go-between in *The Conquest of New Spain*, the role played by the remarkable Indian woman whom the Spanish called Doña Marina.

Montezuma bade him welcome and our Cortés replied through Doña Marina wishing him very good health. And it seems to me that Cortés, through Doña Marina, offered him his right hand. . . . (ii. 40)

Cortés answered with a pretense of lightheartedness, and said through Doña Marina who was always with him during all these conversations. . . . (ii. 173)

Then Cortés embraced Montezuma twice, and Montezuma also embraced Cortés, and Doña Marina, who was very sagacious, said to him artfully that he was pretending sadness at our departure. (ii. 174)

Cortés replied somewhat angrily through our interpreters Doña Marina and Aguilar that they deserved death for having begun the war. (iv. 64)

Cortés flattered these two chieftains who had been captured and gave them beads, and made them many promises that when Mexico was taken he would give them territory, and through our interpreters Doña Marina and Aguilar, he asked them where the piraguas were stationed. . . . (iv. 131)

When Cortés spoke to them amicably through Doña Marina, they brought much maize and poultry and pointed out the road we had to follow. . . . (v. 15)

Before they were hanged the Franciscan Friars confessed them through the interpreter Doña Marina. (v. 27)

There are dozens of such passages, along with recurrent tributes to the interpreter's intelligence, alertness, and courage. Doña Marina spoke both the Aztec and Mayan tongues fluently and quickly learned Spanish; without her, Bernal Díaz writes, 'we could not have understood the language of New Spain and Mexico' (i. 135). And she is of more than instrumental importance; in Bernal Díaz's account, Doña Marina is the principal agent of the circulation of cultural representations elsewhere blocked in the Spanish perception of their experience. She is so, according to Bernal Díaz, because she is already a being in a state of circulation. Doña Marina is at once a figure on the margins and at the center, both an outcast and a great lady (what the Indians called a Teleciguata—'a great chieftainess and the daughter of great Caciques and the mistress of vassals' [i. 128–9]). The daughter of Aztec lords–and hence a native speaker of Nahuatl—she was given away by her parents when her mother remarried and bore her new husband a son. The people to whom she was given lived in Xicalango, an outlying stronghold of the Aztec empire, and they in turn gave her to the Tabascans, a subject people whose language was Chontal Maya. The Tabascans subsequently gave her to Cortés. This history is directly linked to her gender: she was first given away, we are told, in order to facilitate her stepbrother's accession to the lordship, and then given away once again as one of twenty women presented as part of a peace-offering ('four diadems and some gold lizards, and two ornaments like little dogs, and earrings, and five ducks, and two masks with Indian faces and two gold soles for sandals,' etc.) to the Spanish. In response, the Spanish promptly set up a cross on an altar and the sacred image of Our Lady—the caciques politely declared that 'they liked the look of the great Teleciguata (for in their language great ladies are called Teleciguatas)' (i. 127). Then, through Aguilar, Cortés expounded the holy faith to the twenty women who were duly baptized and presented by him as gifts to his principal captains. Bernal Díaz writes that he does not remember the names of nineteen of these women, 'and it is not worth while to name any of them' (i. 129). But one of them, 'good looking and intelligent and without embarrassment,' was christened Doña Marina. She was given to Alonso Hernandez Puertocarrero, an important gentleman. When he returned to Spain, she became Cortés's mistress and bore him a son, Don Martin Cortés. Eventually she was given in marriage to a gentleman named Juan Jaramillo.

Object of exchange, agent of communication, model of conversion, the only figure who appears to understand the two cultures, the only person in whom they meet—Doña Marina is a crucial figure in *The Conquest of New Spain*. For virtually everyone in Bernal Díaz's history—Indians and Spaniards alike—the site of the strategic symbolic oscillation between self and other is the body of this woman. Already in contemporary accounts, Doña Marina has some of the attributes of a mythic figure, and it is not surprising that she has continued to function in our own time as a resonant, deeply ambivalent symbol, half-divinity, half-whore, the savior and the betrayer.[30] Bernal Díaz claims that he was an eyewitness to the moving scene when Doña Marina, now the most powerful woman in Mexico, forgave her mother and brother for having given her away as a child; he remarks that her life resembles that of Joseph—an inevitable analogy, given the way he has chosen to tell the story, but peculiar in implying that Cortés is somehow like Pharaoh. The unsettling reversal is a further sign of the cultural oscillation that is released in and through the figure of Doña Marina.

The Indians called her Malintzin or La Malinche. For them as for the Spanish she was the figure in whom all communication between the two opposed cultures was concentrated, the figure whose actions, as Adelaida Del Castillo writes, 'syncretized two conflicting worlds causing the emergence of a new one—our own.'[31] To be sure, the communication did not signal toleration of difference: Doña Marina delivers threats and exhortations to convert, and she does so as an image of Cortés. But Bernal Díaz clearly believes that she had her own agenda, a program of revenge and triumph, and there is an odd sense in which Cortés becomes for the natives an image of Doña Marina: their name for him was also Malinche.[32]

For Cortés, whose military strategy relied as much on rhetoric as on

Cultural hybridity: Brazilians, with jewelry, feathers, and maracas, brought to France, clothed, and baptized. Joachim Duviert, 1613. Bibliothèque Nationale, Paris.

force, Doña Marina was a critically important tool; if eventually he could give her away as used goods, for more than a year he was almost entirely dependent upon her, not only for her linguistic ability but for strategic information and for her grasp of Mesoamerican reality. Cortés understood next to nothing about the complex culture which he had violently penetrated, and everything he could hope to learn, beyond the enigmatic and opaque visual evidence, had to be conveyed through Doña Marina. She could have chosen to tell him virtually anything, and the deeply skeptical Cortés would have been forced to believe her or remain in the dark.[33] In all his dealings with the peoples of the Yucatán and Mexico she was his principal access to language—at once his tongue and his ears—and hence the key to his hope for survival and success. In 1492, in the introduction to his *Gramática*, the first grammar of a modern European tongue, Antonio de Nebrija wrote that language has always been the partner (*compañera*) of empire. Cortés had found in Doña Marina his *compañera*.

Doña Marina is an extreme figure for the place of language at the center of the technology with which Europeans in the late fifteenth and sixteenth centuries responded to the discovery of new lands. In her enigmatic power, she serves not only as the supreme instance of the go-between in the New World but as an emblem of the vast process of cultural translation that the discovery initiated. For European adventurers not only depended upon go-betweens, but were themselves go-betweens, servants of the great representational machine. Journals, letters, memoranda, essays, questionnaires, eyewitness accounts, narrative histories, inventories, legal depositions, theological debates, royal proclamations, official reports, papal bulls, charters, chronicles, notarial records, broadsheets, utopian fantasies, pastoral eclogues, dramatic romances, epic poems—there is in the sixteenth century a flood of textual representation, along with a much smaller production of visual images,[34] that professes to deliver the New World to the Old.[35]

When I contemplate this torrent of words and images, I feel overwhelmed—a lifetime would not suffice to grasp what was disseminated throughout Europe in the first few generations alone. And there are, of course, even vaster silences—the silences of the unlettered and of those who, though literate, did not have occasion, license, or motive to leave a record of their thoughts. The responses of the natives to the fatal advent of the Europeans survive only in the most fragmentary and problematical form; much of what I would like to learn is forever lost, and much of what is not lost exists only through the mediation of those Europeans who for one reason or another—missionary, commercial, military, literary, historical, or philosophical—saw fit to register the voices of the other.[36] The natives themselves often seem most silent at those rare moments in which they are made to speak.

It is not only the native Americans whose voices are distorted or unrecorded: if anything, there are even fewer traces of the European lower classes, the common seamen and soldiers, the servants and artisans, who endured the greatest hardships and perils of the voyages. Sometimes they are only represented by a number—in casually imprecise remarks like 'som 60 or 70 other soudiars slayn and hurte'[37] or, still less directly, in phrases like 'no one of note was killed or wounded'—sometimes by a simple list of occupations and names. On occasion there is a glimpse of something further, though rarely individuated: a mention of sailors who grumble and threaten to mutiny, or of terrified voices raised in supplication and prayer, or of ferocious, uncontrollable wielders of pikes and swords against naked men and women.

We may tell ourselves that the ordinary seaman and the gentleman adventurer shared the same experiences, and hence that the silence of the former is not especially significant, but there are signs of major differences in perception. When an English serving-woman who had been held captive by the Algonquians reports that her life was hard but no harder than that of a serving-woman at home, or when a Spanish soldier runs away to live with the Mayans and then leads the tribe in attacks against his former countrymen, or when colonists in Virginia establish with the natives illegal trade relations that upset the official rates of exchange, then we are evidently dealing with a different way of construing the otherness of the others than that dominant in the discourse of the European ruling élite.

A few Renaissance writers partially acknowledge this difference. 'I mention Authors sometimes, of meane qualitie,' writes Samuel Purchas, 'for the meanest have sense to observe that which themselves see, more certainly then the contemplations and *Theory* of the more learned.'[38] Similarly, Montaigne claims that his principal source of information about the New World was his servant, 'a simple, crude fellow' and for that very reason a reliable observer:

for clever people observe more things and more curiously, but they interpret them; and to lend weight and conviction to their interpretation, they cannot help altering history a little. They never show you things as they are, but bend and disguise them according to the way they have seen them; and to give credence to their judgment and attract you to it, they are prone to add something to their matter, to stretch it out and amplify it. We need a man either very honest, or so simple that he has not the stuff to build up false inventions and give them plausibility; and wedded to no theory. Such was my man; and besides this, he at various times brought sailors and merchants, whom he had known on that trip, to see me. So I content myself with his information, without inquiring what the cosmographers say about it.[39]

For Montaigne, in this passage at least, the crucial distinction is between the simple who render 'veritable tesmoignage' and the clever (*les fines gens*) who gloss and interpret and rhetorically shape what they have observed until 'les choses pures' disappear beneath 'inventions fauces.' The display of hermeneutical and rhetorical skills—the hallmark of Renaissance education—distorts the representation of whatever has been witnessed, and Montaigne suggests that among the learned this distortion is virtually unavoidable. The educated class cannot help themselves—'ils ne se peuvent garder d'alterer un peu l'Histoire'—because the tendency to warp and mask is an integral part of their interpretive method and rhetorical technique.

In the period's travel literature, the texts written by those who claim to have seen the new lands for themselves, it is style that plays the authenticating and legitimating role played by Montaigne's servant. For the most part the style is humble, unimaginative, uninventive, and hence by implication reliable. For the style to call attention to itself would be as indecorous as for a servant boldly to enter the conversation of his betters or to dress in elaborate finery and sit down at the table.[40] In Renaissance poetry, style is frequently understood as an elegant garment and hence as a mark of the author's status.[41] But what Renaissance readers (and institutions like trading companies) generally want in travel literature is an accurate account of the other, a clear view of the naked truth. For this one needs not a garment but a reliable witness, a trustworthy servant. For the servant, it is thought, is not disposed to interpose himself between the naked object of perception and the representation of that object; he is the agent of simple reporting rather than interpretation. The élite's ability to look through their servants, to ignore them, to assume that they have no independent interpretive judgment underwrites this conception of the discursive project and its appropriate style.

Discursive authority in the early literature of travel then derives from a different source than it would in other forms of poesis—not from an appeal to higher wisdom or social superiority but from a miming, by the élite, of the simple, direct, unfigured language of perception Montaigne and others attribute to servants. If we can assume that most servants were illiterate, we can go further and suggest that this stylistic modesty is a miming by the lettered of the voices of the unlettered, in order to articulate the substance and condition of a world without literacy.

Montaigne's own language, of course, is by no means simple and direct, but he is not claiming to have himself witnessed the New World. Rather he claims to rely on his principal source, his servant, along with other sailors and merchants and the Indians with whom he was able to speak.[42] Frank Lestringant and other scholars have demonstrated that Montaigne had read widely in the texts about the New World—Lopez de Gomara, Jean de Léry, Urbain Chauveton, and others[43]—but, contrary to his usual practice in the *Essays*, he suppresses all mention of these texts, as if he regarded printed sources by recognized intellectuals as tainted regardless of the affected artlessness of their style. Writing at home, thousands of leagues from Brazil, Montaigne uses his servant as his source of pure eyewitness authenticity, and if this servant had not existed, Montaigne might well have made him up to serve his rhetorical purposes. Indeed there is no firm evidence that the servant did exist outside of the essays in which he appears, but he helps to establish a discursive principle: if a gentleman's professed ethnographic source is a servant, he can afford to write in a rich and complex style; if the gentleman is himself the observer, then his style must be his own servant.

The essay 'Of Cannibals' suggests that the testimony of Montaigne's servant—a man to whom he refers as a kind of possession ('Cet homme que j'avoy')—is the naked truth of the New World, the same truth that we would find if we could strip away the interpretive and rhetorical accretions from the discourse of the élite. Such a notion is rhetorically attractive because Montaigne wishes at moments at least to identify the cannibals themselves with the naked truth, with a natural state of humanity stripped of the false adornments of a corrupt civilization: 'Those people are wild, just as we call wild the fruits that Nature has produced by herself and in her normal course' (p. 152). The cannibals have not been adulterated by the artifices of intellect and imagination: 'they have been fashioned very little by the human mind, and are still very close to their original naturalness' (p. 153). And where the purity of nature shines forth, Montaigne writes, 'she wonderfully puts to shame [*une merveilleuse honte*] our vain and frivolous attempts.'[44]

I have suggested that the servant in nobleman's text is a rhetorical figure of transparency, but as so often in Montaigne figures refuse to keep their place. It is not Montaigne's custom to look through people or to encourage his readers to do so. And we may propose that in his insistence on the eyewitness mediation of the servant, Montaigne is going out of his way to register a class-specific interpretation of the New World, what we may call the America of the underlings (or perhaps, more precisely, the America that the underlings describe in response to questions from their noble employers). Montaigne, of course, was entirely capable of generating a heterodox account of the New World without the help of a real or imaginary servant. But I don't think that we should be too quick to dismiss the servant: there is in the essay on the cannibals a particular insistence on the absence of class structure and servitude in the New World and on the misery of oppression in the Old World that is subtly associated with the man Montaigne calls 'simple et grossier.'[45] What we encounter in 'Of Cannibals' is not Montaigne's response to the New World discoveries, but a more complex discourse: a French servant's reaction to or projection upon Brazil, highly charged by his position in his culture's social structure, then mediated by Montaigne's classicizing Utopian fantasies, his profound intelligence, his abhorrence of cruelty.[46] Inscribed in the French nobleman's imaginary conversation with the Greek philosopher about the American Indians is the trace of the unnamed servant, real or imagined eyewitness to a culture without 'custom of servitude.'

Montaigne's essay implies a further link between servant and Indian: it is as if the class otherness of the simple and crude servant (and therefore his poverty, vulnerability, and distance from the literary and philosophical traditions in which Montaigne himself is steeped) mirrored the cultural otherness of the Brazilian. 'Between my way of dressing and that of a peasant of my region,' writes Montaigne in another essay, 'I find far more distance than there is between his way, and that of a man dressed only in his skin.'[47] Montaigne's understanding of the vast cultural differences between Europe and the New World grows out of a meditation upon the vast social differences within his own country, a meditation mediated and in some sense figured by his servant. Near the close of the essay 'Of Cannibals,' Montaigne explicitly articulates these differences, not, however, expressing them directly but placing them in the mouth of one of the Brazilians who had been brought to France. Now the cannibal has become a go-between, bearing Montaigne's own perceptions to his readers. The Brazilians had noticed, Montaigne reports,

> that there were among us men full gorged with all sorts of good things, and that their other halves were beggars at their doors, emaciated with hunger and poverty; and they thought it strange that these needy halves could endure such an injustice, and did not take the others by the throat, or set fire to their houses. (p. 159)

Where we expect to find two terms in Montaigne—subject and object—we find a third: subject, object, and go-between. And if in the history we have been examining the go-between has served often as the agent of betrayal, Montaigne's essay suggests that the go-between can also serve as the agent for a marvelous dispossession, a loss of the fiercely intolerant certainty that licensed unbearable cruelty. For like Mandeville, Montaigne conjures up a world that is always rolling, turning, slipping away, a world of perennial, inescapable circulation. To be sure, this circulation is paradoxically intertwined in Montaigne with a powerful sense of what it means to possess the estate and the title of Montaigne. But that possession, constitutive of his name and essential to his identity, is none the less shot through with intimations of loss, intimations linked perhaps to the insecurity of land tenure during the years of bitter religious conflict in France or even to the shadowy counter-identity embodied by his mother, born of a Jewish family, of whom Montaigne rarely wrote. In these intimations of loss, Montaigne, like Mandeville, is a knight of non-possession.[48] Wonder in Montaigne's discourse on the New World turns not toward fantasies of ownership and rule but toward shame—'une merveilleuse honte.' For he acknowledges the 'barbarous horror' of New World cannibalism only as a means of articulating the horror at home:

> I think there is more barbarity in eating a man alive than in eating him dead; and in tearing by tortures and the rack a body still full of feeling, in roasting a man bit by bit, in having him bitten and mangled by dogs and swine (as we have not only read but seen within fresh memory, not among ancient enemies, but among neighbors and fellow citizens, and what is worse, on the pretext of piety and religion), than in roasting and eating him after he is dead. (p. 155)

This astonishing sentence is written by one who has abjured the desire to possess the souls of others and, for that matter, to possess himself. In this renunciation Montaigne manages to articulate and to realize what the text of Mandeville's travels could only set forth under the cover of a fraud. We are incomplete and unsteady, we are go-betweens, we do not know whom God loves and whom He hates.

I want to close with a final image of circulation in which I must act as the go-between. There is in the valley of Oaxaca (a place redolent with memories of Cortés, who ended his life as the Marques del Valle de Oaxaca) an obscure village called Tlacochahuaya. The village church has changed little since the sixteenth century when it was built as part of the Dominican monastery of Santo Domingo. It has a charming painted interior with interesting wooden effigies, carved by local Indian sculptors instructed by the friars who had converted them.[49] The effigies are placed in recessed niches. Out of curiosity once I peered into one of the niches in which lay the figure of the dead Jesus. There, fixed in the plaster of the ceiling, out of view from the nave, was a stone carving of the Mixtec god of death. The image looked down directly at the face of the crucified god.[50] The divinities have exchanged this sightless gaze, this perpetual circulation, for more than four hundred years.

Notes

Notes to Chapter One

1. Walter Benjamin, 'The Storyteller: Reflections on the Works of Nikolai Leskov,' in *Illuminations*, ed. Hannah Arendt, trans. Harry Zohn (New York: Schocken, 1968), 86.
2. Michel de Certeau, *The Practice of Everyday Life*, trans. Steven Rendall (Berkeley: University of California Press, 1984), 110.
3. For reflections on anecdotes and history, see Joel Fineman, 'Fiction and Fiction: The History of the Anecdote,' in *The New Historicism*, ed. H. Aram Veeser (New York: Routledge, 1989), 49–76.
4. Obviously, we are not very far here from the politics and economics of world domination, but there are surprises, if we only know how to look. It won't do to ignore that politics, but there is a kind of sentimental pessimism that simply collapses everything into a global vision of domination and subjection. To recognize and admire local accommodations is not uncritically to endorse capitalist markets, but it is to acknowledge imaginative adaptations to conditions that lie beyond the immediate control of the poor.

   On the ambiguities of possession, see the suggestive remarks of Greg Dening, 'Possessing Tahiti,' *Archaeol. Oceania* 21 (1986):

   > Possessing Tahiti was a complicated affair. Indeed, who possessed whom? Native and Stranger each possessed the other in their interpretation of the other. They possessed one another in an ethnographic moment that got transcribed into text and symbol. They each archived that text and symbol in their respective cultural institutions. They each made cargo of the things they collected from one another, put their cargo in their respective museums, remade the things they collected into new cultural artefacts. They entertained themselves with their histories of their encounter. Because each reading of the text, each display of the symbol, each entertainment in the histories, each viewing of the cargo enlarged the original encounter, made a process of it, each possession of the other became a self-possession as well. Possessing the other, like possessing the past, is always full of delusions. (p. 117)

5. I should add that I felt welcome, not in any very special way but simply as a member of the crowd. I remarked repeatedly that the Balinese not only tolerate but even seem to enjoy the confusion that goes with large groups, and

tourists are incorporated easily into those groups as they are incorporated (often very comically) into Balinese temple carving.

6. Homi K. Bhabha, 'The Commitment to Theory,' in *New Formations* 5 (1988), 5–23.
7. The Wayang, in any case, should not be understood only as an archaic form, an atavism, nor should we think of it as the 'authentic' Balinese art form. Wayang was widely used for political propaganda during the Indonesian struggle for independence. And its roots lie in Java. I might add that in Java, according to Miguel Covarrubias, 'it is a rule that the men look at the puppets, while the women see only the shadows' (*Islands of Bali* [London: KPI, 1986], 238). In Bali, by contrast, mobility appeared to be universal, and women (along with men and many children) crowded in behind the screen to see the puppets. (The contrast may no longer be valid; Covarrubias's book was first published in 1937, and Javanese Wayang may have changed radically.)
8. Thomas Harriot, *A Briefe and True Report of the New Found Land of Virginia* (New York: Dover, 1972; reprint of the 1590 Theodor de Bry edn.), 64. The Flemish engraver, De Bry, seems to have intensified the resemblance, but it is already apparent in White's original (in Paul Hulton and David Beers Quinn, *The American Drawings of John White* [Chapel Hill: University of North Carolina Press, 1964]). Jean de Léry, *History of a Voyage to the Land of Brazil, Otherwise Called America*, trans. Janet Whatley (Berkeley: University of California Press, 1990). I am grateful to Professor Whatley and the University of California Press for allowing me to see a prepublication copy of this translation. In her introduction Whatley calls attention to the polemical comparison and notes that 'the anthropophagic metaphor had moved to the center of Protestant polemic in the harrowing controversies over the Eucharist and transubstantiation' (p. xxvii).
9. For a sensitive introduction to these issues, see Janet Whatley, 'Savage Hierarchies: French Catholic Observers of the New World,' in *The Sixteenth Century Journal* 17 (1986), 319–30; and id., 'Une Révérence réciproque: Huguenot Writing on the New World,' in *University of Toronto Quarterly* 57 (1987–8), 270–89. See also Bernadette Bucher, *Icon and Conquest: A Structural Analysis of the Illustrations of de Bry's Great Voyages*, trans. Basia Miller Gulati (Chicago: University of Chicago Press, 1981).
10. Barbara Kiefer Lewalski, *Protestant Poetics and the Seventeenth-Century Religious Lyric* (Princeton, NJ: Princeton University Press, 1979).
11. Samuel Purchas, 'A Discourse of the diversity of Letters used by the divers Nations in the World; the antiquity, manifold use and variety thereof, with exemplary descriptions of above threescore severall Alphabets, with other strange Writings,' in *Hakluytus Posthumus, or Purchas His Pilgrimes*, 20 vols. (Glasgow: James MacLehose & Sons, 1905), i. 486.
12. For a brilliant discussion of this assumption, see Michel de Certeau, *The Writing of History*, trans. Tom Conley (New York: Columbia University Press, 1988), 209–43. See also the fine essay by Michael Harbsmeier, 'Writing and the Other: Travellers' Literacy, or Towards an Archaeology of Orality,' in *Literacy and Society*, ed. Karen Schousboe and Morgens Trolle Larsen (Copenhagen: Akademisk Forlag, 1989).

13. The European sense that the Indians are so different as to make them seem like beasts is widely reiterated. See e.g. Villegagnon's letter to Calvin about the Tupinamba of Brazil: 'they were wild and savage people, remote from all courtesy and humanity, utterly different from us in their way of doing things and in their upbringing: without religion, nor any knowledge of honesty or virtue, or of what is just or unjust; so that it seemed to me that we had fallen among beasts bearing a human countenance' (quoted by Jean de Léry in the preface to the *History of a Voyage*, p. xlix). For initial reactions to Europeans by native observers, see Mary W. Helms, *Ulysses' Sail: An Ethnographic Odyssey of Power, Knowledge and Geographical Distance* (Princeton, NJ: Princeton University Press, 1988), 172–210.
14. Not altogether, however. Leonardo Olschki, writing of the Spanish actions in the Antilles, sees 'a human activity which transformed within a short lapse of time a rudimentary stone-age society into a lively colonial organization' ('What Columbus Saw on Landing in the West Indies,' *Proceedings of the American Philosophical Society* 84 [1941], 635). And Samuel Eliot Morison ends his monumental *European Discovery of America: The Southern Voyages, A.D. 1492–1616* (New York: Oxford University Press, 1974) with the following summary judgment, 'To the people of this New World, pagans expecting short and brutish lives, void of hope for any future, had come the Christian vision of a merciful God and a glorious Heaven. And from the decks of ships traversing the two great oceans and exploring the distant verges of the earth, prayers arose like clouds of incense to the Holy Trinity and to Mary, Queen of the Sea' (p. 737). I prefer to recall that the island Columbus called Santa Maria de la Concepcíon is now known as Rum Cay.
15. *The Conquest of America: The Question of the Other*, trans. Richard Howard (New York: Harper & Row, 1984), 80. See also his edn., with Georges Baudot, of *Récits aztèques de la conquête* (Paris: Seuil, 1983). Baudot briefly mentions the pre-Columbian writing system of the *tlacuiloque*, or Mexican scribes, but does not address the question of whether this should be regarded as 'true' writing.

    I should emphasize that Todorov does not at all share Purchas's belief that the possession of writing is a moral advantage; the central concern of his book is the struggle to link an instrumental grasp of reality with ethical responsibility and tolerance. Todorov has now extended and deepened his moral and political reflections on otherness in the recent *Nous et les autres: La Réflexion française sur la diversité humaine* (Paris: Seuil, 1989).
16. In Todorov's original, unlike the translation, there is no second use of the term without the qualifying quotation marks: 'les Espagnols sont plus "avancés" que les Aztèques (ou pour généraliser: les sociétés à écriture, que les sociétés sans écriture)' (*La Conquête de l'Amérique: La Question de l'autre* [Paris: Seuil, 1982], 165).
17. On the crucial role of interpreters, see Emma Martinell Gifre, *Aspectos Linguisticos del Descubrimiento y de la Conquista* (Madrid: Consejo Superior de Investigaciones Científicas, 1988), 59–99.
18. The closest one can come to imagining such a figure in the service of Montezuma is Gonzalo Guerrero, who had with Aguilar survived a shipwreck on an earlier Spanish expedition and had been assimilated to Mayan culture. According to

Bernal Díaz, Guerrero incited the Maya to attack the Spaniards and drive them from the land. Cortés realized that he was dangerous: 'I wish I could get my hands on him,' he is said to have exclaimed, 'for it will never do to leave him here.' But then Guerrero's adopted people were not Aztecs but Maya, so there was never any real likelihood that he would serve Montezuma in the way that Aguilar and Doña Marina served Cortés. Bernal Diáz thinks that Guerrero was eventually killed in an attack on the Spanish invaders.

19. See the critique of Todorov in Inga Clendinnen, 'Fierce and Unnatural Cruelty: Cortés, Signs, and the Conquest of Mexico,' in A. Grafton and A. Blair (eds.), *The Transmission of Culture in Early Modern Europe* (Philadelphia: University of Pennsylvania Press, 1990), 84–130.
20. *The 'Diario' of Christopher Columbus's First Voyage to America, 1492–1493*, transcribed and trans. Oliver Dunn and James E. Kelley, Jr. (Norman, Okla.: University of Oklahoma Press, 1989), 243–5.
21. Jean de Léry, *History of a Voyage*, 141. Léry voyaged to Brazil in 1556–8, but he did not publish the first edn. of the *History* until 1578; five other edns., with substantial additions and revisions, appeared during his lifetime. See Frank Lestringant, 'L'Excursion brésilienne: Note sur les trois premières éditions de l'*Histoire d'un voyage* de Jean de Léry,' in *Mélanges sur la littérature de la Renaissance à la mémoire de V.-L. Saulnier* (Geneva: Droz, 1984), 53–72. Lestringant has published a series of astute and learned studies of Léry to which I am indebted.
22. He remarks similarly that the 'false prophets' whom the Tupinamba call *caraïbes* go from village to village 'like popish indulgence-bearers' (p. 140), bearing in each hand a maraca or rattle like 'the bell-ringers that accompany those impostors who, exploiting the credulity of our simple folk over here, carry from place to place the reliquaries of Saint Anthony or Saint Bernard, and other such instruments of idolatry' (p. 142).
23. Quoted by Whatley in Jean de Léry, *History of a Voyage*, 248.
24. Albertus Magnus, *Opera Omnia*, ed. Augustus Borguet (Paris, 1890), vi, 30*a*–31*a*; trans. in J. V. Cunningham, *Woe and Wonder* (Denver: Denver University Press, 1951), 79. See Chap. 2, pp. 16 ff.
25. Michael Camille, *The Gothic Idol: Ideology and Image-Making in Medieval Art* (Cambridge: Cambridge University Press, 1989), 78–81.
26. *The Writing of History*, 213.
27. In the Middle Ages, Jacques Le Goff has observed, there are endless references in both popular and learned writing to 'marvels' (*mirabilia*) but little or no discussion of 'the marvelous' as a category (Jacques Le Goff, *L'Imaginaire médiéval* [Paris: Gallimard, 1985], 18 ff.). Le Goff argues that this is because there is something disturbing to the dominant ideology about marvels, something unpredictable and alien, as if the proliferation of wonders bespoke a tacit, unorganized, but tenacious resistance to Christian orthodoxy, an atavistic survival of the old pagan marvels and the belief in a plurality of spiritual forces. Gradually, through the concept of the miraculous, supernatural and strictly Christian elements are separated out: in the Christian marvelous, there is only one author, one source of all spiritual power. Thus the Church was able to make predictable, to legitimate, and to colonize some of the old

marvels, while at the same time pushing what remained toward the domain of magic. Le Goff suggests that in the later Middle Ages there were other strategies for containing the marvels, including what he calls its 'aestheticization.' I will argue below that in Columbus we will find further strategies for Christianizing and colonizing the marvelous in the very place—the East—that had long been its great reservoir.

28. Descartes, *Philosophical Works*, trans. Elizabeth Haldane and G. R. T. Ross, 2 vols. (Cambridge: Cambridge University Press, 1911), i. 363.

29. Baruch Spinoza, *Chief Works*, trans. R. H. M. Elwes, 2 vols. (London: George Bell & Sons, 1884), ii. 174. 'The thought of an unusual thing, considered in itself, is of the same nature as other thoughts, and for this reason I do not count wonder among the emotions; nor do I see why I should do so, since this distraction of the mind arises from no positive cause that distracts it from other things, but only from the lack of a cause for determining the mind, from the contemplation of one thing, to think of other things' (Baruch Spinoza, *The Ethics and Selected Letters*, trans. Samuel Shirley, ed. Seymour Feldman [Indianapolis: Hackett, 1982], 143). Unlike Descartes, Spinoza thought that wonder does have an opposite: contempt.

30. In *The Poems of John Milton*, ed. John Carey and Alastair Fowler (London: Longman, 1968). David Quint kindly called my attention to the relevance of this passage. Milton is, at least by implication, a brilliant reader of the discourse of discovery and the uses of wonder. See, for example, the passage in which Satan, on the lowest stair of heaven, 'Looks down with wonder at the sudden view|Of all this world at once':

> As when a scout,
> Through dark and desert ways with peril gone
> All night; at last by break of cheerful dawn
> Obtains the brow of some high-climbing hill,
> Which to his eye discovers unaware
> The goodly prospect of some foreign land
> First-seen, or some renowned metropolis
> With glistering spires and pinnacles adorned,
> Which now the rising sun gilds with his beams.
> Such wonder seized, though after heaven seen,
> The spirit malign, but much more envy seized,
> At sight of all this world beheld so fair. (*PL* 3. 542–54)

31. Sir Walter Ralegh, *The Discoverie of the Large, Rich, and Beautifull Empire of Guiana*, in Richard Hakluyt, *The Principal Navigations, Voyages, Traffiques and Discoveries of the English Nation*, 12 vols. (Glasgow: J. MacLehose & Sons, 1903–5), x. 406.

Notes to Chapter Two

1. Columbus's copy of Marco Polo, with his annotations, has survived. We know of his familiarity with *Mandeville's Travels* from Andrés Bernaldez, *Memorias del*

reinado de los Reyes Católicos, ed. M. Gómez Moreno and J. de Mata Carriazo (Madrid: Real Academia de la Historia, 1962), 270, 307, 315, 319. Columbus's son Fernando also wrote that among the reasons that led his father to undertake his voyage were the works of 'Marco Polo, a Venetian, and John Mandeville.'

See Neil J. S. Renni, 'Fact and Fiction in the Literature of Travel, Real and Imaginary, with Particular Reference to the South Seas' (University of London Ph.D. thesis, 1986); Alexandre Cioranescu, *Colón humanista* (Madrid: Prensa Española, 1967), esp. 54–7.

2. Christopher Dawson (ed.), *The Mongol Mission: Narratives and Letters of the Franciscan Missionaries in Mongolia and China in the Thirteenth and Fourteenth Centuries* (London: Sheed & Ward, 1955), 117.
3. *Mandeville's Travels: Texts and Translations*, ed. Malcolm Letts, Hakluyt Society 2nd ser., vols. 101–2 (London: Hakluyt Society, 1953), i. 25. Letts uses *The Buke of John Maundeuill, being the Travels of Sir John Mandeville, Knight (1322–1356)*, ed. George F. Warner (London: Roxburghe Club, 1889), which is based on the Egerton text, an early 15th-century MS in the British Museum. All citations of *Mandeville's Travels* will be to this text, unless otherwise noted. In my notes, where I think the differences are significant, I will give the reading from the Cotton text, another early 15th-century MS in the British Museum. In Cotton, the text I have just quoted reads as follows: 'And he wolde haue maryed me fulle highly to a gret princes doughter yif I wolde han forsaken my lawe and my beleue, but I thanke God I had no wille to don it for no thing that he behighte me' (*Mandeville's Travels*, ed. M. C. Seymour [Oxford: Clarendon Press, 1967], 24).
4. Cotton MS: 'because that the deueles ben so subtyle to make a thing too seme otherwise than it is for to disceyue mankynde, and therfor I towched none; and also because that I wolde not ben put out of my deuocoun' (pp. 204–5). As a gifted liar Mandeville knows too that from time to time he must claim not to have witnessed some marvel or other. And in appropriating a complex story, like that of the Vale Perilous which he took from Odoric, he can weave various authentication strategies together. Where Odoric writes that he picked up some of the silver only to throw it down, Mandeville reports seeing the riches but then raises the whole question of illusion.
5. Cotton MS: 'for I was more deuout thanne than euere I was before or after' (p. 205).
6. *Digest* 41. 2. 1 (4. 502b). It seems likely that the derivation of property from occupation is itself an inversion of a prior phenomenology of possession: placing one's body on an object is posited as 'possessing' it by analogy with placing an object on one's body.
7. On the centrality of Jerusalem in the discourse of pilgrimage and crusade, see Paul Alphandéry, *La Chrétienté et l'idée de croisade*, 2 vols. (Paris: Albin Michel, 1954), esp. i. 9–56. For Robert le Moine and others in the early 12th century, Alphandéry writes,

> Jérusalem est le nombril de la terre. Motifs et attraits s'emmêlent autour de cette Jérusalem, dont la réalité spirituelle est d'ailleurs hautement saisie par le moine scripteur. Cette cité royale en effet, placée au centre du monde, c'est celle que le

Rédempteur du genre humain a illustrée de sa venue, de sa présence, qu'il a consacrée de sa passion, rachetée par sa mort, rendue insigne par sa sépulture. L'exaltation de Jérusalem culmine à cette historicité du mystère rédempteur. Toute la découverte laborieuse des pèlerinages s'impose maintenant dans ce sentiment, capital, d'un centre au milieu de la terre: ce nombril est aussi le lieu où s'est accompli le plus haut, le plus total mystère qui concerne l'univers chrétien et son salut' (pp. 37–8).

8. There is a peculiar emphasis in the texts of the late Middle Ages and Renaissance on Jesus' perambulation of the Holy Land. See, for example, Shakespeare's Henry IV calling for a crusade

> To chase these pagans in those holy fields
> Over whose acres walked those blessed feet
> Which fourteen hundred years ago were nailed
> For our advantage on the bitter cross.
> (*I Henry IV* I. i. 24–7)

9. This move from the rhetoric of Crusade to vehement, often radical social criticism is characteristic of the eschatological discourse of the late Middle Ages and early Renaissance. Alain Milhou observes that from the 14th to the 16th centuries, millenarian movements frequently translated the struggle to retake Jerusalem into a national campaign against the enemies of the people: the crusading rhetoric was adapted for very different social ends. 'La referencia a la conquista—*mítica*—de Jerusalén siguió confiriendo a la lucha—*real*—de los pobres contra sus enemigos (supestos o reales: moros, conversos, ricos, malos clérigos) el prestigio de la lucha escatológica por la Ciudad Santa' (*Colón y su mentalidad mesiánica en el ambiente franciscanista español* [Valladolid: Casa-Museo de Colón, 1983], 301).
10. Late in the work there is an allusion to Halaon, the brother of Mango Khan, who went 'with a great host for to win the Holy Land out of the Saracens' hands into Christian men's hands, and for to destroy Mahomet's law. . . . He, this ilk Halaon, conquered and won all the Holy Land into Christian men hands' (i. 159–60). Mandeville does not explain how the Holy Land passed again into the control of the sultan.
11. Cotton MS: 'And because that thei gon so ny oure feyth, thei ben lyghtly conuerted to Christene lawe whan men preche hem and schewen hem distynctly the lawe of Ihesu Crist and tellen hem of the prophecyes' (p. 98).
12. Cotton MS: 'Now sith I haue told you beforn of the Holy Lond and of that contree abouten and of many weyes for to go to that lond and to the Mount Synay and of Babyloyne the More and the Less and to other places that I have spoken [of] beforn; now is tyme yif it like you for to telle you of the marches and iles and dyuerse bestes and of dyuerse folk beyond theise marches. For in tho contrees beyonden ben many dyuerse contrees and many grete kyngdomes that ben departed by the iiii. flodes that comen from Paradys Terrestre' (p. 105).
13. 'The "Marvels of the East" determined the western idea of India for almost 2000 years, and made their way into natural science and geography, encyclopaedias and cosmographies, romances and history, into maps, miniatures and sculpture.' Rudolf Wittkower, 'Marvels of the East: A Study in the History of Monsters', *JWCI* 5 (1942), 159.

14. On the complex history of the marvels of the East, see Wittkower, art. cit. 159–197; John Block Friedman, *The Monstrous Races in Medieval Art and Thought* (Cambridge, Mass.: Harvard University Press, 1981); Henri Estienne, *Introduction au traité de la conformité des merveilles anciennes auec les modernes. ou traité preparatif à l'Apologie pour Herodote* (Geneva, 1579); Giuseppe Nenci, 'A concezione del miracoloso nei poemi omerici,' *Atto della Accademia delle Scienze di Torino* 92 (1957–58), 275–311; Leonardo Olschki, *Storia Letteraria delle Scoperte Geografiche* (Florence: Olschki, 1937); John Spencer, *A Discourse Concerning Prodigies* (London, 1665); Claude Kappler, *Monstres, Démons et Merveilles à la fin du Moyen Age* (Paris: Payot, 1980); Jacques Le Goff, *L'Imaginaire médiéval* (Paris: Gallimard, 1985); Daniel Poirion, *Le Merveilleux dans la littérature française au Moyen Age* (Paris: P.U.F., 1982); Jean Céard, *La Nature et les prodiges: L'Insolite au 16e siècle en France* (Geneva: Droz, 1977).
15. Leland, in Bishop Tanner's *Bibliotheca Britannico-Hibernica* (London, 1748), quoted by Malcolm Letts, *Sir John Mandeville: The Man and his Book* (London: Batchworth, 1949), 34. Purchas (xi, 363–4) cited in Josephine Waters Bennett, *The Rediscovery of Sir John Mandeville* (New York: Modern Language Association, 1954), 250.
16. Quoted in C. W. R. D. Moseley, 'The Metamorphoses of Sir John Mandeville,' *Yearbook of English Studies* 4 (1974), 8.
17. Mandeville's admission that he hadn't actually entered Paradise, writes Warner, 'is to the author's credit, for it must have cost him something to make it' (*The Buke of John Maundeuill*, pp. 220–1).
18. Cf. C. W. R. D. Moseley, 'The Metamorphoses of Sir John Mandeville,' *Yearbook of English Studies* 4 (1974), 5–25.
19. Christopher Dawson (ed.), *The Mongol Mission: Narratives and Letters of the Franciscan Missionaries in Mongolia and China in the Thirteenth and Fourteenth Centuries* (London: Sheed & Ward, 1955), 95.
20. *Mandeville's Travels*, ed. M. C. Seymour (Oxford: Clarendon Press, 1967), pp. xv–xvi. 'None of the various attempts to pierce the author's anonymity, which began in the fourteenth century at Liège and which have successively associated the book with Jean de Bourgogne, a Liège physician (d. 1372), and Jean d'Outremeuse, a Liège notary (d. 1399), as well as with the author's adopted name, will bear critical examination' (p. xiii).
21. Ibid., p. xvii. See, likewise, Warner: 'After the disingenuous manner in which . . . the work was compiled, the few pious and touching words with which it finally concludes sound incongruous, not to say revolting. But it would be a hasty assumption that the writer merely added conscious hypocrisy to his other sins. With the evidence before us of fraud and mendacity, appearances are against him, and it is easy to explain his expressions of humble faith as intended to keep up to the end the character of devout pilgrim and simple-minded traveller which he assumes all along. But . . . as likely as not his words were the outcome of genuine religious feeling, united though it was with a blunted moral sense which saw nothing reprehensible in an elaborate literary imposture' (*The Buke of John Maundeuill*, p. xxix). I think the whole force of *Mandeville's Travels* is to complicate a phrase like 'genuine religious feeling.'
22. 'The more one questions Mandeville's truthfulness, the higher one has to rate

his literary ability,' C. W. R. D. Moseley, *The Travels of Sir John Mandeville* (Harmondsworth: Penguin, 1983), 13. See also Mary B. Campbell, *The Witness and the Other World: Exotic European Travel Writing, 400–1600* (Ithaca, NY: Cornell University Press, 1988): Mandeville 'was writing realistic prose fiction—for the first time since Petronius' (p. 122). The most important and revealing accounts of Mandeville's literary skill are by Donald Howard: 'The World of *Mandeville's Travels*,' *Yearbook of English Studies* 1 (1971), 1–17; *Writers and Pilgrims: Medieval Pilgrimage Narratives and Their Posterity* (Berkeley: University of California Press, 1980).

23. Jonathan Haynes, *The Humanist as Traveler: George Sandys's 'Relation of a Journey begun An. Dom 1610'* (Rutherford, NJ: Fairleigh Dickinson University Press, 1986), 31. Haynes compares Odoric's account of his voyage to China: 'Odoric closes with a sworn, dated, and witnessed statement—required by his monastic superior—that everything he said is true. But even this does not solve the problem. Anxiously he repeats again and again: "Thus much concerning those things which I beheld most certainly with mine eyes, I frier Odoricus have heere written; many strange things also I have of purpose omitted, because men will not beleeve them unless they should see them."' Odoric's uneasiness is characteristic of his age; medieval writers commonly avoid any implication of autonomy and appeal to 'auctoritates' even if they have to invent them. See Michel Zink, 'Une Mutation de conscience littéraire: Le Langage romanesque à travers des examples français du XIIe siècle,' *Cahiers de Civilisation Médiévale* 24 (1981), 3–27.

24. If *Mandeville's Travels* is to be linked to the literary at all, it is not to the medieval masters of personae, to Dante or Chaucer, but rather to post-modern artists bent on dismantling stable structures of literary identity and meaning. The works closest in spirit to Mandeville's, with its complex, self-reflexive mirrorings, its elusiveness, its fascination with otherness, its narrative disjunctions, and its refusal to take possession are Calvino's *Invisible Cities* and Barthes's *Empire of Signs*. But Calvino's cities are the fantastic projections of the emblematic imagination, while Barthes's signs, even as they gesture toward Japan, are explicitly cut off from any mimetic claim: 'to me the Orient is a matter of indifference,' Barthes writes at the opening of his book, 'merely providing a reserve of features whose manipulation—whose invented interplay—allows me to "entertain" the idea of an unheard-of symbolic system, one altogether detached from our own.' (Roland Barthes, *The Empire of Signs*, trans. Richard Howard [New York: Farrar, Straus, & Giroux, 1982], 3.) Now the manipulation of a reserve of features in order to produce a sense of the faraway is very close to Mandeville, but where *The Empire of Signs* depends upon the idea of invented symbolic systems, *Mandeville's Travels* depends upon the idea of alternative realities, that is, of features that are not invented but witnessed. There is a substantial difference—about six hundred years of complex cultural work—between alternative realities and invented symbolic systems, and I have no interest in collapsing one into the other. My purpose is not to make *Mandeville's Travels* post-modern but to make it strange.

25. See Warner's *The Buke of John Maundeuill*, p. xxvii. Warner adds, 'Nor was the translator (or copyist) even satisfied with this, for he plainly considered the

case was one that required hard swearing. At the end of the story therefore he makes the author solemnly affirm its truth and declare that he and his fellows had dwelt a long time with Prester John himself at his own court.'

26. *The Travels of Sir John Mandeville*, ed. Josef Krasa, trans. Peter Kussi (New York: Braziller, 1983), 13. The scene seems to be a parody of the monastic community gathered to listen to a reading from Scriptures or the Fathers. I have not, however, been able to verify Krasa's claims.
27. Marco Polo, *The Travels*, trans. Ronald Latham (Harmondsworth: Penguin, 1958), 34.
28. See, likewise, from this account of Kinsai, the following: 'You may take it for a fact that the salt of this city yields an average yearly revenue of 80 *tomauns* of gold: as a *tomaun* is equivalent to 70,000 *saggi* of gold, this brings the total to 5,600,000 *saggi*, of which every *saggio* is worth more than a gold florin or ducat. This is indeed a thing to marvel at and an inordinate sum of money' (p. 228).
29. The Cotton MS adds, 'And of that moneye is som of gretter prys & som of lasse prys, after the dyuersitee of his statutes' (p. 172). Hamelius cites as sources Odoric and Hayton. 'The diversity of his statutes' is apparently a mistranslation of the French (based on Hayton), 'solone la diuersite de seinal qi y est,' i.e. according to the variety of the marks upon it.
30. The fusion of the materialized and disembodied could be said to describe the very idea of the corporation. There is a strange relation between Mandeville as the knight of non-possession—a radical, utopian model of non-appropriation—and Mandeville as the site of the appropriation of dozens of texts. It is possible that this relation figures the emergence of a merchant *class*, a class represented not by the great merchant *princes* (like the Fuggers) but by the disembodied, fabricated realism of the fictive narrator.
31. Cotton MS: 'But the Sarazines wole not suffre no Cristene man ne Iewes to come therein, for thei seyn that none so foule synfulle men scholde not come in so holy place. But I cam in there and in othere places there I wolde, for I hadde lettres of the Soudan with his grete seel, and comounly other men had but his signett; in the whiche lettres he commanded of his specyalle grace to alle his subgettes to lete me seen alle the places and to enforme me pleynly alle the mysteries of euery place . . .' (p. 60).
32. Cotton MS: 'And the folk of the contree don gret worschipe and reuerence to his signett or his seel and knelen thereto as lowly as wee don to *Corpus domini*' (pp. 60–1).
33. Mandeville is drawing upon a complex web of associations that are played out in Jewish, Christian, and Muslim sources. There is, to my knowledge, no Biblical reference to the rock in the Temple, but in the wake of the destruction of the Temple there developed a body of legend and rabbinical commentary. According to the Mishnah Yoma, 'After the Ark was taken away a stone remained there from the time of the early prophets, and it was called "Shetiyah" (foundation).' The Zohar makes the rock the foundation stone of the world and its center:

   When the Holy One, blessed be he, was about to create the world, He detached one precious stone from underneath His throne of glory and plunged it into the abyss; one

> end of it remained fastened therein, whilst the other end stood out above . . . out of which the world started, spreading itself to the right and left into all directions.
>
> That stone is called in Hebrew Shetiyah—Foundation.
>
> Now the earth's expansion around the central point was complete in three concentric rings . . . The second expansion embraces the whole of the land of Israel, the land which was declared holy. The third expansion comprehends the rest of the earth.

(Cited in Zev Vilnay, *Legends of Jerusalem* [Philadelphia: Jewish Publication Society of America, 1973], 7–8.)

I am indebted to references given to me by Professor Harold Fisch and an unpublished paper by Hannah Davis, 'Jerusalem as the Center of the World.'

34. The medieval Jewish commentary of Rashi casts an interesting light on Mandeville's conception. The rabbis noted that the passage in Genesis first states that Jacob 'took of the stones of that place, and put them for a resting-place for his head' but then states that Jacob 'took the stone that he had put for a resting-place for his head, and set it up for a pillar' (Genesis 28: 11, 18): the 'stones' have become a single 'stone.' Rashi writes that the stones 'began quarreling with one another. One said, "Upon me let this righteous man rest his head," and another said "Upon me let him rest *it*." Whereupon the Holy One, blessed be He, straightway made them into one stone!' In the Midrash Rabbah, R. Judah is reported to have said, 'He took twelve stones, saying: "The Holy One, blessed be He, has decreed that twelve tribes should spring forth. Now neither Abraham nor Isaac has produced them. If these twelve stones cleave to one another, then I know that I will produce the twelve tribes." When therefore the twelve stones united, he knew that he was to produce the twelve tribes.' I am indebted to Professor Dov Spolsky for these references.
35. The Cotton MS adds several other events associated with the rock. I might add that Muslims have comparable associations, including the belief that Mohammed, ascending into heaven, left the trace of his foot on the Dome of the Rock.
36. The Rawlinson MS notes, 'And thys they arn bothe in doute wiche it is, and I my selfe also am in doute, for the soth can no man telle' (quoted in *Mandeville's Travels*, ed. Letts, i. 10 n.4).
37. It would be possible to argue that the Holy Land is rather the place of sacred metaphor—that is, of the biblical typology that views events in the Hebrew Scriptures as figures for the events in Jesus' life in which their ultimate signification is revealed and fulfilled. *Mandeville's Travels* clearly assumes such typological understanding—for example, in referring to Melchisedek's offering of bread and wine as a token of the sacrament—but the events are so jumbled and the area in which they are said to take place so small that the temporal and spatial distances across which metaphor normally travels are collapsed.
38. Cotton MS: 'For he that wil pupplishce ony thing, to make it openly knowen he wil make it to ben cryed and pronounced in the myddel place of a town, so that the thing that is proclaimed and pronounced may euenly strecche to alle parties. Right so He that was formyour of alle the world wold suffre for vs at Jerusalem, that is the myddes of the world' (pp. 1–2).

39. Hence the Savior both created the world and took possession of it *a pedibus quasi positio*.
40. 'The geometry of a tripartite world was compared to T and O in 1422 by Leonardo Dati in his poem *Della sphera*': Hildegard Binder Johnson, 'New Geographical Horizons: Concepts,' in *First Images of America: The Impact of the New World on the Old*, ed. Fredi Chiappelli, 2 vols. (Berkeley: University of California Press, 1976) ii. 622.
41. See Alain Milhou, *Colón y su mentalidad mesianica* (Valladolid: Casa-Museo de Colón, 1983), 404–5: 'si la "tierra cosmográfica" era . . . un globo, el ecúmeno (o sea la tierra habitable) no representaba más que una mínima parte de la superficie de la Tierra y podía, por lo tanto, ser considerado como un disco llano, colocado encima de la esfera.' See also W. G. L. Randles, *De la terre plate au globe terrestre: Une mutation épistémologique rapide (1480–1520)*, Cahier des Annales (Paris: Armand Colin, 1980).
42. Michel de Certeau, *The Practice of Everyday Life*, trans. Steven Rendall (Berkeley: University of California Press, 1984), 103. Certeau speaks of 'a universe of rented spaces haunted by a nowhere or by dreamed-of places.'
43. For a similar late-14th-century account of the Antipodes (based on Isidore of Seville), see Bartholomaeus Angelicus, *De proprietatibus rerum* (1398; trans. Trevisa, 1495): 'yonde ben the Antipodes, men that haue theyr fete ayenst our fete' (xv. 52. 506). Cf. in the mid-16th century, Robert Recorde:

> When the sonne riseth to vs in the spring tyme, it is noone with them that dwell aboute Calecut, and when the son is in our Meridian line, then doth he set to them: so that when the son doth set to vs, it is midnight to them about Calecut, & then is it noone to the famous cuntry of Peru: Again at that time the son riseth to them that be in the isles of Molucca. Whereby you may gether that Peru & Calecut be in 2. contrarye coasters of the earthe, and therfore seeme to go wyth their feet the one against the other, and their heddes the one fromwarde the other, whiche sorte of people therefore are called of the Greeks and Latines also . . . Antipodes, as you myght say Counterfooted, or Counterpasers. (*The Castle of Knowledge* [London, 1556], 93)

44. Thus, for example, the Samaritans 'were converted and baptized through the apostles. But they hold not the apostles' teachings, and so they are fallen in errors and hold a sect by themselves and a law diverse from the law of Christians and of Jews, Saracens, and Paynims. Nevertheless they trow in a God and saw there is none but he that made all, and all shall deme' (i. 76–7).
45. On the use of the term 'mawmet' (i.e. Mohammed) as a synonym for 'idol,' see Michael Camille, *The Gothic Idol* (Cambridge: Cambridge University Press, 1989), 129–65.

    Mandeville is very close to Odoric who writes, 'in questa città [Llasa in Tibet, which Odoric quite possibly never reached] dimora lo Abiffo, cioè lo Papa in sua lingua; et questo si è el capo di tutte quelle idole, a'quali secondo la lora usanza dà et distribuisce tutti gli lor benefici, e quali egli hanno' (Odorico da Pordenone, *Relazione del Viaggio in Oriente e in Cina (? 1314–1330)* (a cura della Camera di Commercio Industria, Artigianato e Agricoltura, Pordenone)—the texts follow Teofilo Domenichelli, *Sopra la vita e i viaggi del beato Odorico da Pordenone dell'ordine de'Minori* [Prato: Ranieri Guasti, 1881], 64). It is possible to argue that here and elsewhere Mandeville has more of a sense of the oscillation between homology and antithesis than Odoric, but the argument should not obscure Odoric's own considerable complexity.

46. Cotton MS: 'And after that, as preestes amonges vs syngen for the dede *Subuenite sancti dei, et cetera* right so tho prestes syngen with high voys in hire langage, "Beholdeth how so worthi a man and how gode a man this was, that the angeles of God comen for to sechen him and for to bryngen him into Paradys." And thanne semeth it to the sone that he is highliche worschipt whan that manye briddes and foules of raveyne comen and eten his fader. And he that hath most nombre of foules is most worschiped. And thanne the sone bryngeth hoom with him alle his kyn and his frendes and alle the othere to his hows and maketh hem a gret feste . . . . And whan thei ben at mete, and sone let bryne forth the hede of his fader and thereof he yeueth of the flesch to his most specyalle frendes instede of entremess or a sukkarke. And of the brayn panne he leteth make a cuppe, and thereof drynketh he and his other frendes also with gret deuocoun in remembrance of the holy man that the aungeles of God han eten. And that cuppe the sone schalle kepe to drynken of alle his liftyme in remembrance of his fadir' (p. 225).

47. Among the many vivid examples of this piety analyzed by Caroline Walker Bynum, consider the ancient Irish hymn, *Sancti uenite*: 'Come, holy people, eat the body of Christ, drinking the holy blood by which you are redeemed. We have been saved by Christ's body and blood; having feasted on it, let us give thanks to God' (in *Holy Feast and Holy Fast: The Religious Significance of Food to Medieval Women* [Berkeley: University of California Press, 1987], 50; cf., likewise, 49, 59, 66 ff.).

48. The passage continues, 'And therefore when I pray for the dead and say my *De Profundis*, I say it for all Christian souls and also for all the souls that are to be prayed for.' This passage is explicitly linked to a refusal of possessions by the naked and virtuous Gynoscriphe who have been offered riches by Alexander the Great.

49. I want to acknowledge here the searching interventions of Professor Arnold Davidson and Professor Janel Mueller, when I delivered this chapter as a lecture in Chicago.

50. *The Legitimacy of the Modern Age*, trans. Robert M. Wallace (Cambridge, Mass: MIT Press, 1983), 229–456.

51. 'The early-modern renewal of the pretension to unrestricted theoretical curiosity turned against the exclusion of pure theory, and of the pure happiness that was bound up with it, from the realm of what could be reached in this world, just as it turned against the medieval God's claim to exclusive insight into nature as His work,' ibid. 232.

52. 'The whole trend of the *Mandeville's* argument is obviously as heterodox as was possible in his day,' remarks Hamelius, who regards the work as 'an anti-Papal pamphlet in disguise' (i. 15).

53. Carlo Ginzburg, *The Cheese and the Worms: The Cosmos of a Sixteenth-Century Miller*, trans. John and Anne Tedeschi (Baltimore: Penguin Books, 1980), 41–2.

54. Quoted in Certeau, *Practice of Everyday Life*, 107.

55. We cannot have *our* disillusioned recognition of Mandeville's radical empti-

ness *and* include a sense of this emptiness as part of the intended meaning of the text. That is, the text initially does not seem to have given indications of its own bad faith; readers appear to have assumed that Mandeville existed and that his travels actually took place. It can be said, perhaps, that we are now able to recognize that the alienation—the fictive nature of the performing self—was part of the achievement of *Mandeville's Travels*; but this alienation does not seem to have been available to the early readers and in this sense is not likely to have been intended. At the same time, it is obviously problematical to impose upon a 14th-century text a conception of the self or of empirical verifiability such as Warner displays. And as Roger Dragonetti has shown, the medieval relation to sources and to citation is quite different from our own (see *Le Mirage des sources: l'Art du faux dans le roman médiéval* [Paris: Seuil, 1987]).

56. 'The Task of the Translator,' in *The Resistance to Theory* (Manchester: Manchester University Press, 1986), 91.

57. They are mentioned once in the first half of the book, in relation to Islam. The Saracens, Mandeville writes, 'do not understand the Holy Writ spiritually, but according to the letter, as do the Jews. . . . Therefore some Saracens say that the Jews are wicked men, and cursed, because they have broken the Law that God gave them through Moses; and they say Christian men are wicked and evil because they do not keep the Commandment of the Gospel, which Jesus Christ ordained for them' (p. 107).

58. *The 'Diario' of Christopher Columbus's First Voyage to America, 1492–1493*, transcribed and trans. Oliver Dunn and James E. Kelley, Jr. (Norman: University of Oklahoma Press, 1989), 291. (Citations of the *Diario* in my book will be to this bilingual parallel text.) On Columbus's Messianic dream of the conquest of Jerusalem, a dream shared by many in Spain and elsewhere in Europe in the late 15th and early 16th centuries, see e.g. Alain Milhou, *Colón y su mentalidad mesianica en el ambiente franciscanista español*, esp. 289–474. Milhou argues that while the references in Columbus to the rebuilding of the 'arx Sion' and the restoration of the 'Casa Santa' may be meant literally, this literal sense, in the context of Columbus's Joachite Messianism, may serve as a metonymic reference to Christian holy places far from Jerusalem. See also Pauline Moffitt Watts, 'Prophecy and Discovery: On the Spiritual Origins of Christopher Columbus's "Enterprise of the Indies,"' *American Historical Review* 90 (1985), 92 ff.

A hitherto unedited cache of Columbus's letters has recently been unearthed in Seville's Archive of the Indies. Among these is a letter of 1493 to the king and queen asking—characteristically—for more money and for a cardinalship for his son. The favors are small in relation to what Columbus promises: in seven years, he writes, the gold of the Indies will finance the raising of an enormous army, an army capable of capturing Jerusalem and restoring to Christendom the holy places, 'los Santos Lugares, entre ellos la *Casa Santa*.' Román Orozco, 'Colón sí tiene quien le escriba,' in *Cambio* 16 (1988), 99.

Notes to Chapter Three

1. *Select Documents Illustrating the Four Voyages of Columbus*, trans. and ed. Cecil Jane, 2 vols. (London: Hakluyt Society, 1930), i. 2. 'Señor, porque sé que avréis plazer de la gran vitoria que Nuestro Señor me ha dado en mi viaje, vos escrivo esta, por la qual sabréys como en .xxxiii. días pasé de las islas de Canaria á las Indias con la armada que los ilustrísimos rey é reyna nuestros señores me dieron, donde yo fallé muy muchas islas pobladas con gente sin número; y d'ellas todas he tomado posesión por Sus Altezas con pregón y vandera real estendida, y no me fué contradicho. á la primera que yo fallé puse nombre "San Salvador", á comemoración de Su Alta Magestad, el qual maravillosamente todo esto ha dado; los Indios la llaman "Guanahaní"; á la segunda puse nombre "la isla de Santa María de Concepción"; á la tercera "Fernandina"; á la quarta "la Ysabela"; á la quinta "la isla Juana", é así á cada una nombre nuevo.' Quotations from Columbus's letters, unless otherwise noted, will be from this edn.
2. Santangel, the *escribano de ración*, had helped Columbus find the money to finance his voyage. Santangel was a member of a family of *conversos*. A copy of the letter was also sent to Gabriel Sanchez, the treasurer of Aragon and also from a family of *conversos*.
3. Over whom does Columbus imagine that he has achieved a victory: over the Indians? over the destructive power of the sea? over his detractors in Europe? over the classical geographers and indeed the whole classical world? At the close of the letter, Columbus returns to the language of victory. He speaks of 'the eternal God, our Lord, Who gives to all those who walk in His way triumph [*victoria*] over things which appear to be impossible,' and he urges all of Christendom to share this sense of triumph: 'So that, since Our Redeemer has given this victory to our most illustrious king and queen, and to their renowned kingdoms, in so great a matter, for this all Christendom ought to feel delight and make great feast and give solemn thanks to the Holy Trinity with many solemn prayers for the great exaltation which they shall have, in the turning of so many peoples to our holy faith, and afterwards for temporal benefits, for not only Spain but all Christians will have hence refreshment and gain' (Jane, i. 18).

   Theodore J. Cachey, Jr. points out that the Latin translation of Columbus's letter, by Leandro de Cosco (a chancellor in the Roman Curia, an Aragonese at the court of Alexander VI), omits Columbus's martial rhetoric. Instead of 'la gran victoria,' the Latin renders the sentence, 'Since I know that it will please you that I have carried to completion the duty which I assumed. . .' ('The Earliest Literary Response of Renaissance Italy to the New World Encounter, in *Columbus*, ed. Anne Paolucci and Henry Paolucci [New York: Griffin House for the Council on National Literatures, 1989], 28). Cachey calls attention to the recurrence of the verbal motif of the *victoria* at the close of the letter (so that the motif, in effect, frames the narrative): 'since, thus Our Redeemer has given this victory to our most illustrious King and Queen. . . .' 'The martially connotated language of Columbus's *exordium*,' Cachey writes, 'is based upon the link in Columbus's mind (established explicitly in the dedicatory letter to the *Diario*) between his Discovery and the "victoria" at Granada, the final act of the Reconquest' (p. 28).

4. 'Mittimus in presenciarum nobilem virum Christoforum Colon cum tribus caravelis armatis per maria oceania ad partes Indie pro aliquibus causis et negotiis seruicium Dei ac fidem ortodoxe concernentibus' (Jane, p. lxx).
5. *The 'Diario' of Christopher Columbus's First Voyage to America, 1492–1493*, transcribed and trans. by Oliver Dunn and James E. Kelley, Jr. (Norman: University of Oklahoma Press, 1989), 109.
6. An often-repeated modern theory is that no one had really thought ahead of time about the difficulties. 'Surely, the reader will ask, you do not suppose that Ferdinand and Isabella (and Henry VII) were so simple as to suppose that three small vessels (or one still smaller) with ninety (or eighteen) men could sail into a harbor of Japan or China and simply take over? The answer is, yes, they were as simple as that' (Samuel Eliot Morison, *Admiral of the Ocean Sea: A Life of Christopher Columbus* [Boston: Little, Brown, 1942], 106–7). This view is supported by the recent study of Spanish practices before 1492: In the Spanish invasion of Majorca, we are told, 'A pattern was established which remained influential throughout the history of the expansion of the Crown of Aragon—indeed, in some respects, throughout the history of western Mediterranean expansion generally. The problems were not considered in advance' (Felipe Fernández-Armesto, *Before Columbus: Exploration and Colonization from the Mediterranean to the Atlantic, 1229–1492* [Philadelphia: University of Pennsylvania Press, 1987], 18). I might add that in his letter to Santangel, Columbus supplements the language of legal possession with the language of occupation.
7. In an important unpublished paper, Patricia Seed suggests that the Spanish term *tomar posesión* (and the Portuguese *tomar posse*) did not have the same meaning as the English 'to take possession.' 'Possession' in Elizabethan royal patents such as that granted to Sir Humphrey Gilbert and Sir Walter Ralegh means to 'have, hold, occupy and enjoy,' and to wield over the territory so held 'full power to dispose thereof . . . according to the lawes of England.' In Spanish usage, Seed argues, the phrase 'tomar posesión' referred to the repertory of symbolic actions and formulaic pronouncements. The difference is reflected in Elizabeth's response to Spanish complaints against Francis Drake. According to William Camden, the queen denied that the Spanish had established 'possession': Spaniards, she said, 'had touched here and there upon the Coasts, built Cottages, and given Names to a River or Cape which does not entitle them to ownership; . . . Prescription without possession is worth little [*cum praescriptio sine possessione haud valeat*]' (William Camden, *Rerum Anglicarvm et hibernicarvm Annales regnante Elisabetha* [London: Ludwig Batavorvm, 1639], 328). The actions that Elizabeth characterizes as mere 'prescription' are precisely what the Spanish seem to have meant by 'taking possession.'
8. Christopher Dawson (ed.), *The Mongol Mission: Narratives and Letters of the Franciscan Missionaries in Mongolia and China in the Thirteenth and Fourteenth Centuries* (London: Sheed & Ward, 1955), 93.
9. The Sahara is in some way a similar obstacle, but there had been, of course, many contacts over the centuries, esp. along the coasts of Africa.

10. *Diario*, 63–5. Morison translates *escrivano* as 'secretary'; other translations render it 'ship's clerk,' 'recorder,' and 'purser.' The *escrivano* was also an 'officer of the court'; as such, his testimony was equal to that of three other witnesses (see Stanley S. Jados, *Consulate of the Sea and Related Documents* [Tuscaloosa: University of Alabama Press, 1975], art. 330).
11. Quoted in Arthur S. Keller, Oliver J. Lissitzyn, Frederick J. Mann, *Creation of Rights of Sovereignty through Symbolic Acts, 1400–1800* (New York: Columbia University Press, 1938), 39–40. For the Spanish text, see 'Instrución que dió el Rey á Juan Diaz de Solís para el viage expresado,' 24 de Nov., 1514, in Don Martin Fernandez de Navarrete (ed.), *Colección de los viages y descubrimientos que hicieron por mar los Españoles*, 5 vols. (Buenos Aires: Editorial Guarania, 1945; orig. pub. 1825), iii. 149–50.
12. Keller *et al.* 41.
13. Ibid. 35.
14. On Hispaniola, on December 12, Columbus had his men raise 'a large cross at the western side of the entrance to the harbor on a conspicuous height, as a sign, he says, that Your Highnesses claim the land as your own, and chiefly as a sign of Jesus Christ Our Lord and in honor of Christianity' (*Diario*, 219).
15. *Journals and Other Documents on the Life and Voyages of Christopher Columbus*, trans. and ed. Samuel Eliot Morison (New York: Heritage Press, 1963), 27.
16. After describing the ritual, the log-book entry goes on to say, 'Soon many people of the island gathered there' (*Diario*, 65). Given the Arawaks' timidity, it is possible that they kept their distance at this point.
17. Michel de Certeau, *The Writing of History*, trans. Tom Conley (New York: Columbia University Press, 1988), 212.
18. It is remotely conceivable that the phrase was intended to include the Spanish as well as the natives, since it was certainly possible for Columbus to imagine a Spaniard who would dispute his authority. But the principal reference must be to the inhabitants of the land whose possession is being claimed.
19. For a useful collection of legal texts bearing on the possession of Indian lands in North America, see Charles M. Haar and Lance Liebman, *Property and Law* (Boston: Little, Brown, 1977).
20. *Institutes* II. i. 40. This passage is cited by Francisco de Vitoria in his brilliant review of the Spanish (and, more generally, the European) claims to the Indies. See James Brown Scott, *The Spanish Origin of International Law: Francisco de Vitoria and His Law of Nations* (Oxford: Clarendon Press, 1934), p. xxxiii.
21. *Digest* 41. 2. 6.
22. Accursius, *Glossa ordinaria*, on *Digest* 41. 2. 6. I am indebted for this reference to Laurent Mayali.
23. *The Letter of Columbus on the Discovery of America* (New York: Lenox Library, 1892), 19.
24. This is an instance of the situation Jean-François Lyotard has called the 'differend': 'the case where the plaintiff is divested of the means to argue and becomes for that reason a victim' (*The Differend: Phrases in Dispute*, trans. Georges Van Den Abbeele [Minneapolis: University of Minnesota Press, 1988], 9). A differend—rather than simply a difference—between two parties takes place, Lyotard explains, 'when the "regulation" of the conflict that

opposes them is done in the idiom of one of the parties while the wrong suffered by the other is not signified in that idiom' (p. 9). Columbus and the Arawak are an extreme version of such a case. But it would not necessarily have been better had Columbus recognized the incommensurability of Spanish and native cultural constructions of reality. For such a recognition was in the early 16th century precisely the argument of those who sought to deny the natives any right to have rights. Thus, as Anthony Pagden points out, the jurist Palacios Rubios had argued in 1513 that a society that did not possess property relations (and hence did not live within a legitimate civil community) could not for that reason claim on behalf of any of its individuals *dominium rerum* when confronted by invaders attempting to seize their lands. In other words, a full recognition of the profound disparity between the indigenous culture and that of the invaders would not necessarily lead to what we regard as equity: on the contrary, it could lead to a justification for seizure. See, similarly, the argument made in 1550 by Juan Ginés de Sepúlveda that 'since no Indian society had had a monetary economy, no Indian could be said to have exercised any rights over any precious metal. These were, therefore, still a common part of Adam's patrimony, to which the Spaniards had a high moral claim by having traded metals which had been useless in the ancient Indian world for such useful things as iron, European agricultural techniques, horses, donkeys, goats, pigs, sheep, and so on' (Anthony Pagden, 'Dispossessing the Barbarian: the Language of Spanish Thomism and the Debate over the Property Rights of the American Indians,' in *The Languages of Political Theory in Early-Modern Europe*, ed. Anthony Pagden [Cambridge: Cambridge University Press, 1987], 81, 92).

25. For an illuminating discussion of the problem of cultural incompatibility, see Don F. McKenzie, 'The Sociology of a Text: Oral Culture, Literacy and Print in Early New England,' *The Social History of Language*, ed. Peter Burke and Roy Porter (Cambridge: Cambridge University Press, 1987), 161–96.
26. Vitoria's refutation of the claim in the 1530s is worth quoting:

> This title, too, is insufficient. This appears, in the first place, because fear and ignorance, which vitiate every choice, ought to be absent. But they were markedly operative in the cases of choice and acceptance under consideration, for the Indians did not know what they were doing; nay, they may not have understood what the Spaniards were seeking. Further, we find the Spaniards seeking it in armed array from an unwarlike and timid crowd. Further, inasmuch as the aborigines, as said above, had real lords and princes, the populace could not procure new lords without other reasonable cause, this being to the hurt of their former lords. Further, on the other hand, these lords themselves could not appoint a new prince without the assent of the populace. Seeing, then, that in such cases of choice and acceptance as these there are not present all the requisite elements of a valid choice, the title under review is utterly inadequate and unlawful for seizing and retaining the provinces in question. (xxxiii–xxxiv)

27. See Richard Epstein, 'Possession as the Root of Title,' in *Georgia Law Review* 13 (1979), 1221–43; Carol M. Rose, 'Possession as the Origin of Property,' *University of Chicago Law Review* 51 (1985), 73 ff.
28. Closed formalism is in fact one step beyond the marriage ritual whose

formulaic phrases after all are actually spoken in the presence of those who could, if they wished, 'speak now.' Columbus's required declarations are presumably made in the present tense, but their actual orientation is the future perfect: they are directed to those who will have heard that they were already made. The future perfect tense is a highly serviceable, if often unacknowledged, device in legal ritual.

29. 'Narrative,' writes Lyotard, 'is perhaps the genre of discourse within which the heterogeneity of phrase regimens, and even the heterogeneity of genres of discourse, have the easiest time passing unnoticed. . . . The narrative function is redeeming in itself. It acts as if the occurrence, with its potentiality of differends, could come to completion, or as if there were a last word' (*The Differend*, 151).
30. Francisco de Vitoria, in *The Spanish Origin of International Law*, ed. Scott, pp. xxiv–xxv.
31. See Anthony Pagden, *The Fall of Natural Man: The American Indian and the Origins of Comparative Ethnology* (Cambridge: Cambridge University Press, 1982). Pagden's remarkable book makes it clear that the most sustained and intellectually coherent challenge to the Spanish claim to possession was mounted on formal principles by Spanish jurists and theologians.
32. Gonzalo Fernandez de Oviedo y Valdes, *General and Natural History of the Indies*, trans. Earl Raymond Hewitt and Theodor Terrones, 2 vols. (Madrid: Royal Academy of History, 1851), i. 36–40 [I. 1. 1. iii].
33. Pagden, *The Fall of Natural Man*, 30.
34. Giuliano Gliozzi, *Adamo e il nuovo mondo. La nascita dell'antropologia come ideologia coloniale: dalle genealogie bibliche alle teorie razziali (1500–1700)* (Florence: La nuova Italia editrice, 1976), 47. 'O the profound wisdom and knowledge of the Most High,' writes Rocha, 'that after so many centuries ordained that these islands would be returned by Columbus to the Spanish crown.'
35. See ibid. 15–48. The evidence for the Welsh claim includes Montezuma's testimony that he and his people are descended from foreigners, along with what seemed to a Welsh observer the obvious linguistic parallels. (Cf. *New American World, A Documentary History of North America to 1612*, ed. David Beers Quinn, 5 vols. [New York: Arno Press and Hector Bye, 1979], i. 66–8.)
36. Montezuma is said to have asked Cortés why the strangers had such a hunger for gold, and Cortés is said to have replied that Spaniards had a disease about the heart, for which the only cure was gold.
37. The drive to bring experience under discursive control is inseparable from the task of ethical justification and legitimation. The disastrous epidemic diseases that afflicted the Indians may ultimately have proved a more decisive historical factor than the Spanish atrocities, but the ethically compelling concern is an inner account of what guides actions, that is, an account of intentions. I should add that 16th-century observers attempted to moralize the epidemic diseases in a variety of ways: as God's punishment of pagan unbelief, for example, or as the horrible consequence of Spanish cruelty. These moralizations may be understood as attempts to understand and hence imaginatively control the natural. Post-Enlightenment strategies for achieving such control have centered on science rather than religious polemic and have characteristically involved

searching for cures (or at least medical causes) on the one hand and searching for means to inflict disease (through biological agents) on the other.

38. J. L. Austin, *How to Do Things with Words*, ed. J. O. Urmson and Marina Sbisà (Cambridge, Mass.: Harvard University Press, 1975). See also the remarks of John Searle about the conditions that must be met for a declaration, proclamation or any speech act that involves a 'double direction of fit' (the world to the word and the word to the world) to be valid (John Searle and Daniel Vanderverken, *Foundations of Illocutionary Logic* [Cambridge: Cambridge University Press, 1985], 52 ff.)
39. It is not entirely clear whom the Spanish imagined the Grand Khan to be or how they conceived of his rule, but it is clear that they imagined that there was some kind of empire with a centralized authority structure.
40. *Select Documents*, ed. Jane, i. 14 (*su mayoral ó rey*). Men, Columbus writes, appear generally to be content with one woman, but the chief is given as many as twenty wives. And these wives, he implies, have economic value: 'It appears to me that the women work more than the men.' Columbus is uncertain, however, if this social arrangement entails a notion of private property: 'I have not been able to learn if they hold private property [*bienes propios*]; what seemed to me to appear was that, in that which one had, all took a share, especially of eatable things' (i. 14).
41. Quoted in Etienne Grisel, 'The Beginnings of International Law and General Public Law Doctrine: Francisco de Vitoria's *De Indiis prior*,' in *First Images of America: The Impact of the New World on the Old*, ed. Fredi Chiappelli, 2 vols. (Berkeley: University of California Press, 1976), 1. 309. See also Pagden, for a wonderfully detailed and intelligent discussion of the categories at issue here.
42. *Select Documents*, ed. Jane, ii. 66.
43. For the texts of the two drafts of this famous papal bull, see *Bullarum diplomatum et privilegiorum sanctorum romanorum pontificum* (Rome: Franco and Henrico Dalmazzo, 1858).
44. *Politics*, 1253a, 28–9.
45. In the letter to Santangel, Columbus mentions an island he calls 'Quaris,' which is inhabited 'by a people who are regarded in all the islands as very fierce and who eat human flesh' (i. 14). On Columbus's perceptions of cannibalism, see the remarkable book by Peter Hulme, *Colonial Encounters: Europe and the Native Caribbean, 1492–1797* (London: Methuen, 1986); Michael Palencia-Roth, 'Cannibalism and the New Man of Latin America in the 15th- and 16th-century European Imagination,' in *Comparative Civilizations Review* 12 (1985), 1–27.
46. Earlier in the letter he casually mentions that he 'understood sufficiently from other Indians, *whom I had already taken*, that this land was nothing but an island' (i. 4) (emphasis added). And in his journal entry for October 12, 1492, he writes, 'Our Lord pleasing, at the time of my departure I will take six of them from here to Your Highnesses that they may learn to speak' (*Diario*, 69). For a discussion of the policy of kidnapping, see Chapter 4.
47. See Bartolomé de Las Casas, *History of the Indies*, trans. Andrée M. Collard (New York: Harper & Row, 1971), 127.
48. See Alain Milhou, *Colón y su mentalidad mesianica*, 289: 'El "negocio" o la

"negociación" de las Indias tiene, como la palabra "empresa," unas connotaciones dobles: una mercantil, la del mundo de los "negocios" en que se crió Colón, pero también otra religiosa, la del *negotium crucis* de los cruzados as cual equiparaba su "negocio" ultramarino. . . .'

49. For the paradoxicality of Christian imperialism, see the letter on the 3rd voyage: 'I came with the mission to your royal presence, as being the most exalted of Christian princes and so ardently devoted to the Faith and to its increase. . . . On this matter I spent six or seven years of deep anxiety, expounding, as well as I could, how great service might in this be rendered to the Lord, by proclaiming abroad His holy name and His faith to so many peoples, which was all a thing of so great excellence and for the fair fame of great princes and for a notable memorial for them. It was needful also to speak of the temporal gain therein. . . .' (ii. 1). It is possible, of course, to see such passages as evidence not of paradox but of unresolved tension, comparable to the class tension explored with great intelligence by David Quint in 'The Boat of Romance and Renaissance Epic' (*Romance: Generic Transformation from Chrétien de Troyes to Cervantes*, ed. Kevin and Marina Brownlee [Hanover, NH: University Press of New England, 1985], 178–202). Quint argues that the central contradiction was between an aristocratic account of the voyages of discovery and a 'bourgeois' account; the former allied itself with epic, the latter with romance. Columbus seems to me to combine both with a reckless disregard for literary decorum.

50. Claude Lévi-Strauss quotes (or paraphrases) the finding of the commission of the monks of the Order of St. Jerome in 1517: the Indian 'is better off as a slave, among men, than as an animal on his own' (*Tristes Tropiques*, trans. John Russell [New York: Atheneum, 1961; orig. pub. 1955], 80).

51. 'Because we wish to be informed by civil lawyers, canonists and theologians whether we may, with a good conscience, sell these Indians or not' (Pagden, *Fall of Natural Man*, 31). Pagden notes that one year later the queen 'ordered all the Indian slaves in Seville to be taken from their masters and sent back to their former homes.'

52. In his log-book entry for October 12, Columbus also emphasizes that the Indians were friendly, so friendly in fact 'that it was a marvel' [*quedarō tạnto nro(s?) q̄ era maravilla*] (*Diario*, 64–5).

53. There are obviously some parallels between the role of the marvelous in the early literature of discovery and the stylistic feature of contemporary Latin American writing, known as the 'real maravilloso.' See J. Edgardo Rivera Martínez, 'La literatura geografica del siglo xvi en Francia como antecedente de lo real maravilloso,' in *Revista de Critica Litteraria Latinoamericana* 5/9 (1979), 7–19. But my aim is to insist on the very specific purposes served by the marvelous in late 15th- and early 16th-century writing.

54. Columbus appears to have been fluent in Castilian (all of his surviving writings, including letters he wrote to Italian correspondents, are in Castilian), and he had what by our standards would be reasonably impressive linguistic gifts. See Pauline Watts, 'Prophecy and Discovery': 'Columbus did not have the advanced, specialized education of a professional academic. But he did read and annotate works composed in Latin (for example, d'Ailly's *Imago*

mundi and Pius II's *Historia*), Castilian (Alfonso de Palencia's translation of Plutarch's *Lives*), and Italian (Cristoforo Landino's translation of Pliny's *Naturalis historia*),' 75. See likewise V. I. Milani, *The Written Language of Christopher Columbus* (Buffalo: State University of New York at Buffalo [for *Forum Italicum*], 1973) and Paolo Emilia Taviani, *Christopher Columbus: The Grand Design*, trans. Taviani and William Weaver (London: Orbis, 1985). It is very unlikely that Columbus could not, if he had wished, have found a synonym for 'marvelous.'

55. Jane's rendering of 'maravillarme' as 'to cause you to wonder' may be misleading. The phrase appears to mean 'to show or perform my wonder.'
56. Jacques Le Goff, *L'Imaginaire médiéval* (Paris: Gallimard, 1985), 17–39.
57. See esp. Baxter Hathaway, *Marvels and Commonplaces: Renaissance Literary Criticism* (New York: Random House, 1968), 133–51. See also Hathaway's *The Age of Criticism: The Late Renaissance in Italy* (Ithaca, NY: Cornell University Press, 1962). Le Goff, however, denies the ultimate compatibility of Christianity and the marvelous: 'Si je simplifiais ma réflexion sur le merveilleux dans l'Occident médiéval jusqu'à la caricature, je dirais qu'en définitive il n'y a pas de merveilleux chrétien et que le christianisme, en tout case le christianisme médiéval, est allergique au merveilleux' (*L'Imaginaire médiéval*, 37).
58. i. 12; cf. the skeptical remark by Andrés Bernáldez, who believes that these stories are told by some Indians in mockery of others who wear clothing (i. 128).
59. Samuel Eliot Morison's translation of this passage (*Admiral of the Ocean Sea: A Life of Christopher Columbus* [Boston: Little, Brown, 1942], 309–10) is rather more flattering to men: the mermaids 'were not as beautiful as they are painted, although to some extent they have a human appearance in the face.'
60. In the *Diario*, Columbus repeatedly uses the term 'maravilla' and its variants to characterize the natural features of the world he has discovered: the trees and fish (Oct. 16), the groves and the birdsong, and the diversity, size, and difference of the birds (Oct. 21), the sheer number of islands (Nov. 14), the harbors (Nov. 26), the fields and the general beauty of the lands and the trees (Nov. 27), the beauty of a harbor (Dec. 6), the beauty of a river (Dec. 7), the valleys, rivers, and good water (Dec. 16), the green mountains (Dec. 21), the green and cultivated mountains (Jan. 9).
61. In fact the highest peak on Teneriffe is considerably higher than the highest peak on Hispaniola.
62. Columbus (or, alternatively, Las Casas) evidently regards the point as worth repeating. In the same entry, he writes, 'all or most of the Indians began to run to the town, which must have been near, to bring him more food and parrots and other things of those that they had, with such open hearts that it was a marvel' (*Diario*, 259).
63. There is at least a latent polemical irony in this passage that makes one suspect that Las Casas is exercising a more active, shaping presence in the transcription than he admits, but in the absence of the original text there is no way of confirming the suspicion.
64. Several log-book entries record this Indian belief and thereby seem to indicate that Columbus had some curiosity about the native view of the encounter. On

Oct. 21, Columbus notes that 'it is true that any little thing given to them, as well as our coming, they considered great marvels; and they believed that we had come from the heavens' (*Diario*, 109). Columbus does not quite put the two observations together and reflect that they might well treasure even almost worthless articles—bits of broken crockery, cheap cloth, rusted nails—if they believe that the givers come from the heavens. Why doesn't he put them together? Perhaps because it would have led to the ironic self-recognition so characteristic of Mandeville—just as we collect the relics (bits of wood supposedly from the cross, nails, shrivelled pieces of skin, and so forth) associated with those we regard as sanctified, so do these people collect relics from us.

On Nov. 5, Columbus notes similarly, 'The Indians touched them and kissed their hands and feet, marveling [*maravillandose*] and believing that the Spaniards came from the heavens, and so they gave them to understand' (*Diario*, 137). The last phrase, in Las Casas's transcription, is ambiguous, but it would seem to mean that the Spanish gave the Indians to understand that they, the Spanish, came from the heavens; if so, we are dealing not with a naïve misapprehension on the part of the natives but with an improvisatory lie.

In an important article on Cabeza de Vaca's *Naufragios* (in *Representations* 33 [1991], 163–99), Rolena Adorno suggests that the misapprehension was Spanish rather than Indian. She observes that the 'interpreters of Columbus's text, from Las Casas to Don Hernando Colón and Hernán Perez de Oliva, all claim that the natives meant that the Spaniards "came down from heaven."' But she notes that in a phrase dropped from later editions Cabeza de Vaca offers a more plausible gloss; he writes that 'Among all these peoples, it was held for very certain that we came from the sky, because about all the things that they do not understand nor have information regarding their origins, they say that such phenomena come from the sky' (183).

65. Columbus does not seem greatly interested in disabusing the natives of their mistaken beliefs about the Spanish, though he does tell them that he comes from another kingdom and not from heaven. When, on the second voyage, he explains to an Indian cacique that he serves the rulers of that kingdom, the cacique is surprised: 'And the Indian, greatly marvelling [*muy maravillado*], replied to the interpreter, saying: "How? Has this admiral another lord, and does he yield obedience?" And the Indian interpreter said: "To the king and to the queen of Castile, who are the greatest sovereigns in the world." And forthwith he recounted to the cacique and to the old man and to all the other Indians the things which he had seen in Castile and the marvels of Spain, and told them of the great cities and fortresses and churches, and of the people and horses and animals, and of the great nobility and wealth of the sovereigns and great lords, and of the kinds of food, and of the festivals and tournaments which he had seen, and of bull-fighting, and of that which he had learned of the wars' (i. 154). It is possible that Columbus regarded the arousal of wonder in the Indians as a potential source of power. Other writers in the period anticipate that such an arousal would lead to domination: see, for example, Hieronymus Müntzer's letter to D. Joao II (1493): 'O what glory you would gain, if you made the habitable Orient known to the Occident, and what

profits would its commerce give you, for you would make those islands of the Orient tributaries, and their kings amazed [*sus reyes maravillados*] would quietly submit to your sovereignty!' (in Morison, *Admiral of the Ocean Sea*, 77).

66. We can also cite Andrés Bernáldez, with whom Columbus stayed on his return from the second voyage, and to whom he supplied information about the discoveries. Bernáldez notes that the Spanish saw 'more than a million and a half cormorants' all together in the sky and were amazed (*obieron por maravilla*) (i. 148). See, likewise, the 'marvelous' pastoral scene by the fountain (i. 132).
67. On Columbus and the location of Paradise, see Alain Milhou, *Colón y su mentalidad mesianica*, 407 ff.
68. Vitoria considers the possibility of a Spanish title to the Indies based upon a 'special grant from God.' He concludes that 'it would be hazardous to give credence to one who asserts a prophecy against the common law and against the rules of Scripture, unless his doctrine were confirmed by miracles.' Columbus, of course, explicitly claims that the discovery of the Indies had been prophesied by Isaiah and others, but he seems wary of claiming miraculous confirmation. Vitoria does not believe anyone has made the latter claim: 'Now, no such [miracles] are adduced by prophets of this type' (p. xxxiv). See Etienne Grisel, 'The Beginnings of International Law,' in *First Images of America*, i. 312.

    Las Casas does, however, quote Columbus as saying, upon the discovery of Trinidad, that God's 'exalted power guides me, and in such manner that He receives much service and your highnesses much pleasure, since it is certain that the discovery of this land in this place was as great a miracle as the discovery of land on the first voyage' (Jane ii. 13 n.). In Spanish writing of the period, however, 'maravilla' could on occasion function as the equivalent of miracle. See, for example, the anti-Semitic passage by the Franciscan Juan de Pineda: 'Llegado a Jerusalén, restaurará el templo de Salomón, en el cual . . . se sentará blasfemando de la divinidad del Redentor; y con esto se le darán los judios sus parientes muy obedientes, y habiendo él destruido los lugares sanctos, donde nuestro Redentor hizo sus maravillas, enviará sus mensajeros por el mundo. . .' (quoted in Milhou, 446).
69. Quoted in J. V. Cunningham, *Woe or Wonder: The Emotional Effect of Shakespearean Tragedy* (Denver: Denver University Press, 1951), 82.
70. *Enneades*, 1. 6. 4, quoted in Cunningham, 67.
71. Hathaway, 66–9. Hathaway's account of Patrizi is taken largely from Bernard Weinberg, *A History of Literary Criticism in the Italian Renaissance*, 2 vols (Chicago: University of Chicago Press, 1961). See Francesco Patrizi, *Della poetica*, ed. Danilo Aguzzi Barbagli (Florence, Istituto nazionale di studi sul Rinascimento, 1969–71), vol. ii. For Patrizi, the poet is not only a 'facitore del mirabile' but also a 'mirabile facitore' (Weinberg, ii. 773).
72. For Robortelli, Weinberg writes, 'in the last analysis, the poet is virtually permitted to discard all concern for credibility in order to exploit all the available means of achieving the marvelous and the pleasure connected with it' (Weinberg, i. 397–8)..
73. *Poetica d'Aristotele vulgarizzata et sposta* (1570), quoted in Weinberg, i. 69. Castelvetro's theory, like that of many of his contemporaries, is centrally

concerned with the problem of obtaining the credence of the audience—this rhetorical motive is what makes their analysis so interesting in the context of the New World discourse, concerned as it was with a comparable problem and willing to alter the truth to achieve its effect: 'In all such considerations of historical truth or natural probability or necessity and verisimilitude, the primary aim is not the imitation of nature for the sake of making the poem resemble nature but rather the resemblance to nature for the sake of obtaining the credence of the audience' (ibid., i. 58).

74. *Discorso in difesa della 'Commedia' del divino poeta Dante* (1572), in Allan H. Gilbert, *Literary Criticism: Plato to Dryden* (Detroit: Wayne State University Press, 1962), 371. Cf. Lorenzo Giacomini: tragedy 'pleases through the marvelous, demonstrating that a thing not believed can readily come to pass' (*Sopra la purgazione della tragedia* [1586]), in Weinberg, i. 628.

75. *Discorsi del poema heroico* (*c.*1575–80), in Weinberg, i. 341. Tasso, Weinberg writes, 'thinks of the marvelous as consisting of those events which do not enter into natural probability. How, then, can they be credible and acceptable in the poem? The answer is in the beliefs, even the faith, of the audience. For Christians believe the miracles of the Bible, know them to be true even though they are improbable. This is the only kind of credibility which the poet seeks' (i. 630). One might note, for a pagan precedent, Aristotle's remark that 'there is a probability of things happening also against probability' (*Poetics* 25. 1461^{b}15).

76. All of these positions may be found in Hathaway, *passim*.

77. It is important to recognize that this use of the term 'marvelous' is not Columbus's individual signature; it is the mark of a shared emotional effect and a common rhetoric. Hence, for example, Dr Chanca who accompanied Columbus on the second voyage notes that the natives 'have many tools, such as hatchets and axes, made of stone, so handsome and so fashioned, that it is marvelous how they are able to make them without iron' (i. 68). Even when Chanca expresses distaste for the natives, he does so in the idiom of the marvelous. 'These people,' he writes, 'are so degraded (*tan bestial*) that they have not intelligence enough to seek out a suitable place in which to live. As for those who live on the shore, it is marvelous how barbarously they build [*es maravilla cuan bestialmente edifcan*]' (i. 52). It is striking, however, how infrequently Columbus uses the language of the marvelous to express, as Chanca does here, his disapproval or disdain.

78. In the years that followed, both were in fact called forth: the tears of Las Casas, on the one hand; the laughter of those stories of Indians declaring that the Pope was drunk or mad to think that he could give away what was not his.

79. Albertus Magnus, trans. in J. V. Cunningham, *Woe and Wonder* (Denver: Denver University Press, 1951), 79–80. I am greatly indebted to Cunningham's account of wonder. The intensity of the experience Albertus Magnus is attempting to define seems to me somewhat greater in the original:

> Nam omnes homines qui nunc in nostro tempore et primum ante nostra tempora philosophati sunt, non sunt moti ad philosophandum nisi admirative. Admirationem autem vocamus agoniam et suspensionem cordis in stuporem prodigii magni in sensum apparentis, ita quod cor systolem patitur. Proper quod etiam admiratio aliquid simile habet timori in motus cordis, qui est ex suspensione. Hujus igitur motus admirationis in

agonia et systole cordis est ex suspensione desiderii ad cognoscendam causam entis quod apparet prodigii: et ideo a principio cum adhuc rudes philosophari inceperunt, mirantes erant quaedam dubitabilium quae paratiora erant ad solvendum, sicut Pythagorici de numerorum passionibus, est de pari et impari, et perfecto et abundanti et diminuto numero. . . . Qui autem dubitant et admiratus, ignorans videtur: est enim admiratio motus ignorantis procedentis ad inquirendum, ut sciat causam ejus de quo miratus: cujus signum est, quia ipse Philomithes secundum hunc modum Philosophus est: quia fabula sua construitur ab ipso ex mirandis. (vi. 30)

(In Albertus Magnus, *Opera Omnia*, ed. Augustus Borgnet, 20 vols. [Paris: Ludovicus Vives, 1890] vi. 30 [I Metaphysicorum, tract. II, caput vi].)

80. In a response to the version of this chapter that I delivered at the University of Chicago, Professor Arnold Davidson suggested that it is important not to confound the theology of the marvelous in Albertus Magnus with the aesthetics of the marvelous that I have earlier discussed. For the poet, the arousal of wonder is one of the ends of art; for Albertus wonder is used up and vanishes when the mind actually comes to understand those phenomena by which it has been seized. The distinction seems to me significant, but I have argued here that it is deconstructed by the actual historical circumstances in which Columbus found himself. We may, in effect, take the vanishing of wonder to be a model for the way in which legal title absorbs the potentially disruptive power of the marvelous, a power that in these extraordinary circumstances legal formality none the less needs in order to make up for the deficiency at its center.

81. George R. Stewart, *Names on the Land: A Historical Account of Place-Naming in the United States*, rev. edn. (Boston: Houghton Mifflin, 1958), 12. Stewart cites the 'Instrucción dada por el Rey à Pedrarias Dávila': 'Arrived there by good providence, first of all you must give a name to the country as a whole, and to the cities, towns, and places.'

82. *Luther's Works*, vol. i: 'Lectures on Genesis,' chaps. 1–5, ed. Jaroslav Pelikan (St Louis: Concordia Publishing House, 1958), 119.

83. Francis Bacon, in *A Selection of His Works*, ed. Sidney Warhaft (New York: Odyssey, 1965), 21.

84. It is then a renaming such as the renaming of Jacob after his struggle with the mysterious man. 'He said to Jacob, "What is your name?" and he answered, "Jacob." The man said, "Your name shall no longer be Jacob, but Israel, because you strove with God and with men, and prevailed" ' (Gen. 32: 27–9). Such a context would place Columbus in the position of the messenger of God.

85. See Rudolf Schnackenburg, *Baptism in the Thought of St. Paul*, trans. G. R. Beasley-Murray (New York: Herder & Herder, 1964), 20: 'The naming of a person had the meaning of attaching the baptized to this person so that the baptized belonged to him. This is confirmed by exegesis; for the consequence and effect of baptism "in the name" of Christ may be gathered from a consideration of Paul's assertion, "you belong to Christ." ' (I owe this reference to Michael Ragussis.)

86. Morison, *Admiral*, 360.

87. See Paolo Emilio Taviani, *Christopher Columbus* (Paris, 1980), 38–40. Columbus's son Ferdinand wrote about the 'mystery' of his father's name and linked that

mystery to the original baptism: 'If we consider the common surname of his forebears, we may say that he was truly Columbus or Dove, because he carried the grace of the Holy Ghost to that New World which he discovered, showing those people who knew Him not Who was God's beloved son, as the Holy Ghost did in the figure of a dove when St. John baptized Christ; and because over the waters of the ocean, like the dove of Noah's ark, he bore the olive branch and oil of baptism, to signify that those people who had been shut up in the ark of darkness and confusion were to enjoy peace and union with the Church' (quoted in Pauline Moffitt Watts, 'Prophecy and Discovery', 101).

88. *First Images*, ii. 619.

89. See Columbus's *Libro de las profeciás*, in *Raccolta di documenti e studi pubblicati dalla R. Commissione Colombiana pel quarto centenario dalla scoperta dell'America* (Rome: Ministero Sella pubblica istruzione, 1894), pt. 1, vol. ii, *Scritti di Cristoforo Colombo*, ed. C. de Lollis, 76–160. In the unfinished letter to the Catholic monarchs with which he intended to introduce the *Book of Prophecies*, Columbus says that his decision to sail westward was inspired by the Holy Ghost:

> Animated by a heavenly fire, I came to your highnesses: all who heard of my enterprise mocked at it; all the sciences I had acquired profited me nothing; seven years did I pass in your royal court, disputing the case with persons of great authority and learned in all the arts, and in the end they decided that all was vain. In your highnesses alone remained faith and constancy. Who will doubt that this light was from the Holy Scriptures, illuminating you as well as myself with rays of marvelous brightness? [*con rrayos de claridad maravillosos*]

(Trans. in John Leddy Phelan, *The Millennial Kingdom of the Franciscans in the New World*, 2nd rev. edn. [Berkeley: University of California Press, 1970], 20. For the original see *Raccolta di documenti*, 79–80.)

On Columbus and prophecy, see Pauline Moffitt Watts, 'Prophecy and Discovery,' 73–102; Marjorie Reeves, *Joachim of Fiore and the Prophetic Future* (London: SPCK, 1976), 128–9. On his deathbed, Columbus took the habit of a Franciscan.

90. For the notion of the land 'conforming' to the name, see Columbus's relation of his third voyage: 'I called this place there *Jardines*, for it corresponded to that name [*porque así conforman por el nombre*]' (Jane ii. 24). See, similarly, the naming of Trinidad (ii. 12). There is, of course, in such naming an element both of magical hope and of tactical cunning. For a candid glimpse of the latter, see Lopez Vaz (1586), in Purchas xii. 292: 'The discoverer of these islands named them the Isles of Solomon, to the end that the Spaniards supposing them to be those Isles from whence Solomon fetched Gold to adorne the Temple at Jerusalem, might be the more desirous to goe and inhabit the same.'

91. ii. 90–2. The reference to the keys is paraphrased from Seneca's *Medea*. On Columbus and the figure of David there is a substantial literature, including a long-standing debate about the status of Judaism in Columbus's thought. See Alain Milhou, *Colón y su mentalidad mesianica*, esp. 230–51; Juan Gil, *Colón y la Casa Santa*, 'Historiografía y Bibliografía Americanistas,' E.E.H.A., 21 (1977), 125–35.

Notes to Chapter Four

1. Las Casas quotes Columbus: 'It pleased Our Lord, by His exalted majesty, that there were first seen three mountains, I say three mountains, all at one time and at one view. Of His goodness, His exalted power guides me, and in such manner that He receives much service and your highnesses much pleasure, since it is certain that the discovery of this land in this place was as great a miracle as the discovery of land on the first voyage' (*Select Documents*, ed. Jane, ii. 13).
2. See Todorov, *The Conquest of America: The Question of the Other*, trans. Richard Howard (New York: Harper & Row, 1984; orig. French edn. 1982), 14–50.
3. In David B. Quinn (ed.), *New American World: A Documentary History of North America to 1612*, 5 vols. (New York: Arno Press & Hector Bye, 1979), i. 77, 134, 76.
4. There are interesting differences between the signs Columbus collected in the years before his voyage and those collected on the voyage itself, signs coded to the place in which the signs are found: the piece of wood picked up off Cape St Vincent was interesting because it did not appear to be worked by iron and hence suggested a culture other than Europe; the piece of wood picked up on October 11 was interesting because it appeared to be worked by iron and hence suggested the proximity of the Indies.
5. Todorov, *Conquest of America*, 17. I should emphasize that Todorov is describing a tendency rather than an invariable habit of mind. On occasion Columbus was indeed able to use unexpected signs to form new hypotheses. Hence, for example, in the face of an apparently anomalous reading on the ships' magnetic compasses, Columbus proposed that it was the North Star that moved and not the needles.
6. Richard Mulcaster, *The First Part of the Elementarie* [1582] (Menston: Scolar Press, 1970), chap. 22. For a remarkable deconstructive reading of Mulcaster's *Elementarie*, see Jonathan Goldberg, *Writing Matter: From the Hands of the English Renaissance* (Stanford, Cal.: Stanford University Press, 1990), 28–55.
7. If such a view of travel seems implausible, consider Ben Jonson's epigram to William Roe:

> Roe (and my joy to name) thou'rt now to go
> Countries and climes, manners and men to know,
> To extract and choose the best of all these known,
> And those to turn to blood and make thine own.
> May winds as soft as breath of kissing friends
> Attend thee hence; and there may all thy ends,
> As the beginnings here, prove purely sweet,
> And perfect in a circle always meet.
> So when we, blest with thy return, shall see
> Thyself, with thy first thoughts, brought home by thee,
> We each to other may this voice inspire:
> This is that good Aeneas, passed through fire,

Through seas, storms, tempests; and embarked for hell,
Came back untouched. This man hath travailed well.

8. Perhaps in excitement or exhaustion, Columbus ran the log-book entry for October 12 together with that for October 11.
9. There are frequent mentions in Marco Polo of the wearing of elaborately worked cotton or silk strips of cloth, both as scarves around the head and as loin-cloths. See, for example, the description of the people of Maabar, in India (Marco Polo, *The Travels*, trans. Ronald Lathan [Baltimore: Penguin, 1958], 262).
10. Cf. the scene of mutual dancing in Africa, reported in Vasco da Gama's *Roteiro* (1497–8): The inhabitants of what is now Port Elizabeth, South Africa, 'forthwith began to play on four or five flutes, some producing high notes and others low ones, thus making a pretty harmony for negroes who are not expected to be musicians; and they danced in the style of negroes. The captain-major [i.e. da Gama] ordered the trumpets to be sounded, and we, in the boats, danced, and the captain-major did so likewise when he rejoined us' (*A Journal of the First Voyage of Vasco da Gama 1497–99*, trans. and ed. E. G. Ravenstein, Hakluyt Soc. 99 [London: Hakluyt Society, 1898], 11).
11. Columbus seems here to be suppressing, in order to attract royal support, the linguistic diversity that he himself notes in his log-book entries near the end of his first voyage: 'He says that he understood some words, and through them he says he found out other things, and that the Indians he brought with him understood more, although they found differences between the languages, because of the great distance between the lands' (*Diario*, 331 [Jan. 13]); 'There, he says, they have no iron or other metal that has been seen, although in a few days one cannot learn much about a country, both because of the difficulty of the language, which the Admiral did not understand except by guessing, and because the Indians did not know, in a few days, what he was trying to do' (*Diario*, 339 [Jan. 15]).
12. *New American World*, i. 287.
13. 'Jacques Cartier's First Account of the New Land, Called New France, Discovered in the Year 1534,' in *New American World*, i. 299.
14. Dionise Settle, in Richard Hakluyt, *Principal Navigations*, vii. 230.
15. 'By this meanes and other witchcrafts, which he teacheth them,' Hawkins continues, 'he possesseth them, and causeth them to doe what pleaseth him.' See Sir Richard Hawkins (1593–4), in Samuel Purchas, *Hakluytus Posthumus, or Purchas His Pilgrimes*, trans. R. S. Pine-Coffin (Baltimore: Penguin, 1961), xvii. 117–18.
16. *Confessions* (Penguin), 29. On the use of gestures in communicating with the Indians, see the useful collection of passages in Emma Martinell Gifre, *Aspectos Lingüisticos de Descubrimiento y de la Conquista*, 21–42.
17. See also Cicero, *De oratore*, 3. 59. 223. For a 15th-century version, see Guillaume Tardif, *Rhetorice artis ac oratorie facultatis compendium* (with other works by G. Tardif) [Paris, ?1475], fo. [75r]. In a richly documented paper, 'Ideas on Gesture and Universal Languages *c.*1550–*c.*1650,' Dilwyn Knox, to whom I owe these references, argues that the notion of gesture as a universal

language was only developed theoretically and methodologically in the wake of Ramism in the later 16th century (in *New Perspectives on Renaissance Thought: Essays in the History of Science, Education and Philosophy, in Memory of Charles B. Schmitt*, ed. John Henry and Sarah Hutton [London: Duckworth, 1990], 101–36).

18. See my 'Learning to Curse: Aspects of Linguistic Colonialism in the Sixteenth Century,' in *First Images of America*, ii. 561–80; Tzvetan Todorov, *The Conquest of America*, esp. 25–33.
19. The Algonquians, like many peoples in both North and South America, seem to have been devoted to oratory. On 'the duty to speak,' see Pierre Clastres, *Society against the State*, trans. Robert Hurley (New York: Zone Books, 1987; orig. French pub. Paris: Minuit, 1974), esp. 151–5.
20. In Richard Hakluyt, *Principal Navigations*, viii. 300–1.
21. Cabeza de Vaca, in *New American World*, ii. 51. It is in this same passage that Cabeza de Vaca remarks that had he and his companions been able to explain themselves perfectly, they should have converted all the Indians. The acknowledgement of linguistic distance and the collapse of that distance exist side by side, without an apparent awareness of contradiction.
22. Peter Martyr, *The Decades of the Newe World* (*De orbe novo*), trans. Richard Eden, decade 3, bk. 9, in *The First Three English Books on America*, ed. Edward Arber (Birmingham: Turnbull & Spears, 1885), 117.
23. Bartholomé de Las Casas, *History of the Indies*, trans. and ed. Andrée Collard (New York: Harper & Row, 1971), 241.
24. Cf. Las Casas, 50–2, 130–1. See also my extended discussion (from which I have drawn several sentences in this account) in 'Learning to Curse: Aspects of Linguistic Colonialism in the Sixteenth Century'; and Inga Clendinnen, 'Fierce and Unnatural Cruelty: Cortés, Signs, and the Conquest of Mexico,' in A. Grafton and A. Blair (eds.), *The Transmission of Culture in Early Modern Europe* (Philadelphia: University of Pennsylvania Press, 1990), 84–130.
25. 'Memorial of Hernando de Escalante Fontaneda on the Florida Indians,' in *New American World*, v. 11–12.
26. Text in Sir Arthur Helps, *The Spanish Conquest of America and its Relation to the History of Slavery and to the Government of Colonies*, ed. M. Oppenheim, 4 vols. (London, 1855–61; rpt. New York: AMS Press, 1966), i. 269.
27. Bartolomé de Las Casas, *History of the Indies*, 196. For a further discussion of linguistic transparency, see my 'Learning To Curse: Aspects of Linguistic Colonialism in the Sixteenth Century,' ii. 561–80.
28. Escalante is reiterating the policy of the commander under whom he had served, Pedro Menéndez de Avilés.
29. Jean de Léry, *History of a Voyage*, trans. Janet Whatley, 164.
30. One of the advocates of the Indians, Bernadino de Minaya, recalls that on his return to Spain from the New World, 'I went on foot, begging, to Valladolid, where I visited the cardinal and informed him that Friar Domingo [de Betanzos, an exponent of the theory that the Indians were beasts] knew neither the Indians' language nor their true nature. I told him of their ability and the right they had to become Christians. He replied that I was much

deceived, for he understood that the Indians were no more than parrots' (quoted in Lewis Hanke, 'Pope Paul III and the American Indians,' *Harvard Theological Review* 30 [1937], 84).

31. For a people who seemed to lack a concept of economic value or an interest in exchange, see Joseph Banks, *The Endeavour Journal of Joseph Banks, 1768–1771*, ed. J. C. Beaglehole (Sydney: Angus & Robertson, 1962), ii. 125: 'These people [at the Endeavour River, east coast of Australia] seemed to have no Idea of traffick nor could we teach them; indeed it seemd that we had no one thing on which they set a value equal to induce them to part with the smallest trifle; except one fish which weighd about 1/2 a pound that they brought us as a kind of token of peace no one in the ship I beleive procurd from them the smallest article. They readily received the things we gave them but never would understand our signs when we askd for returns.'
32. 'Discoverie made by John Guy [of Bristow] in Newfoundland in anno 1612,' British Library MS, fos. 54–5; a version is published in Purchas, xix. 410–24.
33. The fact that the Indian signs are not self-evidently peaceful is indicated by the touch of hermeneutical self-consciousness in the phrase 'we took to be for . . . .' At the same time, by the early 17th century there had been a history of contact between Bristol merchants and the natives of Newfoundland.
34. Herodotus writes of the Carthaginians trading in West Africa that when they

> come there and disembark their cargo, they range it along the seashore and go back again to their boats and light a smoke signal. The natives, as soon as they see the smoke, come down to the shore and then deposit gold to pay for the merchandise and retreat again, away from the goods. The Carthaginians disembark and look; if they think that the price deposited is fair for the merchandise, they take it up and go home again. If not, they go back to their boats and sit there. The natives approach and bring more gold in addition to what they have put there already, until such time as the Carthaginians are persuaded to accept what is offered. They say that thus neither party is ill-used; for the Carthaginians do not take the gold until they have the worth of their merchandise, nor do the natives touch the merchandise until the Carthaginians have taken the gold.

(In *The History*, trans. David Grene [Chicago: University of Chicago Press, 1987], 352–3.) This mode of exchange—without personal contact, without go-betweens, without the necessity of language learning—is, in the context of the exchanges I have been describing, a kind of utopian model. For its continuation into the modern period, see Lars Sundström, 'The Trade of Guinea,' *Studiea Ethnographica Upsaliensia* 24 (1965), 22–31.

35. This was not, we should add, the beginning of a model intercultural history. The Indians and the English had agreed to meet in a year's time, but at the appointed time, when the Indians were waiting, a fisherman came to the place and being alarmed at the sight of the Indians he shot at them—the Indians ran off, thinking that the shot came from one of Guy's ships, and they subsequently refused to trade. The British Library's keeper of MSS, C. R. Dodwell, notes that Guy's account is 'the only record of friendly relations between Englishmen and the Beothucks.'
36. *New American World*, i. 299.
37. This is why it is singularly appropriate that missionaries begin by learning

languages, but the whole Christian ethos involves the proposition that one must submit in order to transcend or, as we might rather say, dominate.

38. Used as the epigraph to Inga Clendinnen, *Ambivalent Conquests: Maya and Spaniard in Yucatan, 1517–1570* (Cambridge: Cambridge University Press, 1987).
39. Purchas, xvi. 56.
40. Purchas, xviii. 317–18.
41. Columbus casually mentions that the *Niña* was pulling a dugout at her stern (*Diario*, 81), so evidently he had ordered several of the boats taken. The early log-book entries call the native boats *almadias*, a term for West African dugouts; Columbus did not learn the native term *canoa* until Oct. 6. He also noted that the larger boats were 'worked marvelously in the fashion of the land' (*Diario*, 69).
42. Later, after Columbus's departure, they will have another politics, if we are to assume that the deaths of all the Spaniards left by Columbus did not take place exactly as reported.
43. *Select Documents*, ed. Jane, i. 88.
44. Inga Clendinnen, *Ambivalent Conquests*, 52.
45. For another instance of the Christians forced to rely on unreliable Indians as interpreters and guides, see the account of De Soto in Florida, where an Indian boy, who asked to be baptized and was named Pedro, proves himself a liar but is nevertheless kept on because of his knowledge of various dialects: 'No credit was given to him because of the lies in which he had been found; but everything was endured in him because of the need of him to tell what the Indians said' (*New American World*, ii. 116).
46. Michael Lok, in Richard Collinson (ed.), *The Three Voyages of Martin Frobisher* (London: Hakluyt Society, 1867), 82.
47. To cite a single example out of hundreds: 'The King of these Orethusien, gave our Captaine foure Plates of gold, and foure silver Rings, which they put about their armes: but the Indians weare the Plates of gold on their foreheads for ornament, as our Nobles doe their Chaines, or Collars of Esses hanged about their neckes. For these things our Captaine gave the King of the Indians an Hatchet, Knives, and Beades, or Pater-Nosters, Barbar Scizzars, and such like' (Hulderike Schnirdel [1534–54], in Purchas, xvii. 35–6).
48. See the Earl of Cumberland on the Dominican natives, 'men wholly naked, saving that they had chaines and bracelets and some bodkins in their eares . . . the cause of their comming was to exchange their Tabacco, Pinos, Plantins, Potatoes, and Peppers with any trifle if it were gawdie' (in Purchas, xvi. 52).
49. One Englishman, Sir Humphrey Gilbert, even proposed to use this savage taste for trinkets as a means to put the English unemployed to work; the New World voyages, he suggests, provide the occasion 'to set poor men's children, to learn handy crafts, and thereby to make trifles and such like, which the Indians . . . do much esteem: By reason whereof, there should be none occasion, to have a country cumbered with loiterers, vagabonds, and such like idle persons.' (I am indebted for this reference, and for reflections on English 'trifling,' to Jeffrey Knapp, *Island Empire* [Berkeley: University of

California Press, forthcoming].) In reality, of course, the exchanges were not controlled by public policy but by the avidity of the sailors and adventurers.

50. George Best, in Collinson (ed.), *Three Voyages*, 73.
51. Cf. Dionise Settle: 'What knowledge they have of God, or what Idoll they adore, we have no perfect intelligence, I thinke them rather Anthropophagi, or devourers of mans flesh then otherwise: for that there is no flesh or fish which they find dead (smell it never so filthily) but they will eate it, as they find it without any other dressing. A loathsome thing, either to the beholders or hearers' (in Hakluyt, *Principle Navigations*, vii. 227). This sits strangely with the other observation, that their captives could not digest English food (vii. 223).
52. Best reports that Eskimos wounded in skirmishes with the English would drown themselves rather than allow themselves to be caught: 'And when they founde they were mortally wounded, being ignorant what mercy meaneth, with deadly furie they cast themselves headlong from off the rocks into the sea, least perhaps their enemies shoulde receive glory or praye of their dead carcasses; for they supposed us be like to be canibales, or eaters of mans flesh' (in Collinson [ed.], *Three Voyages*, 142).
53. The scope of the travel was suggested by a globe bought by Michael Lok, and displayed on the bowsprit of Frobisher's boat when it entered London. (See Kenneth Andrews, *Trade, Plunder, and Settlement: Maritime Enterprise and the Genesis of the British Empire, 1480–1630* [Cambridge: Cambridge University Press, 1984], 173). On the Eskimo's language as a token of extreme otherness, see my 'Learning to Curse,' in *First Images of America*, ii. 563; on the 'investigation of cultural distance,' see the interesting discussion in Mary Helms, *Ulysses's Sail*, esp. 66–130.
54. See, for example, the MS account, probably by Lok, of the first voyage:

> 'And because that I have heard report of many strange tales and fayned fables touching the personage and manners of this strange man, I have thought good therefore to declare the very truthe thereof to satisfy the world and allso to expres his picture as well as may be done with ink and paper. He was a very [ ] good shape [ ] and strongly pight . . . a very brode face and very fat and fu[ll] his body. But his legs shorter and smaller [than the pro]portion of his body required, and his hands [ ] his heare [cole] blak and long hanging and "tyer" tyed [in a knot] above his forehead. His eyes little and a little cole blak beard. His cullor of skyn all over his bo[dy and fa]ce of a dark sallow, much like to the tawny Mores, [or ra]ther to the Tartar nation, whereof I think he was. [His] countenance sullen or churlish and sharp withall.' (Collinson, 87)

55. Hence, for example, the chronicler Fabian notes that the savages brought back from Newfoundland by Cabot were 'clothed in beasts skin, & did eate raw flesh, and spake such speech that no man could understand them, and in their demeanour like to bruite beastes.' Two years later, he reports, he saw them, 'apparelled after the maner of Englishmen in Westminster pallace, which that time I could not discerne from Englishmen' (in Hakluyt, *Principal Navigations*, vii. 155).
56. There are, of course, other motives that may be served by each of these pictures. The naked portrait, for example, could satisfy curiosity about what lies beneath the clothes of the Eskimo; or alternatively, it could reflect the

conviction that savages are best represented without clothes, in their 'essential' nakedness.

57. On Columbus's fourth voyage, his men thought that they had been bewitched.
58. Norman Graburn, of the University of California, Berkeley, Anthropology Department, tells me that the wrist bones of a seal are frequently used by the inhabitants of Baffin Land as representations of people, indeed, the Innuit word for these bones means 'imitation people,' and each one is understood to represent (according to size) a man, woman, or child.
59. In an important essay that uses this passage in a discussion of Shakespeare's *Merchant of Venice*, Steven Mullaney suggests that we think of this scene in terms of the Renaissance 'dramatic expedient of holding the mirror up to nature.' But we have, he says, to complicate our usual sense of reflection theory:

> Reflection here hardly reaffirms what is reproduced but instead produces a moment of cultural feedback such as might be described in information, as opposed to reflection, theory. . . . His comrade in captivity changes before his eyes, transformed into an image of the Other as this betrayal is first projected onto his 'disdaynful' companion and then reproduced and acted out by the native himself, in a choler directed not at his captors but at an emblem of his own cultural identity. . . . What has indeed lived and died at the pleasure of these Elizabethans . . . is nothing less than the native's sense of himself, of those tribal loyalties which had, up until this moment, defined him and produced in him any sense of self he possessed. Far from naïve, his unceasing wonder is in fact the enduring sign of his alienation: produced at the moment when he realizes his error, it marks the distance between his former naïveté and a new perspective that comes from seeing himself, in error, through the eyes of his captors.

(In *Cannibals, Witches, and Divorce: Estranging the Renaissance* [Selected papers from the English Institute; new ser., no. 11], ed. Marjorie Garber [Baltimore: Johns Hopkins University Press, 1987], 68–9.)

These are richly suggestive speculations, but, as I have argued elsewhere in this book, I think we should be extremely wary of drawing any conclusions about native experience from the accounts of early European observers. For George Best (who speculates that the natives live as 'hordes and troupes'), the 'captive' never awakens to any meaningful subjectivity, only to subjection. And with that consciousness of subjection, Best thinks, the captive 'confesses' his complicity in (or at least his awareness of) the kidnapping of the Englishmen. What we learn, that is, is not something about the native's 'sense of himself'; we learn something rather about Elizabethan representational technology, something closely linked to Hamlet's conviction that the play would catch the conscience of the king.

60. There are powerful reflections on this phenomenon in Jeffrey Knapp's *Island Empire* (forthcoming).

Notes to Chapter Five

1. And what of the natives? Do they consider the Europeans or, for that matter, do they consider themselves to be representations, 'tokens' of something? Did they value the trifles they seemed so eager to possess as *signs*? It is difficult at this distance to say—and I am not inclined to attempt to speak for them. What my discipline professes to know something about is how Europeans of the early modern period conceived of their tokens, images, witnesses, and representations. I am skeptical about projecting this knowledge, such as it is, on non-European peoples.
2. This account is complicated, in the case of Judaism and Islam, by hostility to visual representation and, in the case of Rabbinical Judaism at least, by a resistance to the project of conversion. Christian universalism—the conviction that its principal symbols and narratives are suitable for the entire population of the world—commits it to the unconstrained circulation of its mimetic capital.
3. Many of the texts that we are considering express powerfully this desire for access to the real—it is one of the motives that leads to kidnapping human 'tokens'. And we may speculate at least that this desire for access to the real in the other culture is in part a deflection of desire for access to the real within one's own. Always instead of such access there is mediation—a set of texts, or eyewitness accounts, or objects to be viewed. The dream would be to get past the interpretation of these objects, and seize the things themselves: one of the satisfactions in the discovery of gold is the apparent escape from the uncertainty of mediation, since for Europeans of this period gold has an innate cultural value. But with gold, of course, one cannot claim to have discovered the other but rather the same—just as one can get blood and bone in the body of the other, but hardly direct access to the culture of the other.
4. The *Histories* had fallen into oblivion in the Middle Ages; they were rediscovered and translated into Latin by Lorenzo Valla only in the mid-15th century, and then into Italian by Boiardo in the later 15th century. They did not appear to influence practical discourse.
5. Christian Meier, 'Historical Answers to Historical Questions: The Origins of History in Ancient Greece,' in *Arethusa* ('Herodotus and the Invention of History') 20 (1987), 44. The spatial extension Herodotus achieves is comparable to the temporal extension that he elegantly invokes: 'If the Nile should now turn its stream into the Arabian Gulf, what would hinder it from being silted up inside of twenty thousand years? For myself, I could well believe that it would do so within ten thousand' (Herodotus, *The History*, trans. David Grene [Chicago: University of Chicago Press, 1987], 2. 11. 135). All citations of Herodotus are to this translation.
6. A. Momigliano, 'The Fault of the Greeks,' *Daedalus* 104 (1975): 'It was not for them [the Greeks] to converse with the natives in the natives' languages . . . . There was no tradition for translating foreign books into Greek . . . . There was no temptation to yield to foreign civilisations. In fact, there was no desire to get to know them intimately by mastering foreign languages' (pp. 12–15). But see

also Ivan M. Linforth, 'Greek Gods and Foreign Gods in Herodotus,' *University of California Publications in Classical Philology* (1926). Herodotus 'did not deny the existence of the gods of foreigners. However barbarous and grotesque the foreigner's conception of his gods may be, it never seems to occur to the Greek traveler to doubt their objective existence. Furthermore, he never makes derogatory remarks or disparaging comment about them. He follows his own principle, that none but a fool will laugh at the customs of strangers. He never once evinces the belief that there are no gods but the gods of the Greeks, nor even that the gods of the Greeks are superior to the gods of other peoples. His polytheism is of unlimited capacity, and admits quietly and without criticism whatever gods are worshipped by men anywhere in the world' (p. 2). 'Herodotus and his Greek readers instinctively believed that foreign gods were not different beings from the gods whom they knew under Greek names, but identical with them. It was indifferent whether the Greek or the foreign name was used, but it was altogether more natural to use the familiar Greek name. When Herodotus gives us the foreign name as well as the Greek, it seems to be because he regards it as an example of the difference between the customs of one nation and the customs of another. The difference in name is a curiosity which is interesting for its own sake' (pp. 10–11). In effect then Herodotus separates a universal religious essence (called for convenience and naturalness by Greek names) and religious practices or customs which vary widely.

7. The little that we know of Herodotus' life would seem consonant with this interest in travel and in marginality. He was born in Halicarnassus (now southwest Turkey) and hence grew up at a point of intersection of Greek culture with the culture of the 'barbarians.' After the tyrant who ruled the town consolidated his power, Herodotus went into exile. He traveled extensively, lived for some time in Athens, and eventually settled in Thurii, in southern Italy, where he died.

8. 'It is clear that there is far the greatest supply of gold to the north of Europe, but how it is got is . . . something I cannot tell exactly; it is said that the Arimaspi—men with one eye—steal the gold from the griffins. I cannot be persuaded about this either—that there exist in nature men who are just like everyone else except that they have only one eye. Certainly, however, it seems likely that the ends of the earth, which enclose and entirely shut in all the rest, should have in themselves what we think most beautiful and rarest' (3. 116. 260). Herodotus intertwines an apparent skepticism about what someone has not witnessed first-hand with a willingness to relate hearsay: 'North of this land . . . no one knows what there is. For I could not learn from anyone who claimed to be an eyewitness. . . . I shall, however, tell everything as exactly as I can, depending on the further researches to which my hearsay evidence goes' (4. 16. 285–6).

9. David Konstan argues that counting one's people is particularly associated with the barbarians and is implicitly criticized ('Persians, Greeks and Empire,' in *Arethusa* ('Herodotus and the Invention of History') 20 (1987), 59–73). The thesis is an interesting one, but the difference in this respect between barbarians and Greeks seems to me repeatedly to collapse.

10. The threatened punishment, mentioned presumably as a reassurance as to the

effectiveness of the command, in fact suggests that the king himself was not altogether confident of being obeyed.

11. Michel de Certeau, 'Montaigne's "Of Cannibals": The Savage "I"', in *Heterologies: Discourse on the Other*, trans. Brian Massumi, Theory and History of Literature, vol. 17 (Minneapolis: University of Minnesota Press, 1985), 68. In Herodotus, as François Hartog observes, 'autopsy'—the 'I have seen'—is 'an intervention into his narration on the part of the narrator, as a way of providing proof. . . . The "I have seen" is, as it were, an operator of belief.' François Hartog, *The Mirror of Herodotus: The Representation of the Other in the Writing of History*, trans. Janet Lloyd [Berkeley: University of California Press, 1988], 260–4).
12. Hartog, 202.
13. 'If the Athenians had taken fright at the approaching danger and had left their own country, or even if they had not left it but had remained and surrendered to Xerxes, no one would have tried to oppose the King at sea. If there had been no opposition to Xerxes at sea . . . all of Greece would have been subdued by the Persians. . . . So, as it stands now, a man who declares that the Athenians were the saviors of Greece would hit the very truth' (7. 139. 514–15).
14. Plutarch, *On the Malice of Herodotus* (*Moralia*, trans. L. Pearson and F. H. Sandbach, 1965), 868.
15. 'Theses on the Philosophy of History,' in *Illuminations*, ed. Hannah Arendt, trans. Harry Zohn (New York: Schocken Books, 1968), 256. But the terms of this memorable thesis, which seems relevant to what I have written about Herodotus, are completely reversed. By 'barbarism,' Benjamin means the forces that work to annihilate freedom, forces epitomized in Fascism. Hence he argues that the task of the historical materialist is 'to brush history against the grain' so as to dissociate his work from the taint of barbarism. For Herodotus, barbarism in the form of the Persians has something of this sinister meaning—Xerxes' invasion threatens to extinguish Greek freedom—but there is a very different barbarism epitomized in Scythian nomadism: this latter form of barbarism is the implicit model for the victory of civilization, and it must be welcomed by the historian of that victory.

    I should add that it is the echoes of barbarism that keep Herodotus' account of the Greek defeat of the Persians from drifting toward hubris.
16. If there are tantalizing parallels, they are curiously inverted, for the great invading army of a despotic power that threatens to destroy native freedoms belongs to the cultural heirs of classical antiquity. And the story ends badly, of course, not with the heroic repelling of the invaders but with the brutal enslavement and murder of millions of innocents. Montaigne comes close to a sense of this horrible inversion: 'We may well call these people barbarians, in respect to the rules of reason, but not in respect to ourselves, who surpass them in every kind of barbarity' ('Of Cannibals,' in *The Complete Essays of Montaigne*, trans. Donald Frame [Stanford: Stanford University Press, 1957], 155–6. Unless otherwise noted, all citations of Montaigne are to this edn.). But though there is a moment in which Montaigne even toys with the thought that the Brazilians' language is 'somewhat like Greek in its endings' (p. 158), he does not pursue the analogy. Indeed, in his essay 'Of Coaches,' contemplating

the horrible cruelty of the European conquerors, Montaigne wishes that conquest of the New World had fallen rather to Alexander or to the ancient Greeks and Romans, civilized victors who 'would have gently polished and cleared away whatever was barbarous' in the natives (p. 694). Instead the Indian cultures have been destroyed for the basest of motives: 'Who ever set the utility of commerce and trading at such a price? So many cities razed, so many nations exterminated, so many millions of people put to the sword, and the richest and most beautiful part of the world turned upside down, for the traffic in pearls and pepper!' (p. 695).

17. Bernal Díaz del Castillo, *The True History of the Conquest of New Spain*, ed. Genaro García, trans. Alfred Maudslay, 5 vols. (London: Hakluyt Society, 1908), i. 3. For the Spanish text, I have used *Historia Verdadera de la Conquista de la Nueva España*, ed. Joaquin Ramírez Cabañas, 2 vols. (Mexico City: Editorial Porrua, 1960).
18. William H. Prescott, *The Conquest of Mexico* (New York: Random House, 1936), 504.
19. A model for this involvement as witness is the great scene in which the Spanish watch helpless as their comrades are sacrificed.
20. Cf. Cortés's description of the practices which, in his view, distinguish the Mexicans not only from the Spanish (which goes without saying) but from all other natives he has seen:

> Each day before beginning any sort of work they burn incense in these temples and sometimes sacrifice their own persons, some cutting their tongues, others their ears, while there are some who stab their bodies with knives. All the blood which flows from them they offer to those idols, sprinkling it in all parts of the temple, or sometimes throwing it into the air or performing many other ceremonies, so that nothing is begun without sacrifice having first been made. They have a most horrid and abominable custom which truly ought to be punished and which until now we have seen in no other part, and this is that, whenever they wish to ask something of their idols, in order that their plea may find more acceptance, they take many girls and boys and even adults, and in the presence of the idols they open their chests while they are still alive and take out their hearts and entrails and burn them before the idols, offering the smoke as sacrifice. Some of us have seen this, and they say it is the most terrible and frightful thing they have ever witnessed.

(In Hernan Cortés, *Letters from Mexico*, trans. and ed. Anthony Pagden [New Haven: Yale University Press, 1986], 35.)

21. 'When all was melted down that could be,' Cortés writes to the king, 'Your Majesty's fifth came to more than 32,400 *pesos de oro*, exclusive of the gold and silver jewelry, and the featherwork and precious stones and many other valuable things which I designated for Your Holy Majesty and set aside; all of which might be worth a hundred thousand ducats or more. All these, in addition to their intrinsic worth, are so marvelous that considering their novelty and strangeness they are priceless; nor can it be believed that any of the princes of this world, of whom we know, possess any things of such high quality,' in Hernan Cortés, *Letters from Mexico*, 101.
22. 'I find myself poor and very old, with a marriageable daughter and my sons young men already grown up with beards, and others to be educated' (v. 273).

23. 'If you ask me the whereabouts of their tombs,' Bernal Díaz writes of his fellow conquistadors, 'I say they are the bellies of the Indians who ate their legs and thighs, arms and flesh, and feet and hands' (v. 274).

24. On August 19, 1562 in a village in the Yucatán a Mayan schoolboy, Antonio Pech, was interrogated under torture by the Franciscan Diego de Landa, who had been tirelessly leading the missionary enterprise for more than a decade. The boy testified that he had gone to the village church to say matins and had come upon a sacrifice to 'idols and demons.' The elders and *ah-kines* (that is, Mayan priests) had tied two girls to crosses, and the officiating priest declared, ' "Let these girls die crucified as did Jesus Christ, he who they say was our Lord, but we do not know if this is so." And afterwards in saying this, they lowered them from the cross, unbound them, cut them open and took out the hearts and the *ah-kines* offered them to the demons as anciently they were accustomed to' (Clendinnen, *Ambivalent Conquests*, 204–5).

    I do not know if these dark rituals took place as alleged, but the discourse elicited under torture is a nightmare of mimetic circulation, a nightmare in which the interrogators are weirdly complicit.

25. See Jean de Léry, in the Introduction, above. Several similar quotations, from Reginald Scot, John Ridley, and Zwingli, are conveniently assembled by James Nohrnberg in *The Analogy of 'The Faerie Queene'* (Princeton: Princeton University Press, 1976), 712. Zwingli declares that his object 'was to prove that to teach that the bodily flesh and sensible flesh of Christ is eaten when we give thanks to God is not only impious but also foolish and monstrous, unless perhaps one is living among the Anthropophagi.'

26. Indeed there are significant differences, in Bernal Díaz's account, between Cortés's policy and that advocated by Olmedo. Cortés 'ordered all the priests, captains and other chieftains of that city [Tlaxcala] to assemble, and explained to them very clearly all the matters concerning our holy faith, and told them that they must cease worshipping idols, and must no longer sacrifice human beings or eat their flesh. . . . Therefore . . . he begged them to destroy the Idols and break them in pieces. That if they did not wish to do it themselves we would do it for them. He also ordered them to whitewash a temple, so that we might set up a cross there' (ii. 17). According to Bernal Díaz, the Indians, having agreed to follow Cortés's command, delayed carrying it out. There followed a debate about the wisdom of the radical and immediate substitution Cortés demanded: 'Then the Padre de la Merced said to Cortés that it was going too far, in the beginning, to take away their Idols until they should understand things better, and should see how our expedition to Mexico would turn out, and time would show us what we ought to do in the matter, that for the present the warnings we had given them were sufficient, together with the setting up of the Cross' (ii. 18). At this point Cortés appeared to accept the friar's argument, but the subsequent history suggests the triumph of the policy, whenever possible, of immediate substitution.

27. Hernan Cortés, *Letters from Mexico*, 36.

28. Instead he used an Indian woman from Jamaica who had been cast ashore among the Maya several years before and spoke their language. We learn very

little about this woman except that she accompanied the Spanish when they continued their voyage.

29. The phrase is from the letter that Cortés's loyalists sent to Spain from Vera Cruz; in the Cabañas edn., i. 166.
30. See, for example, Octavio Paz, *The Labyrinth of Solitude*, trans. Lysander Kemp (New York: Grove Press, 1961), 65–88; Jaime Delgado, 'La Mujer en la Conquista de América,' in *Homenaje a Jaime Vicens Vives* (Barcelona: Universidad de Barcelona, 1967), 101–11; Américo Paredes, 'Mexican Legend and the Rise of the Mestizo: A Survey,' in Wayland Hand (ed.), *American Folk Legend* (Berkeley: University of California Press, 1971), 97–107; Adelaida R. Del Castillo, 'Malintzin Tenépal: A Preliminary Look into a New Perspective,' in *Essays on la Mujer*, eds. Rosaura Sánchez and Rosa Martinez Cruz (Los Angeles: University of California, 1977), 124–49; Norma Alarcón, 'Chicana's Feminist Literature: A Re-Vision Through Malintzin/or Malintzin: Putting Flesh Back on the Object,' in *The Bridge Called My Back: Writings by Radical Women of Color*, eds. Cherríe Moraga and Gloria Anzaldúa (New York: Kitchen Table, 1981, 2nd edn. 1983), 182–90; Cherríe Moraga, 'From a Long Line of Vendidas: Chicanas and Feminism,' in Teresa De Lauretis (ed.), *Feminist Studies/Critical Studies* (Bloomington: Indiana University Press, 1986), 173–90.
31. 'Malintzin Tenépal: A Preliminary Look into a New Perspective,' in *Essays on la Mujer*, eds. Rosaura Sánchez and Rosa Martinez Cruz (Los Angeles: University of California Press, 1977), 125. Doña Marina is 'the first example, and thereby the symbol, of the cross-breeding of cultures.' (Tzvetan Todorov, *The Conquest of America*, trans. Richard Howard [New York: Harper & Row, 1984], 101).
32. 'The reason why he received this name,' Bernal Díaz writes, 'was that Doña Marina was always with him, especially when he was visited by ambassadors or *Caciques*, and she always spoke to them in the Mexican language. So they gave Cortés the name of "Marina's Captain," which was shortened to Malinche' (p. 172). If this account is correct, then Doña Marina herself was evidently referred to as 'Marina's Captain.'
33. The limits of her understanding—and, as a woman, however high-born, those limits may have been quite substantial—were his limits. At the same time, the fact that she was a woman may have given Doña Marina crucial access to information not otherwise available. Cortés writes to the king that in Cholula, Doña Marina 'was told by another Indian woman and a native of this city that very close by many of Mutezuma's men were gathered . . . All this she told to Gerònimo de Aguilar, an interpreter whom I acquired in Yucatan . . . and he informed me' (*Letters from Mexico*, 73). This leads, Cortés claims, directly to the massacre of Cholula. Note that the circuit begins with women talking to each other.
34. The difference between the production of text and of image should not simply be taken for granted. Even in societies with some literacy, such as the Aztecs, people would be inclined to draw rather than to write; the Europeans had developed in the opposite direction: many people felt that they could describe

accurately and effectively in writing but not in drawing. Recall, for example, William of Rubruck writing to King Louis that if only he could draw, he would send him a picture of certain of the things he had witnessed, but he would have to content himself with a verbal description. ('The married women make for themselves really beautiful carts which I would not know how to describe for you except by a picture; in fact I would have done you paintings of everything if I only knew how to paint' [*The Mongol Mission*, ed. Christopher Dawson (London: Sheed & Ward, 1955), 95].) I should add that with the very important exception of maps and plans writing clearly seemed more instrumentally significant in the early years of discovery.

35. This massive, if irregular and sporadic, discursive activity is from the beginning made up of many distinct strands and represents a wide range of motives and interests. The overwhelming pervasiveness of writing ensured that a large number of these motives would be recorded and that the encounter with peoples and territories unknown to the ancient world would not and could not be organized into a single, ideologically coherent discourse. The rapid development of printing in this period assisted both in the recording of polyvocal interests and in the wide diffusion of textual and visual traces of the New World.

36. Even when it is relatively well-informed and well-intended, such mediation drastically transforms what it records of the native perspective. As I have argued throughout this book, the few textual traces of Indian responses to the Europeans in the earliest years of contact are precious, but principally because they provide unusually candid and revealing access to the Europeans' own self-conceptions.

37. Sir Thomas Baskerville's 'Discourse,' in *The Last Voyage of Drake and Hawkins*, ed. Kenneth R. Andrews, Hakluyt Soc., 2nd ser., vol. 142 (Cambridge: Hakluyt Society, 1972), 121.

38. Samuel Purchas, 'To the Reader,' in *Purchas his Pilgrimage, or Relations of the World and the Religions Observed in all Ages and Places Discovered, from the Creation unto this Present* (London, 1613).

39. 'Of Cannibals', 152.

> [C]ar les fines gens remarquent bien plus curieusement et plus de choses, mais ils les glosent; et, pour faire valoir leur interpretation et la persuader, ils ne se peuvent garder d'alterer un peu l'Histoire; ils ne vous representent jamais les choses pures, ils les inclinent et masquent selon le visage qu'ils leur ont veu; et, pour donner credit à leur jugement et vous y attirer, prestent volontiers de ce costé là à la matiere, l'alongent et l'amplifient. Ou il faut un homme très-fidelle, ou si simple qu'il n'ait pas dequoy bastir et donner de la vray-semblance à des inventions fauces, et qui n'ait rien espousé. Le mien estoit tel; et, outre cela, il m'a faict voir à diverses fois plusieurs matelots et marchans qu'il avoit cogneuz en ce voyage. Ainsi je me contente de cette information, sans m'enquerir de ce que les cosmographes en disent.

(Montaigne, 'Des cannibales,' in *Essais*, ed. Maurice Rat, 3 vols. [Paris, 1948], i. 233–4.) See, likewise, Jacques Cartier, who writes that if the world is now better known, it is not because of the theories of the 'saiges philosophes du temps passé,' but because 'les simples mariniers de present . . . ont congneu le contraire d'icelle opinion des philosophes par vraye experience' (Cartier, 'Au

Roy treschrestien,' *Brief recit* . . . (Paris, 1545). I owe this reference to Neil J. S. Renni, 'Fact and Fiction in the Literature of Travel, Real and Imaginary, with Particular Reference to the South Seas,' Ph.D. dissertation, University College London, 1986, fo. 38.

40. One might note the constant apologies. Bernal Díaz: 'I have observed that before beginning to write their histories, the most famous chroniclers compose a prologue in exalted language, in order to give lustre and repute to their narrative, and to whet the curious reader's appetite. But I, being no scholar, dare not attempt any such preface . . . What I myself saw, and the fighting in which I took part, with God's help I will describe quite plainly, as an honest eyewitness, without twisting the facts in any way.' Or Thomas Maynarde's account of Drake's last voyage: 'Thus I have truly set downe the whole discourse of our voyage usinge therin many Idle wordes and ill compared sentences, It was done on the sea which I thinke can alter any disposition' (*The Last Voyage of Drake and Hawkins*, ed. Kenneth R. Andrews, Hakluyt Soc. 2nd Ser. No. 142 [Cambridge: Hakluyt Society, 1972], 106).

41. The notion of style as garment is central to Rosamond Tuve, *Elizabethan and Jacobean Imagery: Renaissance Poetic and Twentieth-Century Critics* (Chicago: University of Chicago Press, 1947).

42. In 'Of Cannibals' Montaigne writes that he personally met one of the Brazilian natives who had traveled to Rouen and had a very long talk with him. But he appears to have little to relate from this talk—'I had,' he writes, 'an interpreter who followed my meaning so badly, and who was so hindered by his stupidity in taking in my ideas, that I could get hardly any satisfaction from the man' (p. 159).

43. On Montaigne's New World sources, see Frank Lestringant, 'Le Cannibalisme des "Cannibales",' in *Bulletin de la Société des amis de Montaigne*, 9–10 (1982), 27–40; Géralde Nakam, *Les 'Essais' de Montaigne: Miroir et procès de leur temps* (Paris: A.-G. Nizet, 1984), 329–51; and a fine article by Gérard Defaux, 'Un Canniable en haut de chausses: Montaigne, la différance et la logique de l'identité,' in *Modern Language Notes* 97 (1982), 919–57.

44. 'Par tout où sa pureté reluit, elle fait une merveilleuse honte à nos vaines et frivoles entreprinses' (Rat edn., i. 234). For an intelligent discussion of the design of this essay, and in particular of the range of meanings that attach to the word 'barbare,' see Edwin M. Duval, 'Lessons of the New World: Design and Meaning in Montaigne's "Des cannibales" (III:31) and "Des coches" (III:6),' *Yale French Studies* 64 (1986), 95–112.

45. To this insistence I would add the remarks of the visiting Indians that Montaigne quotes—remarks that seem directed only against the king but could easily be extended. A comparable moment of class pressure in Montaigne's essays comes when he has a similar conversation with a peasant 'of his' on the subject of the religious wars.

46. 'This is nation, I should say to Plato, in which there is no sort of traffic, no knowledge of letters, no science of numbers, no name for a magistrate or for political superiority, no custom of servitude, no riches or poverty, no contracts, no successions, no partitions, no occupations but leisure ones, no care for any but common kinship, no clothes, no agriculture, no metal, no use of wine or wheat'

(p. 153). Of course, 'Of Cannibals' is much more complicated than this three- or four-way dialogue (Brazilians–servant–Montaigne–Plato), since there are many more 'sources' invoked.

47. 'Of the Custom of Wearing Clothes,' in *Essays*, trans. Frame, 167.
48. Not surprisingly, Montaigne's position toward possession is extremely paradoxical. See, for example, the illuminating essay by Philippe Desan, 'Quand le discours social passe par le discours economique: Les *Essais* de Montaigne,' in *Sociocriticism* 4 (1988), 59–86.
49. Ronald Spores, *The Mixtecs in Ancient and Colonial Times* (Norman: University of Oklahoma Press, 1984): 'The great religious structures of the Mixteca were designed by Europeans, but they were built and subsequently supported by natives' (p. 156).
50. 'Much of the success of the Christianization of the Mixtec people must be attributed to a preexisting compatibility between native and European religious traditions. Transferences were relatively easy. . . . In some instances only moderate redirection or transference was involved' (Spores, 142–3).

Index